MISSION CAT

Tips, Techniques & Strategies

to Crack CAT & Other MBA Exams

- **Corporate Office :** 45, 2nd Floor, Maharishi Dayanand Marg, Corner Market, Malviya Nagar, New Delhi-110017

  Tel. : 011-49842349 / 49842350

Typeset by Disha DTP Team

For further information about books from DISHA,

Log on to **www.dishapublication.com** or email to **info@dishapublication.com**

Contents

Chapter 1

CAT–GATEWAY TO A SUCCESSFUL CAREER

WHY IS MBA A SOUGHT AFTER CAREER?

Master of Business Administration or MBA is the perfect choice if you want to acquire the knowledge, skills, and ethics which are needed to fit right into the business community. For a safe and secure future, you need to focus on the goals from the very beginning i.e., while doing your graduation.

An MBA program is recognized worldwide and is considered as a major step towards a successful management career. MBA education goes beyond classroom teaching and helps in the holistic development of an individual. An MBA helps in building your network, skills and brand.

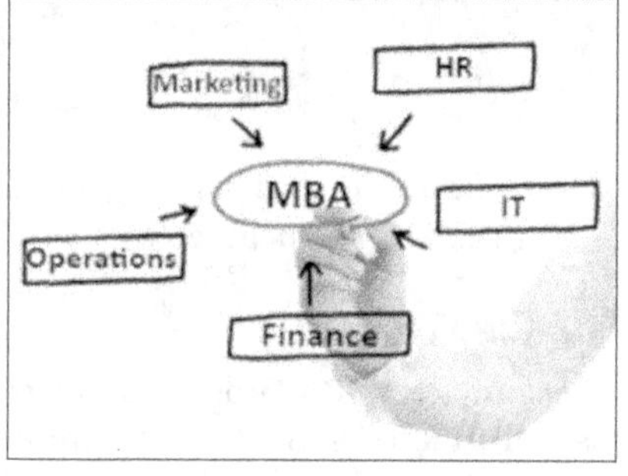

Soft skills of leadership, ethics, team work and communication become the driving force of your life. While you will obviously use hard skills like theory knowledge of HR, IT, Finance, Marketing, Accounting and Operations in your job, your soft skills will help you grow from just an individual to a well rounded individual.

If you are considering money as your prime goal, then MBA is the best option, as it is a short and compact course which with time makes you earn in millions! But if your prime goal is other than money then you need to ask only one question from yourself, *i.e.*

What skills you still lack to achieve your stated goal, and which course will enable you to get each of those skills?

For example: Suppose you lack knowledge "X" which you need to accomplish your goal "Y" and if you think that MBA will let you gain that knowledge "X", then you should do MBA to achieve your goal. As it is very rightly said, *"Real management is developing people through work and not getting work done through people."*

The right program for MBA will teach you exactly this and help you become a manager in its true sense.

MBA is not just about learning key concepts in the field of management. It is about how you apply those concepts and become a successful manager. An MBA from one of the top management institutes will help you develop application skills through several live projects but you become a successful manager only when you are faced with real problems and come out with real time solutions based on your MBA education.

Some of the core reasons are given here which describe why you should go for MBA. They include:

1. Flexibility

Most of the MBA programs are offered as part-time course as well as full-time course, so if you are employed and planning to do post-graduation without leaving your job, then an MBA is the best fit for you. You can easily give full time to your job without being stressed. Even in a part time MBA programme, there are various options available like you can attend the class in the evening, or even in the weekends, so it's up to you, choose which suits you the best!

2. Entrepreneurship

MBA program will give you deep insight into what exactly the business is, how it's operated, how all things are worked in a systematic and organized way, so overall you can acquire the requisite knowledge and practices which are needed to develop and run your own business.

As the program's name suggests, you will learn how to master business administration and if you want to establish your own business and want to contribute to the economic development of the country, go for it without any hesitation.

If you want to become an entrepreneur you will need experience in the sector of preference, and financial backing besides others. Your ability to get seed capital for starting a new business improves tremendously if you have an MBA degree. You also get to interact with the best minds in the country where you can brainstorm your ideas and get a better handle on things.

3. Develop Management Skills

Management is pervasive; it is not as easy as it seems to be, it includes various skills like problem-solving, decision-making, planning, delegation, communication. So, if you are doing an MBA, then you will come across all these skills and finally you will learn the right way of doing management.

4. Job Opportunities

MBA opens the doors to various job opportunities; there are a number of job opportunities available in various sectors, to name a few like -

- ➢ Banking & Finance
- ➢ Information System Management
- ➢ Investment Banking
- ➢ Management Consulting
- ➢ Data Analytics
- ➢ Entrepreneurship

5. Financial Independence

We hear about the ₹ 1 crore plus salary packages that students from the IIMs get every year. Even beyond those, one can expect a package of 8-14 lakhs post an MBA from one of the top 25 B-schools in India. And mind you, these numbers are for a fresh out of B-school graduate. With a few years of work experience the salary levels would only go higher. So, for even an average engineering graduate, MBA offers at least a 3 fold jump over his pre-MBA salary levels.

6. Growth in Career

Those of you who have worked for a few years in an organization will agree that to grow beyond a certain level in your job, you need an additional degree. Also, even as a fresh graduate you can reasonably expect a saving of 2-3 years in reaching the Project Manager level of profiles. An MBA will give a boost to your professional life and hence success in every aspect.

7. Confidence

An MBA will instil in you the confidence to speak about anything, at any time and to anyone even if you don't know a thing about it. You will be better prepared to face interviews or giving presentations. This is an important skill to have, something that'll serve you for life.

8. Foreign Exchange

An MBA from a top B-school gives you the opportunity to experience education in some of the best universities of the world, and hence a nice paying job in an MNC. The whole experience of travelling on your own in foreign land, making new friends, adapting to new culture and managing this drastic change is capable of teaching you more than your two years in classroom.

9. Social respect, Networking and Credibility

You gain access to the extensive alumni network of that particular MBA programme. Your connections will give you a great overview of the business world and a deep understanding of the slightest changes in the business environment. You can reflect on some big business issues, and make connections between various global events and world affairs. The sheer diversity of jobs, the extent of responsibility and ownership that you get as an MBA in your job make it worth your while.

10. Job Security

If you recall the slew of recessions that have hit our country over the past 10 years and how vulnerable every job has become, it'd help also remember that your job as an MBA is one of the safest ones as the senior and talented human resources are relatively difficult to hire and fire.

Also, other than a degree and a lucrative career, let's assure you an MBA provides you with a valuable network which you can cherish for life. A strong alumni, an excellent faculty, brilliant batch mates will help you go places from any remote part of the country. Remember all global businesses need local support. So even if you open a startup and wish to be an entrepreneur, your right contacts at the right places and at the right time will help you do just that.

For reasons given above, more and more people are looking forward to possess a degree in management, that too without compromising on the institute or the quality of education to be received. The first option that strikes their mind is to attempt CAT, as it is possibly the most viable means to achieve the same.

RIGHT TIME TO START THE PREPARATION

CAT aspirants should always start early in preparing for the exams as an early start would benefit them in gaining knowledge about the kind of questions to be asked. Another advantage to it can be spending time in developing extra reading habits and increasing vocabulary.

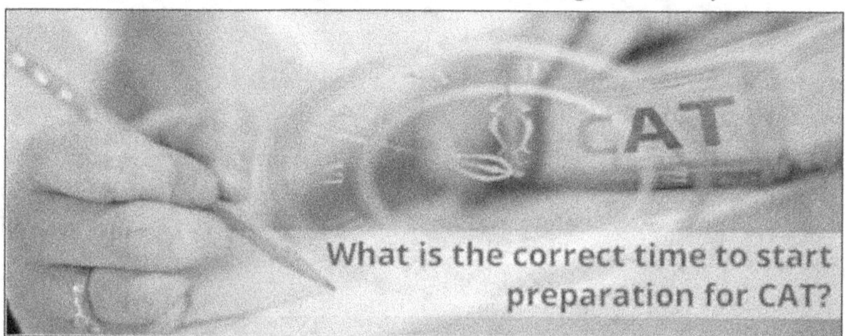

Students often find themselves in a troubled position when they cannot decide as to when they should start with their preparations. Though it may differ from student to student and can be regarded as a subjective topic to comment on. Now let's discuss the time strategy and milestones.

The best time is whenever you decide that you want to crack CAT is all about practice. We can say that the right time to start the preparation is NOW. Once you start, maintain the rhythm.

The second step for preparation for any exam requires you to identify your strengths and weaknesses. This will help you find the amount of time that you need for CAT preparation as it will help you judge how difficult or easy is the level of exam for you individually.

On a standard basis, people recommend second year to be the time when one must start getting sincere about your exam. However, it does not imply that we must get too panicked or overstressed if that time has passed. The only difference is if you have less time, you will have to put in more efforts.

The beginning is the more fun bit of preparation as one attempts his/her hands at numbers, calculations, and article reading and vocabulary expansion. There is ample time left to get to serious business as it is never too late for starting your preparation, unless of course CAT is right at the corner.

An aspirant should at best start by June, comfortably finish all the portions by August, or latest early September, take 20 mock CATs and be ready for CAT by November. This exam is as much about momentum and intensity as it is about knowledge or application.

Ideally, it depends on whether you were equally comfortable in Mathematics and English till class 10th or not. If you were comfortable with both the subjects, then you can start 10-12 months before CAT. If you were not very comfortable, let's say with any one subject - for instance English - you need to spend extra 3–4 months to build command of the subject. The idea is to make sections comparable and then rise up to the CAT level.

So, if one section is very weak compared to the other, you need to spend more time; if both the sections are equally good, then you can do it in 10 months time as well. However, lots of people who have all subjects well covered in high school (class 7 to 10th) crack CAT even in 5–7 months.

So, assess your current status in subjects and accordingly start the preparation.

You must remember that preparing for CAT is an ongoing process. There is no certain rule that a specific number of months of preparation are enough for qualifying the exam. Remember…

> *"Success doesn't come from what you do occasionally. It comes from what you do consistently."*

Some Key Points

➢ Try to read as many diverse topics as possible that include articles ranging from Sociology to Sports, from Philosophy to Politics and from History to Economics.

➢ Interest in non-material preparation (reading blogs, editorials, novels, etc.) also helps.

➢ *The more you read the better*. Although CAT has kept grammar and direct vocabulary questions off the table for the past few years, but still focusing on it always helps.

➢ Keep your detective glasses on every time you read, this will help you gain better hold on the language. Search for any new word you find- its meaning, synonyms, antonym and various usages in different contexts.

➢ Put the formulas and acronyms on your room's wall. Memorize them all.

A Few Important Tips

1. Go through Previous year's questions papers once you have a basic idea of important topics.

2. Mock CATs are important and analyzing them is most important if you want to bell the CAT! Mocks help you develop a strategy to solve problems. That strategy should help you maximize your score.

3. A mock test every 10 days and at least once a week starting August (that makes a total of at least 25-30 tests).

4. For course material if you don't have any, either register with a coaching institute or refer a specialized book.

5. Try to make yourself believe that CAT is not difficult. So, when you approach the exam be calm and composed. This is easier said than done, but you need train yourself to act peaceful. This solves 50% of the problems!

6. Make a study plan for CAT 2018 starting today. It can be similar to or something you're comfortable with. Stick to it!

7. Try the sectionals/solving material/preparation through mail, Facebook groups/forums/etc. (10-15 questions a day on an average).

8. It's important that you have a time table which you follow strictly.

Everything been said, for the last line of wisdom says that CAT is all about being aware *about your strong points and weak points* and investing your time accordingly. *Prudential use of time is of essence, use fewer pens and rely more on brain.* To sum up, the final mantra is "*Keep CALM and bell the CAT*".

This is the best time to prepare for CAT (I mean the month March-April). You get around six-seven months for going through all topics in QA, DILR and VA.

To do this, if you are preparing from home, it is recommended that you buy correspondence material from some coaching. The material should be well designed, go through the concepts and then practise all the questions. That would be enough and you won't need any other material.

If you intend to join some coaching, just follow whatever they tell and do all the sheets and books with full devotion without running for any third party material or such.

Thus by September end, you should be thorough with all the topics and should gain decent speed and accuracy. Now the last two months are the most crucial.

Also, you ought to start some test series around August or September, as a large number of students give that, thus would give you a fair idea of your standings.

In the last two months, you should revisit all the topics as well as keep giving tests, at least 3 a week so that till November-end you have given around 25 tests. Also make sure to do thorough analysis of your tests and work on your weak areas. CAT is all about rejection, getting 150 marks in the previous year's CAT would fetch you 99%. So, it's all about leaving the questions which you don't know and attempting what you are best at. So, all these mock analysis are meant for the same purpose i.e. you find out which questions you have to attempt as well as which questions you definitely don't have to attempt.

Doing all this, you will definitely get above 95%.

Preparation Milestones and Points to Remember

Your preparation milestones should look somewhat like this:

- You should ideally finish off the CAT papers and basics of preparation (all the important concepts, formulas and question types) at least 6 months before the exam, so that you are in fine shape once the mock season starts.

- Then, it will be more of an identify-error-and-work-on-it exercise and you should be plugging the major gaps in your prep.

- By the time the CAT notification comes out (end of July), you should be operating at least 80-85% of your capacity. Post that, the focus would shift to your strategy (considering the changes in pattern, interface, etc.)

- Minor additions to your knowledge base can be made till mid-end October post which, you would spend more time revising and analyzing your previous mocks.

- Do not divert your mind on looking for any new matter or books at this stage. But instead focus only on revising what all you learned till now, concentrate there.

- Follow a timetable and schedule as per your convenience. But try to strictly stick to it.

- Stay motivated by reading and interacting with learned people.

- One important point is also make some time for you, don't overdo. Else you will feel stressed and tired.

COMPUTER BASED TEST

The IIM (Indian Institute of Management) decided to introduce the online format of Common Admission Test in the year 2009. There was lot of apprehensions concerning the same. It also led to a fall in the number of applicants by about 12%.

Choosing the type of test posed a huge dilemma for the aspirants, i.e., *Computer-based or Paper based?* And if the numbers are to be trusted, a majority of the vote goes to the paper based tests. Now, in an era where it seems almost everyone is internet savvy with an active social media presence, reluctance towards CBTs is a little surprising.

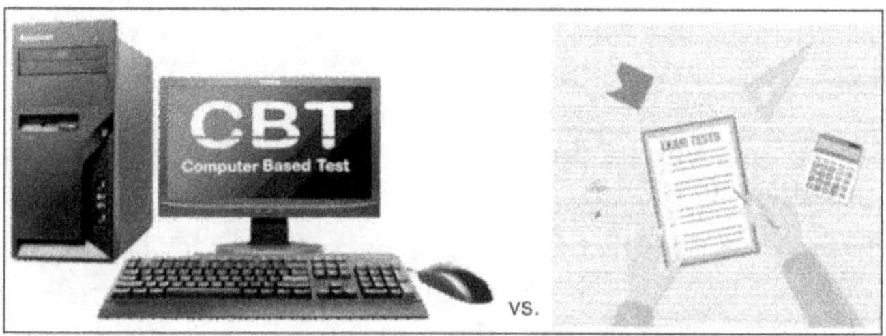

The last one, i.e. CAT 2017 was a computer based or computer delivered exam and not an online exam. There is a difference between computer aided and online. Just like you use a paper and pen to write an exam, which we generally refer as offline mode; similarly in a computer aided examination, a computer is used as the mode of giving answers. An online exam would mean that both the examiner and examinee are connected by an internet connection and the test taker is giving answers directly to the test conducting body via an internet connection.

Let us understand this by the example of paper and pen based test. In a paper pen based test, you are given an OMR sheet and when you are finished with the test, your OMR sheets are collected by the centre and sent to the concerned test conducting body. Similarly, in a CBT (Computer Based Test), you give your answers and those are recorded in the computer system. Those responses are then sent to the test taking authorities. There is no involvement of internet connection as long as you are appearing for the test. It's just a computer that is recording your answers as an OMR sheet would have done.

The History

> Before 2009, CAT was a paper based test conducted on a single day for all candidates.

> The IIMs outsource the exam to a global testing company.

> The American firm Prometric was entrusted with the responsibility of conducting the test from 2009 to 2013.

> Since 2014 onwards, CAT has been conducted by Tata Consultancy Services (TCS).

The Present: In the Examination Hall

- Every candidate is allocated a computer system.
- Candidates are required to login using the ID provided to them at the exam centres. Most of the times your Roll Number is the login ID.
- As soon as you are logged in, few guidelines are displayed regarding the exam mode and the exam.
- Candidates should proceed only after reading the instructions carefully.
- There are two kinds of questions in the test, MCQ and non-MCQ. For non-MCQ type mathematical questions you will need to type the answer using the virtual number-board provided.
- When the exam begins, there will a box displayed on left side with question numbers and buttons beside them marked from 1 to 100.
- Candidates are supposed to mark the answers using the mouse.
- Some of the pros and cons of CBT are:

Pros	Cons
Navigation through the question paper is easy	Technical glitches in the system might cause loss of data and time.
Very easy to change your answer, just go back to the question and change the answer.	Difficult for candidates if one is not familiar with the technology of computers and internet
A test clock is provided on the top to keep track of time left.	A tickling clock always on the screen can be stressful. Also if one is not in a habit of sitting in front of a computer for hours, it can cause headache.

The Fears and the Strategies to Overcome them

The aspirants have a fair share of doubts and arguments against Computer based tests. However, if you are afraid of the Computer Based Exams for any of the following reasons, read on:

i. **You've practised mainly on paper:** This is one of the main reasons students refrain from taking the test online. It is understandable that there is some comfort in the familiar one, but you are provided with rough papers even in the Computer based form of the test. So, while you can work out stuff on paper, you have computers for quickly marking the answers and switching between problems for a quick check, as opposed to worrying about the speed that you need to write, or colour of the ink and the tedious job of properly filling in the bubbles on the paper.

To diversify your preparation, try taking tests online too. This will prepare you for Computer based tests. Online mock tests also offer a much better performance analysis, and you will get a better insight into your strengths and weaknesses. Basically instead of worrying about the CBTs, you should start familiarizing yourself with them.

ii. **CBTs include tougher questions:** This is a myth. In fact, there are articles suggesting that test takers somehow found it easier. There was positive feedback in line with the benefits such as, *'We were able to unmark answers and change them with just a click.'*, *'We could see the questions we skipped for later review'* etc.

Even organizers have denied the view on disparity in difficulty level of questions between CBTs and PBTs (Paper based Test). In fact, CBTs can help you be more organized by allowing you to quickly browse through questions and alert you of any you've missed, unlike PBTs where human error can account for missed questions.

iii. **There may be a power failure:** This is a competent reason to not going for an online test. In fact, if the power situation constantly fluctuates or is really bad in your city, don't go for CBTs. But, if you're basing your decision on a mere possibility of power failure during your exam, you need to think like this.

Having been in the business long enough, your examination centre will definitely have a power backup. If you are in doubt, you can check that with the centre before the exam. One may argue that the time between the power cut and the backup 'kicking in' goes to waste. Well, in that case, for argument's sake, you may drop your pen in a paper based test or worse, spill your stationery on the floor, which you need to re-arrange. This will need the exact amount of time it takes for the power backup to kick in. As the test is online (LAN), your responses will remain unchanged, even if a power failure were to take place.

iv. **What if there are other technical glitches:** If you are worried about technical glitches other than power failure, you can put those fears to rest. The organizers have already thought it through and made the appropriate arrangements for you; some buffer computers (those with a physical memory storage used to temporarily store data while it is being moved from one place to another) are also provided at the centres. With one or two exceptions, there is also evidence that there haven't been any major mishaps during a national level CBT. The reason is the amount of intense situational testing done before the exam by the examination centres.

So there you have it! Now that your biggest fears about CBTs are addressed, all you need to do is make them your best friend – familiarize yourself with the process and give a few mock tests and you'll be all set!

Problems Faced

Apart from the fact that it gives certain advantages, it also poses many challenges in different sections which the candidates find difficult to adapt to. We will discuss some here.

- ➤ The biggest trouble has been with Reading Comprehension passages. It is an entirely different situation reading passages on paper and online, as it will not allow any underlining of key sentences or words. Students need to have enough practice in advance to be comfortable with these during the exam.

- ➤ Not everyone is quick and comfortable using a screen or a visual interface. Many complain that the swiftness and ease of answering papers in written form is much more. For instance, in a DI question, the charts, other data and questions all may come in separate sections causing trouble in using the cursor to shift to each of them again and again.

- ➤ Another disadvantage for students is that they are not able to go through the entire paper in one go, as questions will appear one by one.

- ➤ Also, key challenges accompany the endeavour to move from paper-and-pencil to computer.

- ➤ Another one among the difficulties of computer-based testing is getting access to seat time in front of computers for a large number of students. Candidates have to select only institutes with a big infrastructure.

- ➤ One more issue that could completely shake the strategy of a student is the "sectional time" limits. Most competitive exams have time limits for their various sections, this becomes difficult to administer because of the "logistical" problems in invigilation.

- ➤ In 2017, the students reported that there were some technical glitches due to which they could not appear in Slot I at a Delhi centre. The server was not working due to which about 200 candidates were not able to attend CAT as per their schedule. They had to wait for the next session.

➤ Even similar news was heard from other parts of the country. Students complained that despite heavy examination fees, the authorities didn't provide well equipped examination centres.

➤ Another issue that the students pointed was that many of the questions in the Logical Reasoning and Data Interpretation (LRDI) section remained unsolved. Such issues point a finger at the administration and management; it depicts carelessness on their part.

➤ It has now become very important that such premier institutes focus on the issue of being fair and unbiased to all candidates and take care to steer clear of any such snag.

The impact is the change in the testing environment affecting the performance in the test. The familiarity with the online medium is likely to enhance or hinder performance to a significant extent.

Researches have shown that 'reading speed' drops by as much as 20-30 per cent when shifting from reading from print to that from the computer screens.

The ability to choose questions to attempt could be "limited" by the format of the paper. For instance, if the test format allows one to scroll across the paper from the first question to the last, the ability to choose would be similar to the paper pattern.

On the other hand, if one question can be seen at a time, it completely changes the "paper scanning" process. CBT (Computer based test) is definitely not the friendliest to a student, but most aptitude exams conducted on the computer are in this form.

One more issue that could completely shake the strategy of a student is the "sectional time" limits. Most competitive exams have time limits for their various sections, this becomes difficult to administer because of the "logistical" problems in invigilation.

Familiarity and being comfortable with working on computers becomes key to gaining an edge in test taking. It is likely to play a big role given the nature of the student community that appears for CAT. Finally, though the conceptual learning does not change, the types of questions could. This is in keeping with the new environment.

In experts' opinion, everyone should go for Computer based tests. There are many advantages of the computer based exams over paper based. On a closer look, we find that the cons of a CBT are unlikely and pros of it are most definitely certain.

Also, there are enough reasons to believe that more and more competitive tests are going to be online in the future, given the amount of emphasis being laid on digitalization these days. Your best bet is preparing for what lies ahead without the fear of embracing the new.

MYTHS AND REALITIES RELATED TO CAT

Before we go on to understand the plus points attached with CAT, it is imperative to clarify certain myths and realities that revolve around CAT. CAT is one of the most important exams that any MBA aspirant aims to crack. When there is very little time left for the exam, many aspirants start getting certain doubts or get confused about the exam ques-tions or exam pattern.

There are many preconceived notions about CAT that are heard too often, and that is the reason why some aspirants dread to even think of CAT.

However, most of these notions might just be a myth. If you too have some doubts regarding CAT, go on to see whether they really are a Fact or just a Myth.

(a) **Myth:** ONLY Students with outstanding performance in academics have a chance at top B- schools.

   Reality: Very few B-Schools have more than 10-15% weightage to past academic performance in the overall selection process.

(b) **Myth:** One needs to be a genius to crack CAT.

   Reality: Even an average student can manage 92-95 percentile score with proper planning and hard work and that means getting a call from one of the top-15 colleges.

(c) **Myth:** A lot of money is required to get into an MBA from a prestigious college.

   Reality: Though it is true to an extent that the fees for MBA in a good college may be perceived high for a lot of candidates, however, it does not mean that it is the end of the story. The government provides for various education loans, mostly without collateral that are easy to obtain with very low or negligible interests.

(d) **Myth:** CAT is a game of speed.

Reality: This is one of the biggest myths haunting CAT aspirants who think that someone not too fast cannot tackle CAT questions. However, intelligent approach and concept understanding is more important than speed in this entrance exam unlike others.

(e) **Myth:** The placements have not been very impressive for most B-Schools and for lots there is also no guarantee for jobs.

Reality: Though partially true, it is mostly in the case of low ranked colleges or even for various economic reasons. The top MBA colleges however boast of 100% placements.

(f) **Myth:** It is impossible to get an MBA without some work experience.

Reality: Work experience has weightage only in certain B-Schools that too are not more than 10-15%. For people looking for very high profile jobs right after MBA may opt for some work experience before attempting CAT but for others, it is not a mandatory requirement.

(g) **Myth:** Engineers have an extra edge in comparison to simple graduates.

Reality: Many of us believe that engineers are better at Maths and calculations, thus having an advantage. However, Maths in CAT is not so complicated or of higher degree, it mostly evaluates the understanding of basic concepts and fundamentals.

(h) **Myth:** Aspirants with English background stand great chance to crack CAT.

Reality: Language sure is not something achieved over a few months. But there have been sufficient examples of students with very weak English backgrounds achieving great control over language and enhancing vocabulary with regular reading and learning.

(i) **Myth:** CAT preparation can be done in 3 months.

Reality: Many people suggest that 3 months sure sufficient for preparation but this is only partially true. While these 3 months are the time to prepare rigorously, preparation should start much before in order to improve on languages and vocabulary. Also those weak in Maths definitely need more time to get sufficient practice.

(j) **Myth:** General awareness is not at all important in cracking CAT.

Reality: Since CAT does not have any section on general awareness, aspirants usually leave out on this. However, keeping yourself updated with current events not only helps during GD and PIs but are also many a time the topic for reading comprehensions. This helps to gain a better understanding of the passages.

(k) **Myth:** Vocabulary doesn't hold much importance for CAT.

Reality: This is a baseless myth that surrounds CAT since a strong vocabulary is the key to a good score in CAT. Along with direct questions of vocabulary, knowledge of a vast number of words helps to understand verbal ability questions and RC passages.

(l) **Myth:** Flawless English speaking skills are a must to crack CAT.

Reality: CAT requires more of clear grammatical concepts and a good critical ability. IIMs do not look for high degree of speaking fluency but definitely a high degree of grammar correctness and language control.

(m) **Myth:** Reading comprehension is the toughest nut to crack in the CAT exam.

Reality: Many consider RCs to be very tough; no doubt RCs can be confusing at times and mislead you in terms of options. However, sufficient practice and intelligent choosing can help you get through this.

(n) **Myth:** Cracking CAT assures you a great career.

Reality: People think once they qualify the CAT their career is set, apart from the fact that there are tough levels of GD and PI to cross; all MBA colleges do not provide 100% placements or satisfying job opportunities.

(o) **Myth:** Someone who has taken the CAT multiple times has a better chance at clearing it.

Reality: This is a myth. The very fact that he/she had taken it multiple times is an indication that the preparation has not gone absolutely right. In fact no one can predict what kind of the CAT exam will be the coming year - this unpredictability is what makes the exam tough.

(p) **Myth:** The more shortcuts you know the better your performance.

Reality: Shortcuts are a good way to cut down on time spent per question. But over the past few years, the CAT exam has become more concept-focused and less speed-focused. This has a twin impact. One, the number of questions in the test has reduced significantly, and this would not get additional points for finishing the exam early, so speed is thrown out of the equation to a great extent. Secondly, using shortcuts in the conceptual questions increases the risk of errors. Hence old school methods coupled with crystal clear concepts will hold you in good stead. If you want to go faster improve your calculation speed - that would definitely help.

Now that your inhibitions, if any, may have been removed with respect to CAT to a large extent, we move forward to the career prospects after doing an MBA and also making you aware of the CAT cut-offs along with the list of the B-schools accepting CAT score.

Classification of Sectors based on Placements in Top IIMs

➤ Banking & Financial Services & Insurance
➤ Conglomerates
➤ Consumer Goods
➤ Engineering/Technologies
➤ Logistics
➤ Consulting
➤ General Management & strategy
➤ Sales & Marketing
➤ Operations & IT/ Systems
➤ Strategies and Operations
➤ IT and Analytics
➤ Manufacturing
➤ Media/Communications
➤ Online Services
➤ Pharmaceutical/Health care
➤ Real Estate
➤ Telecom

LIST OF B-SCHOOLS AND CAT CUT-OFFS

CAT scores are used as a primary screening tool by B-Schools for shortlisting candidates for the GD/ PI round. Apart from CAT percentile, other factors which are taken into account for generating calls include academic performance in 10+2, Graduation, duration of work experience. Normally, the cut-offs for old IIMs are higher than those for new IIMs.

B-School Cut-offs on the Basis of Percentiles	
Level (Approx cut-off percentiles Gen.)	**Expected Calls from prominent Institutes**
99.5+	3-8 Calls from IIM A,B,C,L,K,I,S, FMS
99+	1-2 Calls from IIM A,B,C,L,K,I,S And All other IIM calls, IIT B
98+	IIT-D, MDI-PGP, All IIMs except old 7
96.5+	SPJIMR, NITIE, MDI- HR/IM, few new IIMs (Latest 6)
94.5+	IIT-KH, IIT-KN, IIT-C, IIT-R, IISc-B, XLRI-Global BM, MDI-M, IIMA (Abm), IIML (Abm)
90+	MICA, IMT-G/N, XIMB, IMI-D, FSM, IRMA, GIM, TAPMI, KJSIMSR, SIMSREE, UBS-CHD, SPJAIN-D/S, BIM, NIRMA
87+	WIMDR-M, LBSIM, LIBA, IMI-K/B, GLIM, BIMTECH-PGDM/IB, IBS-ICFAI, MFC-DU, IFMR, MIB-DU, MHROD-DU, IMT-H
85+	MISB, ISBM-P, WIMDR-B, BIMTECH-Retail/Insurance, IIFM, MBE-DU,

B-Schools Categorization on the Basis of CAT cut-off

The following table enlists institutes based on CAT Cut-off in which classification of IIMs and B-schools on the basis of the level of cut-offs has been made -

Rating	Level (Approx. CAT cut-off Percentiles for General)	Institutes
A+	I (CAT Percentile 98.5+)	IIM-A, IIM-B, IIM-C, IIM-K, IIM-I, IIM-L, FMS, MDI-PGPM, IIT- B, RGIIMS
	II (CAT Percentile 96.5+)	SPJIMR, IIT-D, NITIE-PGDIM, JBIMS, MDI-PGP HR/IM, IIM-RH, IIM-RN, IIM-RP, IIM-KS, IIM-UP, IIM-T

A	III (CAT Percentile 94.5+)	IIT-KH, IIT-KN, IIT-C, IIT-R, IISc-B, IIM-BG, IIM-N, IIM-V, IIM-Asr, IIM-Sam, IIM-Srm, MDI-M, IIM-A (ABM), IIM-L (ABM)
	I (CAT Percentile 90+)	MICA, IMT-G/N, IMI-D, FSM, IRMA, TAPMI, KJSIMSR, UBS-CHD, SPJAIN-D/S, BIM, NIRMA, PUMBA
B+	II (CAT Percentile 87+)	WIMDR-M, LBSIM, LIBA, IMI-K/B, GLIM, BIMTECH-PGDM/IB, IBS-ICFAI, MFC-DU, IFMR, MIB-DU, MHROD-DU, IMT-H
	III (CAT Percentile 85+)	MISB, ISBM-P, AJKMCRC, IIMC (Mass Com Delhi), WIMDR-B, BIMTECH-Retail/Insurance, IIFM, MBE-DU

B-Schools Accepting CAT Score

Here is a list of Institutes accepting CAT scores (in an alphabetical order). They are:

Institute	Location	Websites
AICAR Business School	MUMBAI	www.aicar.net
Alliance Business Academy	BANGALORE	www.alliancebschool.org
Amrita Institute of Management	COIMBATORE	www.amrita.edu/aim
Aravali Institute of Management	JODHPUR	www.aravali.org
Asia-Pacific Institute of Management	NEW DELHI	www.asiapacific.edu
EMPI Business School	NEW DELHI	www. empiindia.com
EMPI Institute of Advertising, Communication and Management	NEW DELHI	www.empiindia.com
Faculty of Management Studies, Banaras Hindu University	VARANASI	

Fore School of Management	NEW DELHI	www.fsm.ac.in
Foundation for Organizational Research and Education- School of Management	NEW DELHI	
GIDC Rajju Shroff Rofel Institute of Management Studies	VAPI	
Global Business School	NEW DELHI	www.globalbschool.in
Globsyn Business School	KOLKATA	
Goa University	PANAJI	www.unigoa.ac.in
IIM Ahmedabad (IIM A)	AHMEDABAD	www.iimahd.ernet.in/
IIM Bangalore (IIM B)	BANGALORE	iimb.ac.in
IIM Calcutta (IIM C)	KOLKATA	www.iimcal.ac.in
IIM Indore (IIM I)	INDORE	www.iimidr.ac.in
IIM Kozhikode (IIM K)	KOZHIKODE	www.iimk.ac.in
IIM Lucknow (IIM L)	LUCKNOW	www.iiml.ac.in
Indian Institute of Forest Management	BHOPAL	www.iifm.org
Institute of Science and Management	RANCHI	ismr.ac.in
Indian Institute of Social Welfare & Business Management	KOLKATA	www.iiswbm.edu
Indian School of Mines	DHANBAD	www.ismd.ac.in
Institute for Development and Research in Banking Technology	HYDERABAD	www.idrbt.ac.in
Institute for Financial Management & Research	CHENNAI	www.ifmr.com
Institute for Integrated Learning in Management	NEW DELHI	www.iilm.edu
Institute for Technology and Management	NAVI MUMBAI	www.itm.edu

Institute of Business Administration and Training	BHUBANESH-WAR	www.ibat.ac.in
Institute of Engineering and Management	KOLKATA	www.iemcal.com
Institute of Management Development and Research (IMDR)	PUNE	www.imdr.edu
Institute of Management Education (UP)	SHAHIBABAD	www.imesahibabad.org
Institute of Marketing and Management, New Delhi	NEW DELHI	www.immindia.com
Institute of Public Enterprise	HYDERABAD	
Integrated Academy of Management and Technology	GHAZIABAD	www.inmantec.edu
International Management Institute	NEW DELHI	www.imi.edu
International School of Business and Media	PUNE	www.isbm.ac.in
Jaipuria Institute of Management	LUCKNOW	www.jimindia.com
K. J. Somaiya Institute of Management Studies & Research	MUMBAI	www.simsr.somaiya.edu
Kirloskar Institute of Advanced Management Studies	DAVANGERE	www.kiams-hrr.org
Lal Bahadur Shastri Institute of Management (New Delhi)	NEW DELHI	www.lbsim.edu
Management Development Institute (MDI)	GURGAON	www.mdi.ac.in
Montessori Mahila Kala Sala	VIJAYAWADA	www.mnnit.ac.in

Motilal Nehru National Institute of Technology	ALLAHABAD	
Mudra Institute of Communication Ahmedabad	AHMEDABAD	www.mica-india.net
National Institute of Bank Management	PUNE	www.nibmindia.org
National Institute of Industrial Engineering (NITIE)	MUMBAI	www.nitie.edu
National Institute of Management Calcutta	KOLKATA	
New Delhi Institute of Management	NEW DELHI	www.ndimdelhi.org
NIILM Centre for Management Studies	NEW DELHI	www.niilm.com
Nirma Institute of Management	AHMEDABAD	www.nim.ac.in
Prin L N Welingkar Institute of Management Development & Research	MUMBAI	www.welingkar.org
S P Jain Institute of Management & Research	MUMBAI	www.spjimr.org
School of Management Sciences	VARANASI	www.smsvaranasi.com
School of Management Studies, University of Hyderabad	HYDERABAD	uohyd.ernet.in
SDM Institute for Management Development	MYSORE	www.sdmimd.net
T. A. Pai Management Institute	MANIPAL	www.tapmi.org
United Institute of Management	ALLAHABAD	www.unitedcollege.com
University Business School	CHANDIGARH	www.ubschandigarh.org

NOTE: The 6 new IIMs established across the country are also in the list. They also take CAT as the basis of giving admissions.

OVERVIEW OF CAT

STRUCTURE, PATTERN AND COMPONENTS OF CAT

CAT (Common Admission Test) is a premier All India Management Entrance Exam that is conducted once a year by the IIMs (Indian Institutes of Management). The IIMs use the test for selecting students for their business administration programs. CAT, a computer based test, is conducted by one of the IIMs based on a policy of rotation.

The IIMs are the prime management institutes in India established by an act of Parliament. These institutes also provide consultancy and research services in various business and management globally.

Apart from the 20 IIMs including IIM Ahmedabad, Bangalore and Calcutta, and the newest IIMs, IISc and other top rated Management colleges in India namely FMS, SPJIMR, MDI, MI, IMT, NITIE, Management departments of IITs, JBIMS

also accept CAT scores for admission to MBA and other management programs. It means CAT is the entry gate for a Post graduation course in Business Administration of the 20 IIMs and more than 100 B-schools across India.

Masters of Business Administration (MBA) is a post graduate program that, regardless of the specialization, will provide you with conceptual, theoretical and practical training in various aspects of business like economics, operations, marketing, basic accounting, corporate finance etc.

Before 2009, CAT was held in a single day and was a pen paper based test. The first computerized test had lots of technical snags, later some viruses were detected which were named as the culprit for systems getting slow.

Earlier the total time for the test was 170 minutes which got increased to 180 minutes. Another modification is – from earlier two sections i) VALR (verbal ability & logical reasoning), ii) QADI (quantitative ability & data interpretation) to now three sections – i) VARC, ii) DILR and iii) QA.

Below is the compilation of few salient features of the test, which can clear many of your doubts; they include the structure, pattern and the components of the test along with an overview of CAT 2017 and facts of CAT 2018.

CAT 2017

Before moving any further, firstly let's have a look on the last CAT i.e. CAT 2017. Last year almost 2.5 lakhs students competed for around 3200 seats making it the most competitive exam in the country. CAT 2017 was conducted by IIM Lucknow along with Tata Consultancy Services (TCS) as the testing partner.

The results of CAT 2017 were declared in January 2018; 20 candidates had secured 100 percentile in it, out of which two are female candidates and three are male and engineering students.

In the years 2015 and 2016, CAT has been conducted on the same pattern and it was expected that IIM, Lucknow may bring substantial changes in the exam in 2017. And the few changes that were evident in 2017 were:

- There were some non MCQs i.e. questions in which no options were provided. The candidates were required to type in the answer, thus they are called TITA (type in the answer).

- Also, one major change was for the first time the IIMs released the answer keys, this was available online. The students could check their scores, wherein along with the question paper, the correct answer option is marked in green. There is also an objection form, which candidates could apply in case they find any particular answer option incorrect. The test takers also had the option to file objection against one or more questions by paying some amount of fee.

This was the latest initiative by the IIMs which has been applauded by majority of students. With this, the students can understand their errors which will help them a lot by avoiding their previous mistakes in future.

CAT 2018

One of the top six IIMs namely IIM Ahmedabad, IIM Bangalore, IIM Calcutta, IIM Lucknow, IIM Indore and IIM Kozhikode will be assigned the role of CAT convening body. In some time, the convening IIM for 2018 will declare the exact details in the notification.

We are detailing here the structure, pattern and components of CAT which will give you complete information about forthcoming CAT.

- The CAT 2018 will be a computer based test of 3 hours duration. You have to follow the procedure of attempting one section completely and only moving ahead when you are done with that segment.

- Applicants for CAT have grown to more than 2 lakhs during past 3 years and going by the past trends, it is expected that in CAT 2018 also, more than 2 lakh candidates will register and apply.

- It may be noted that even if half of the total questions are attempted correct, they can fetch you a decent percentile. If you are not confident about any answers, don't attempt the questions since there is negative marking. As you might be aware that the percentile goes up to 100, prepare accordingly. What is required is to be consistent and work smartly and honestly towards your desired goal. Let's dive deeper on the CAT.

Eligibility Criteria for CAT 2018

First you need to know the eligibility, who all can apply for the exam; an applicant must possess

- A Bachelor's Degree with at least 50% marks or equivalent CGPA (45% for SC, ST and PWD/DA category).

- Percentage obtained in Bachelor's degree would be calculated on the basis of practice followed by the concerned university/ institution. In case of grades/CGPA, the conversion would be based on the process defined by the concerned university/ institution.

- In absence of any percentage conversion scheme, candidate's CGPA will be divided by maximum possible CGPA and multiplying the result with 100.

- Candidates appearing for the final year of bachelor's degree/ equivalent qualification are also eligible to apply for CAT.

Quick Facts Related to CAT 2018

- Notification for CAT 2018 is proposed to be released around July.

- The exam will be held in December 2018.

- The application fee is required to be paid online only.

- The duration of the examination will be 180 minutes.

- The total number of questions will be 100, which include 34 in VARC, 34 in QA and 32 in DILR.

- Each question will carry 3 marks and there is negative marking of 1 mark for each wrong answer.

- The three sections don't have 100 300 marks divided equally as the number of questions in each section is different.
- DILR segment is of 96 marks, whereas the VARC and QA are of 102 marks each.
- There won't be any negative marking for non-MCQ or TITA type (type in the answer) questions.
- The ratio of MCQs and non MCQs or TITA in CAT is:

Section	MCQs	Non MCQs or TITAs	Total no. of questions in each section
VARC	24	10	34
DILR	24	8	32
QA	27	7	34
Total no. of questions of each type	**75**	**25**	**100**

- There will be no penalty for questions that are left unanswered.
- An on-screen timer will mark remaining minutes for the test.
- Also, a virtual (on-screen) calculator will be available throughout for the purpose of calculation.

Pattern and Components

Despite the number of changes brought about during last 5 years in CAT exam pattern, the basics of the CAT have not changed. The pattern over the past 7 years since it was computerised in 2009 has gone for perceptible changes. CAT paper pattern prior to 2009 was paper-pen based. But CAT exam pattern since 2015 has remained on the same lines. CAT 2018 exam pattern is also expected to remain as per the last 3 years pattern, although there could be some minor changes in number and type of questions and their sectional composition.

Some details related to CAT Exam Pattern are:

- There will be three sections namely, QA (Quantitative Ability or commonly known as Quant), DILR (Data Interpretation and Logical Reasoning) and VARC (Verbal Ability and Reading Comprehension).
- Applicants will be given exactly 60 minutes for answering questions in every section.

- Unlike past few years, now the liberty to switch to any section you like first or to devote more time to any particular section is not allowed. You will have to attend the sections in line for one hour as allotted then only will be able to access the other section. No switching from one section to other is allowed.

The order of the sections is same for all the applicants-

- VARC (Verbal Ability and Reading Comprehension),

- DILR (Data Interpretation and Logical Reasoning), and then

- QA (Quantitative Ability)

- Some questions in each section (Quantitative Ability, Data Interpretation and Logical Reasoning and Verbal Ability and Reading Comprehension) may not be of MCQ type. A few questions in each section of CAT may be of non-MCQs type questions, where you will be required to type in the answers and hence they are called TITA (Type In The Answer).

- It is advised to start with topics which frequently appear in CAT (arithmetic, numbers, geometry) and understand all the basic concepts, question types and applications for the same.

- IIMs additionally use other factors like previous academic performance of the candidates, relevant work experience and other similar inputs in shortlisting and ranking of candidates at various stages of the admission process. If you are still in graduation, try focusing on your performance in the final exams along with the preparation of the entrance.

Though the processes, academic cut-offs and the weights allocated to the evaluation parameters may vary across IIMs, all this information of the admissions policies is available from the IIMs on their respective websites. This will help you make a checklist of which institutes come in your reach; it will be helpful to decide of which other exams you should fill the form.

READING THE EXAMINER'S MIND

Qualifying a national level entrance exam like CAT is not an easy job, one requires putting in a lot of hard work, you have to be patient and do things that keep you motivated for long. To win the battle you need to know the strategy and the skills required to excel.

One very important feature which is going to help you in a great deal is trying to understand what the examiner is willing to test. Attempting an exam which has negative markings is a bit harder, as doing guess work is not allowed it can put you out of the race. In such a case, only the mind power will be rewarding, analyzing and knowing the perspective of the panel on the other side.

As you are aware that CAT is an aptitude test, and through an aptitude test the examiner wants to assess candidate's learning capabilities, they want to understand the quality of your natural abilities to perform a certain kind of work at a certain level or position. It will provide indicators to predict how well a candidate can contribute in a given role.

The CAT exam structure and exam content is reviewed on yearly basis. It is also ensured by IIMs that CAT questions, their contents, type of questions are not repeated in the next year. This is the basic reason due to which CAT has no specific and defined syllabus. The topics on which questions are asked in one year may go missing in next year and after a few years such questions may come up again.

A Review

CAT exam never leaves an opportunity to baffle its test-takers. Its unpredictable nature each year gives cold feet to the candidates due to the varying CAT exam pattern, number of questions and duration over the years.

With more than 2.5 lakhs test-takers each year, CAT tends to give jitters to its aspirants. However, a rigorous practice and a smart preparation along with knowing the most suitable plan of action can help you land in your dream college.

Sharing about why every year CAT is reviewed and changed, Prof Bandyopadhyay was very clear on the objective of doing so and said "One of our concerns is the score in Quant dominates the percentile rank in CAT. As a consequence it brings in a lack of balance to the selection process towards a particular set of candidates from a particular background.

This year we intend to address it by making some changes in the test content and also by rationalizing weights assigned to different components of the test. This we hope will create a level-playing field for all candidates, no matter what educational background they come from, and will remove skewness to a large extent that we referred to above."

Responding to the query in regard to changes in CAT exam pattern and content, Professor Tathagata Bandyopadhyay CAT Exam Convener, Admission chair and faculty at IIM-Ahmedabad shared "Every year we review CAT and make certain changes- both operational and content."

Accordingly, each year CAT exam would be different in one or other way from the earlier one. So the CAT 2018 aspirants should be prepared again to face more changes in the CAT 2018 exam pattern – both in structure and contents. IIMs are now targeting for increase of non-engineers and women students in their class rooms and with this objective before them, the CAT exam is changing every year.

According to the CAT preparation experts at a coaching institute, "The CAT examiners did not spring any major surprises in the CAT exam of 2017. In terms of pattern, structure and difficulty level, the exam was very similar to the exam last year."

"Unlike the common beliefs, the CAT examiners seemed to focus on a candidate's aptitude rather than testing student's ability to handle a disruptive pattern."

CAT 2017 is no exception to the perceptible changes that have taken place in CAT conducted by IIMs in last 7 years. The CAT exam structure and exam content is reviewed on yearly basis to ensure that CAT caters to the need of IIMs like diversity improvement in their class rooms.

CAT 2018

Knowing what all is expected in the coming year, will increase your chances of selection. Though nothing can be interpreted as sure shot but still we can make out a rough draft or idea of what can be expected. The only way out is read more and practise more to avoid disappointment of having missed something relevant and crucial from examiner's point of view.

"The more that you read, the more things you will know. The more that you learn, the more places you'll go."
Dr. Seuss

As per the trends of past years, here is what Common Admission Test 2018 will have in store for you:

- Sectional time-limit was withdrawn in the year 2014 and then reintroduced in 2015. For CAT 2018, candidates will be allotted exactly 60 minutes to attempt each section. They do not have the option of switching sections. Only after completing one section, you go to the other, after an hour.

- More emphasis is likely on the Quantitative Aptitude section, making it easier for candidates to attempt. This is in order to improve the diversity in classrooms, giving a fair chance to all.

- DILR (Data interpretation and Logical Reasoning) can give you a tough time. It can be tricky, time-consuming, so as to check your intelligence and decision-making skills.

- With an influx of more number of CAT test-takers, the testing window is expected to run for 2 days.

- In the year 2016, CAT was conducted in 136 cities. This year, there will be 140 CAT 2018 exam cities across the nation.

Trend of Past Years' Papers

The exam structure and content of CAT is reviewed on yearly basis. They also ensure that CAT questions, their contents, type of questions are not repeated in the next year. That is why the CAT has no specific and defined syllabus. The topics on which questions are asked in one year may go missing in next year and after a few years such questions may come up again.

Hence, CAT exam would be different each year in one or other way from the earlier one. Therefore, the CAT 2018 aspirants should be prepared again to face more changes in the CAT 2018 exam pattern – both in structure and contents. IIMs are now targeting for increase of non-engineers and women students in their class rooms and with this objective before them, the CAT exam is changed every year.

Prior to switching to the computerised format, Common Admission Test (CAT) used to have a very large number of questions, shortest testing window, short time limit but after getting computerised, CAT has not restricted itself either to continue with the same pattern structure or content apart from the testing window and test duration, number of sections and questions.

Number of total questions which were 240 in 1990 to be solved in 120 minutes was reduced to 75 questions in 2007. This number was increased to 90 questions in 2008. Since 2009 to 2013 total questions remained 60 but became more difficult to attempt. Number of questions, although, in comparison to 2008 in CAT, was reduced but the ratio of the same was increased.

The 1st and 2nd computerised CAT exams i.e. CAT 2009 and 2010 had 3 sections on Quant, DILR and VARC with total 60 questions equally divided with 20 questions for each section.

Apart from other type of questions, Grammar and vocabulary based questions in Verbal Ability and Reading comprehension (VARC) section played a major role in scoring high in this section. VARC, after 2010 had to bear the brunt of the most of the changes in CAT exam pattern.

In the partnership of testing agency Prometric, CAT was conducted in a long testing window of 20 – 22 days with 2 sessions on each day making it a long testing window exam with 40 to 44 sessions. Candidates were allowed to choose their preferred date, time slot and test centre.

In 2011, number of sections in the, CAT exam reduced from three to two with same number of 60 questions. Earlier there used to be one section of Quant, one section of Verbal Ability and one section of Data interpretation & Logical reasoning. In 2011 Data Interpretation and Logical Reasoning sections were clubbed to Quantitative and Verbal Ability sections respectively. Now each of the 2 sections had 30 questions making it a total of 60 questions to be solved in 140 minutes.

CAT aspirants were a little relaxed since they had to individually qualify in two sections instead of three. Another benefit they got was that they could compensate the tricky DI or LR questions by attempting more Quant or Verbal questions or vice-versa depending upon their skills. Those who had strong Quant or DI could get through the QADI section. Similarly an aspirant with strong Verbal or LR could get the same benefit.

However, this relaxation was there at the cost of difficulty level. The difficulty level had increased and more accuracy was desired.

Again the testing window for CAT exam remained long enough with 20 days 40 sessions. The choice of preferred date, time slot and test centre remained available for the test takers.

Here, we have made a comprehensive study of the past seven years CAT papers i.e. from 2010 to 2017.

2017

CAT 2017 in both the slots was an extremely student-friendly test!

The overall structure of CAT 2017 was exactly that of CAT 2016. Few salient features are:

- No new question types were seen in any of the sections.
- The test started with the Verbal Section, which had 34 questions - 24 RC and 10 VA.
- The second section was the DI-LR with 32 questions distributed equally between the two areas.
- The third section was the Quantitative Ability section which also had 34 questions. Each section was timed for 60 minutes. One could not go back and forth between sections.
- The marking scheme was also similar to last year with +3 for every correct & -1 for incorrect answers. There was no negative marking for TITA questions. However since the ratio remains the same we do not see this as a major cause of concern.

> "This was my first CAT attempt, and I found the exam easy. VA had around 10 questions, out of which 7 were non MCQs and 3 MCQs. RC had 24 questions. The toughest section was DILR and the questions were majorly based on reasoning. Apart from that, overall I would say that I am expecting a decent percentile."
> Rahul Manna

- Let's have a look at the graph to make out the quantity of the two types of questions of the three sections in the year 2017.
- **Section I** – Verbal Ability and Reading Comprehension
- **Section II** – Data Interpretation & Logical Reasoning
- **Section III** – Quantitative Ability

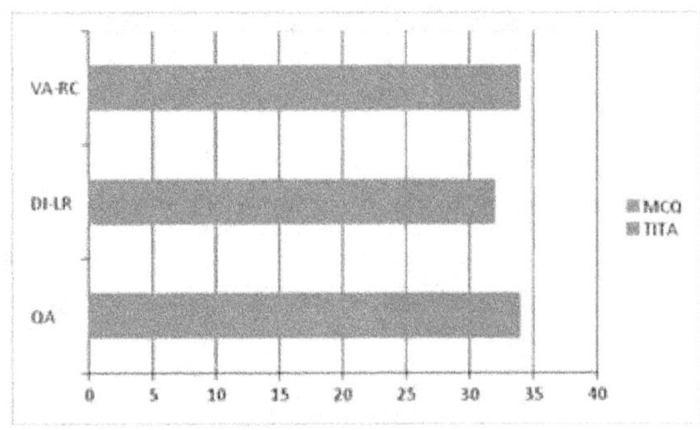

Here is the break-up of questions section-wise:

Section No.	Section Name	Total Number of Questions	Number of Multiple Choice Questions	Number of TITA Questions
I	Verbal Ability & Reading Comprehension	34	27	07
II	Data Interpretation & Logical Reasoning	32	24	08
III	Quantitative Ability	34	23	11
	Total	**100**	**74**	**26**

The test was conducted in two slots. Let's compare the difference between the two slots:

1st slot

- The first slot of CAT 2017 has been reported to be more or less similar to last year with a tougher DI section but an easier QA and VA-RC section.

- An overall attempt of 65+ questions with an accuracy of 80 to 85 percent should be classified as a good performance in this test.

2nd Slot

- Slot 2 offered a comparatively easier DI LR section unlike the slot 1. VA-RC and QA sections were on similar lines (easy) in Slot 2 as in CAT-2016 as well as in Slot-1 of CAT-2017.

- An overall attempt of about 68 to 70 questions with an accuracy of 80 to 85 percent should be classified as a good performance in this test.

Overall Analysis

- According to the analysis of CAT 2017, the overall difficulty level was moderate. Quantitative Ability (QA) was the easiest section and Data Interpretation & Logical Reasoning (DILR) was the toughest section. Verbal and Reading Comprehension (VARC) was of moderate difficulty level.

- CAT 2017 Slot 1 exam paper was on easier side and similar to the previous year's CAT.

- Non-Engineers to benefit from lower difficulty in Quant section
- It was expected that the overall Cut off levels will go up from the previous year.
- Overall, CAT 2017 was slightly easier than CAT 2016.
- Level of difficulty same as last year.
    - ✓ DI-LR: more difficult. 99%ile at 36-37 marks.
    - ✓ Quant was similar to CAT 2015. 99%ile at 62-65 Marks.
    - ✓ Verbal 99% at score of 65+.
    - ✓ Overall 99%ile at 153-155 marks."

Feedback of CAT 2017 by the aspirants

- "I appeared for CAT last year too. The difficulty level of the exam was similar to last year's. There was no change in the exam pattern. English passages were readable, but the options were tricky. The DI-LR was tough. Maths was doable with 9-10 difficult questions. There were no technical glitches."   Gaurav Gupta

- This was Ruchika's second attempt at CAT. While all the candidates found LR-DI on the tougher side, she felt that the section was doable.
- The overall difficulty level of the paper was moderate.
- QA was easy, and Quant was easy to moderate.
- LR-DI was subjective and toughest amongst all the sections, but at the same time the sets were doable, and by making the right choice of questions, one could easily clear off the cut-off.
- The pattern of the exam was more or less on the same alignment as last year's. The actual paper was easier than the mocks.
- No technical glitches were reported during the exam
                                                            Ruchika Bhartiya

2016

CAT 2016 did not throw up any surprises with respect to the paper format. The level of difficulty of the paper changed that year in comparison to the previous year. While VARC continued to be easy, DILR was deceptive with easy looking sets that had difficult questions. Quant threw the biggest curve ball in terms of Level of difficulty and topic distribution.

On first impressions, overall raw score of 155-160 should fetch a student a 99%ile, that year. The overall structure of the CAT paper was as follows:

Section	No. of Questions	No. of non-MCQ questions	Difficulty Level	Good Attempts
Verbal Ability and Reading comprehension	34	10	Easy	27-28
Data Interpretation and Logical Reasoning	32	8	Moderate - Difficult	14-16
Quantitative Ability	34	7	Moderate - Difficult	22-25
Total	**100**	**25**		**68-72**

Verbal Ability and Reading Comprehension Analysis

This section seemed like a repeat of last year's paper. The RCs were from familiar area like Economics and Environmental Studies. The questions in this section were of easy to moderate difficulty level. The trick was to aim for high accuracy by correctly identifying the factual questions in the RC section. However, one must have practised adequately in order to tackle this lengthy session. There were many logical structure questions. The options were extremely tricky. RC's were majorly factual, not being inordinately lengthy or abstract in nature. Only one passage was difficult to read. The others were easy and two passages were also very interesting.

The questions in Verbal ability were dominated by Verbal Logic and did not carry any negative marking, though they needed prior practice to aim for a high percentile. The parajumble section was tough. Even the odd one out questions had close options. Subjective parajumbles should have been attempted without wasting a lot of time. The summary questions were easy.

Surprises: Contrary to popular speculation, the section was a replica of the last year's paper.

With a moderate level of paper many students ended up attempting a lot of questions from RC passages and all questions from Verbal Logic. An attempt of 25-27 would be considered good in this section. Accuracy level will be an issue. As the non-MCQs didn't have any negative marking, a student could have guessed an additional three questions.

Data Interpretation and Logical Reasoning Analysis

In this section four sets were easy (Questions set [5 questions of 4 questions of 10 marks], Folders, T-shirts, movies) and the one based on set theory was of moderate-difficulty level. A couple of sets had 1 question each which were difficult to crack and students would have been wise to leave those questions. Most of the DI sets were calculation intensive. Logical reasoning questions were easy-moderate level of difficulty. There was no DS question. 4 - 5 sets in this section should be attempted, so to get a 99%ile a score of 46-48 (raw score) should suffice.

Picking sets was the key. In general, students would have picked 5 sets out of the 8 above and thus doable questions would be around 15-17.

Quantitative Ability Analysis

There were 34 questions of QA. There were 7-8 Questions of Non MCQ type and the rest were MCQs. The difficulty level was marginally higher than the CAT 2015. The questions were designed to test the grasp of basic fundamentals. In some of MCQs, options were very helpful to get the answer. There were questions from regular topics like Algebra, Geometry, Modern Math, Arithmetic and Number Systems. The number of questions in Geometry showed a spike over previous years.

Questions in Algebra were focused on Inequalities and Quadratic equations. Arithmetic questions were focused on Commercial Math and TSD. There were a good number of questions from Geometry with one question from Pyramids as well. 22-25 attempts with 90% accuracy should suffice for 99 percentile.

2nd Slot

CAT 2016 Slot 2 did not throw up any surprises in comparison to Slot 1. While VARC continued to be easy, DILR was deceptive with easy looking sets that had difficult questions. Like Slot 1, Quant continued to be tricky. Overall DILR seems to have been slightly more difficult as compared to Slot 1 whereas Quant was slightly easier. On first impressions, an overall raw score of 155-160 should fetch a student a 99%ile, this year. The overall structure of the CAT paper was as follows:

Section	No. of Questions	No. of non-MCQ questions	Difficulty Level	Good Attempts
Verbal Ability and Reading comprehension	34	10	Easy	27-28

Data Interpretation and Logical Reasoning	32	8	Moderate - Difficult	14-16
Quantitative Ability	34	7	Medium	22-25
Total	**100**			**68-72**

Verbal Ability and Reading Comprehension Analysis

This section seemed like a repeat of last year's paper. Only one RC was difficult to read. The questions in this section were of easy to moderate difficulty level. The trick was to aim for high accuracy by correctly identifying the factual questions in the RC section. However, one must have practised adequately in order to tackle this lengthy session. The options of some questions were extremely tricky. Time constraint was the major issue. RC's were majorly factual, not being inordinately lengthy or abstract in nature. There was no tone question and only a couple of inference based questions.

The questions in Verbal ability were dominated by Verbal Logic and did not carry any negative marking, though they needed prior practice to aim for a high percentile. The para jumble odd one questions were very easy. Subjective parajumble questions had a lot of linking words and were time consuming. The summary questions were really easy.

Surprises: Contrary to popular speculation, the section was a replica of the last year's paper.

With a moderate level of paper many students ended up attempting a lot of questions from RC passages and all questions from Verbal Logic. An attempt of 25-28 would be considered good in this section. Accuracy level will be an issue. As the non-MCQs didn't have any negative marking, a student could have guessed an additional three questions.

Data Interpretation and Logical Reasoning Analysis

In this section three sets were easy (Organization, Coding/Decoding, Set Theory) and the one based on restaurant rating was of moderate-difficulty level. A couple of sets had 1 question each which were difficult to crack and students would have been wise to leave those questions. Most of the DI sets were calculation intensive. Logical reasoning questions were easy-moderate level of difficulty. There was no DS question. 3 - 4 sets in this section should be attempted, so to get a 99%ile a score of 43-45 (raw score) should suffice.

Picking sets was the key. In general, students would have picked 4 sets out of the 8 above and thus doable questions would be around 13-15.

Quantitative Ability Analysis

There were 34 questions of QA. There were 7-8 Questions of Non-MCQ type and the rest were MCQs. The difficulty level was marginally easier than first slot. The questions were designed to test the grasp of basic fundamentals. In some of MCQs, options were very helpful to get the answer. There were questions from regular topics like Algebra, Geometry, Modern Math, Arithmetic and Number Systems. The number of questions in Geometry showed a spike over previous years.

Questions in Algebra were focused on Inequalities and Quadratic equations. Arithmetic questions were focused on Commercial Math and TSD. There were a good number of questions from Geometry. 22-25 attempts with 90% accuracy should suffice for 99%ile.

2015

The overall structure of CAT-2015 was very different from that of CAT 2014. The exam consisted of 3 Parts. Part 1 consisted of the VARC section. This section was divided into two sub-sections having 24 and 10 questions respectively comprising 34 questions to be attempted in 60 minutes. Further, Part 2 had the DI and LR sub-sections consisting of 32 questions to be answered in 60 minutes while Part 3 had the Quantitative Ability section comprising 34 questions that had to be answered in 60 minutes. Total time for CAT 2015 was 180 minutes. For the first time CAT introduced the TITA (Type in Answer) question type; these were open-ended questions where test-takers would have to type in the correct answer.

The break-up of the sections of CAT 2015 is as follows:

Section	Section Name	Number of questions	TITA Questions	Total Number of questions
Section-I	Verbal Ability & Reading Comprehension	RC-24	10	34
Section-II	Data Interpretation & Logical Reasoning	24	8	32
Section-III	Quantitative Ability	20	14	34
	Total	**68**	**32**	**100**

Reading Comprehension and Verbal Ability

The CAT Reading Comprehension and Verbal Ability sections have been easy and doable for the past couple of years, and this year was no exception. There were 24 RC questions, and 10 Verbal Ability/Reasoning questions. All the Verbal Ability Questions were TITA questions. There were no Grammar questions in the VA section. The exact question distribution was as follows:

Area/Questions	No. of Qs.	Question Type	Level of Difficulty
Reading Comprehension	24	MCQ	
Passage 1	6	MCQ	Easy
Passage 2	6	MCQ	Easy
Passage 3	6	MCQ	Easy-medium
Passage 4	3	MCQ	Easy
Passage 5	3	MCQ	Easy
Verbal Ability	10	TITA	
Jumbled Paragraphs	4	TITA	1 Medium, 3 Difficult
Paragraph Summary	3	TITA	2 Easy, 1 Medium
Odd Sentence Out of the Paragraph	3	TITA	2 Medium, 1 Easy

Data Interpretation & Logical Reasoning

As per students feedback, the Data Interpretation and Logical Reasoning Sets were very time consuming. In particular, the sets in Logical Reasoning were much more difficult than the Data Interpretation Sets . The calculator was useful in solving a few of the DI questions. A rough break-up of most sets is given below.

Area	Set Description	No of Questions	LOD
Data Interpretation	Line graph & Table Set	4	Medium

Data Interpretation	Reasoning & Calculation based Table Set involving percentage calculation and finding missing values of certain variables	4	Medium
Data Interpretation	Reasoning & Calculation based on principles of work	4	Medium
Data Interpretation	Set based on grid arrangements	4	Medium-Difficult
Logical Reasoning	Numerical Puzzle Set based on visualization of a geometrical figure	4	Medium -Difficult
Logical Reasoning	Numerical Puzzle Set Based on finding missing values of the variables	4	Medium -Difficult
Logical Reasoning	Numerical Puzzle Set based on 5 variables to determine missing values	4	Medium -Difficult
Logical Reasoning	Set Based on Groupings & Arrangements	4	Medium

Quantitative Ability

This section was on the easier side and was dominated by Arithmetic, Algebra and Geometry based questions. There were no questions based on Number Properties. Most of the questions in this section tested elementary concepts. A rough break up of the questions is given below:

Area	Topic	No of Questions	LOD
Arithmetic	Profit & Loss	2	Easy
	TSD	1	Medium
	Ratios	1	Easy
	Mixtures & Weighted Average	2	Medium
	Puzzle	2	Medium
	Work ,Pipes & Cisterns	1	Easy /Medium
	Arithmetic Mean	1	Easy
Algebra	Simple Equation	1	Medium
	Inequalities	1	Easy
	Algebraic Solutions	1	Medium
	Algebraic Functions	1	Easy
	Quadratic / Higher Degree Equations	2	Easy
	Surds & Indices	2	Easy
Modern Math	Sequences & Series	1	Medium
	Progressions	1	Medium
	Permutations & Combinations	2	Medium

	Set theory	1	Easy
	Logarithms	1	Easy
Geometry	Functions & Graphs	1	Easy
	Quadrilaterals	2	Easy
	Triangle	1	Easy
	Circles	1	Easy
	Trigonometry	1	Easy
	3-D	1	Easy/Medium

2014

There were surprises in the structure of CAT last year with a fixed number of questions in LR (16) and DI (16) across each slot. Also the pattern was fixed with reference to the question numbers of LR (35-50) and DI (85-100). The QADI section had 34 QA questions along with 16 DI questions in 4 sets of 4 questions each. In the VALR section, Verbal Logic and Usage contributed to 18 questions while LR and RC contributed to 16 questions each (4 sets of 4 questions each). While the QA and VA questions continued to be very easy, LR and DI were difficult and many students would have had a tough time trying to solve these sets. Verbal Logic and RC proved to be life savers in the second section.

Section	No. of Questions	Optimal Time in minutes	Difficulty Level	Good Attempts
Quantitative Ability and Data Interpretation	50	80	Easy	35+
Verbal Ability and Logical Reasoning	50	90	Easy-Moderate	35+
Total	**100**	**170**	**Easy**	**70+**

Quantitative Ability and Data Interpretation

There were 34 questions of QA and 16 questions of DI in the slot. The difficulty level was low and the questions were designed to test the grasp of fundamentals. There were questions from regular topics like Number System, Algebra, Geometry, Modern Math and Geometry. There were two questions from trigonometry as well. Questions in Data Interpretation area did not involve convoluted calculations; however, they continued to be tricky. As has been the norm this year Logic-based

DI was visible again. All the questions in DI came in sets of

Subject	General	OBC	SC	ST
Reasoning (out of 50)	10-13	6-9	6-9	6-9
English Language (out of 40)	6-9	3-6	3-6	3-6
Quantitative Aptitude (out of 50)	6-9	4-6	4-6	4-6
General Awareness (out of 40)	8-11	6-8	6-8	6-8
Computer Knowledge (out of 20)	7-10	5-7	5-7	5-7
Overall cutoff on total score (Out of 200)	**61-70**	**60-68**	**59-64**	**32-38**

With a very easy QA, fairly good students could have attempted about 28-30 questions in QA and 2 sets of DI for a total of 35+ attempts. However, in an easy paper it is accuracy that is the differentiator and anyone with poor accuracy will lose out.

Verbal Ability and Logical Reasoning

The questions in this section were of low difficulty level. The trick here was to aim for high accuracy by correctly identifying the questions that one was confident of solving correctly. RC's were manageable, not being inordinately lengthy or abstract. At most only one of the four given passages was tough. There was a balanced mix of questions from various areas of Verbal Ability. All the questions in LR came in sets of 4. 2 sets were doable while it was best to leave the rest alone.

Surprises: There were not many questions of vocabulary or fill in the blanks. With a difficult LR and easy RC many students ended up attempting three RC passages and only two LR sets. An attempt of 35+ would be considered good in this section.

Area	Topic	No. of Qs.	Description
Reading Comprehension (16 Questions)	Reading Comprehension	16	4 passages of about 550 words and 4 questions each. All the passages were easy to read and comprehend and the difficulty level of the questions varied from easy to moderate. Only one question in one of the passages was a further application question that could have troubled the students.

English Usage (18 Questions)	Sentence Correction	3	Spot the correct sentence, out of five sentences/ parts of a sentence. Easy to moderate but the options gave away the answer.
	Parajumble	4	5 Sentence type. Very easy. One could have solved at least 2 of these by only spotting the first sentence of the sequence and using the options. The language too was not difficult. Except for one questions, sentences were moderate in length.
	Summary	3	Small paragraph of about 200 words followed by four options. Elimination of options made the task easy.
	Critical Reasoning	4	Small passage of about 200-250 words, followed by an inference question - time consuming but easy
	Grammar	3	Simple words, use of phrasal verbs
	Parajumble (Odd sentence out)	4	Very easy sentences to read, the theme was not difficult either, short sentences. Correct answer was easy to spot owing to very obvious pointers - use of pronouns, change in context etc.
Logical Reasoning (16 Questions)	Maxima Minima concept	4	2 LR sets were not very time consuming and doable. 1 set was difficult and time-consuming but doable. The last set was very difficult and left best alone. Students were tested on the concept of maxima minima.
	Arrangement	4	
	Circular arrangement	4	
	Set theory based	4	

2013

Overview of Different Sections

Sr. No.	Sections	No. of Questions	Time Allotted	Difficulty Level
1	Verbal Ability & Logical Reasoning	30	70 Minutes	Moderate
2	Quantitative Ability and Data Interpretation	30	70 Minutes	Moderate to Tough

Sectional Analysis

Verbal Ability & Logical Reasoning

Sr. No.	Area Tested	Description	No. of Questions	Difficulty Level / remarks
1.	Reading Comprehension	3 passages	10 (4+3+3)	Moderate
2.	Verbal Ability	Sentence Correction, Fill in the Blanks, Parajumble, Para Completion, Word Usage	11-14	Moderate
3.	Logical Reasoning	Data Arrangement, Seating Arrangement, Logic based	6-9	Moderate
Over all			30	Moderate

Evaluation: The level of the questions was moderate. Reading comprehension passages were manageable. Only 1 out of the 3 passages was tough. Questions on verbal ability covered entirely every topic of English usage. Logical reasoning witnessed 3 sets with 3 questions each.

Quantitative Ability & DI

Sr. No.	Area Tested	Description	No. of Question	Difficulty Level / remarks
1.	DI: Data Interpretation	Combination of Graphs, Pie Chart, Table	6-10	Moderate-Difficult
2.	Quantitative Ability	Number System, Arithmetic, Algebra, Geometry, Mensuration	20-24	Moderate
Over all			30	Moderate-Difficult

Evaluation: The questions on quantitative ability were based on various topics and involved tough calculations. Overall, this section was difficult and speed, clarity of the fundamentals of DI and immaculate time-management were the key to success in this area.

2012

Overview of Different Sections

Sr. No.	Sections	No. of Questions	Time Allotted	Difficulty Level
1	Verbal Ability & Logical Reasoning	30	70 Minutes	Moderate
2	Quantitative Ability and Data Interpretation	30	70 Minutes	Moderate to Tough

Sectional Analysis

Verbal Ability & Logical Reasoning

Sr. No.	Area Tested	Description	No. of Questions	Difficulty Level / remarks
1.	Reading Comprehension	3 passages	10 (4+3+3)	Moderate

Sr. No.	Area Tested	Description	No. of Question	Difficulty Level / remarks
2.	Verbal Ability	Sentence Correction, Fill in the Blanks, Parajumble, Para Completion, Word Usage	11	Moderate
3.	Logical Reasoning	Data Arrangement, Seating Arrangement, Logic based	9	Moderate
Overall			30	Moderate

Evaluation: The level of the questions was moderate. Reading comprehension passages were manageable. Only 1 out of the 3 passages was tough. Questions on verbal ability covered entirely every topic of English usage. Logical reasoning witnessed 3 sets with 3 questions each.

Quantitative Ability & DI

Sr. No.	Area Tested	Description	No. of Question	Difficulty Level / remarks
1.	DI: Data Interpretation	Combination of Graphs, Pie Chart, Table	9	Moderate-Difficult
2.	Quantitative Ability	Number System, Arithmetic, Algebra, Geometry, Mensuration	21	Moderate
Overall			30	Moderate-Difficult

Evaluation: The questions on quantitative ability were based on various topics and involved tough calculations. Overall, this section was difficult and speed, clarity of the

2011

Overview of Different Sections

Sr. No.	Sections	No. of Questions	Time Allotted	Difficulty Level
1	Verbal Ability & Logical Reasoning	30	70 Minutes	Moderate
2	Quantitative Ability and Data Interpretation	30	70 Minutes	Moderate

Sectional Analysis

Verbal Ability & Logical Reasoning

Evaluation: The level of the questions was moderate. Verbal Ability covered entirely every topic of English usage. Good knowledge of grammar and vocabulary would have helped students to achieve good score in this section. Reading comprehension passages were manageable if a student has done lot of reading. Generally passages were based on science, politics, philosophy and cultural topics. Logical reasoning witnessed sets that were easily manageable as they were more or less logic based only.

Quantitative Ability & DI

Evaluation: The questions on quantitative ability were based on various topics and involved simple calculations. It generally tested ones logic and did not demand a direct application of formula. Speed, clarity of the fundamentals of DI and immaculate time-management were the key to success in this area. DI sets was easier than the previous year. Overall difficulty level of this section was moderate.

2010

Overview of Different Sections

Sr. No.	Sections	No. of Questions	Difficulty Level
1	Verbal Ability	20	Easy-Moderate
2	Quantitative Ability	20	Moderate
3	Data Interpretation/ Logical Reasoning	20	Moderate-Difficult

Sectional Analysis

Verbal Ability

Evaluation: The level of the questions was moderate. Verbal Ability covered entirely every topic of English usage such as Para completion, Parajumble, Fill in the blanks, Correct usage of words, etc. Good knowledge of grammar and vocabulary would have helped students to achieve good score in this section. Also there were 3 Reading comprehension passages with 3 questions each that were manageable if a student has done lot of reading.

Quantitative Ability

Evaluation: The questions on quantitative ability were based on various topics and involved simple calculations. The difficulty level of this section was moderate. There were 3-4 questions on geometry, 7-8 on arithmetic and number theory and few on algebra. Also there were a mix of higher math and modern math even a small application of logarithms. Questions also tested fundamental understanding like ratios and percentages, volumes of solids, permutation & combination, etc.

Section III: Data Interpretation/Logical Reasoning

Evaluation: This section was a bit lengthy as it involved tedious calculations. DI section mainly involved sets on Pie charts, Bar graphs, Tables, Line graphs, 3D charts, Maxima & minima, etc. Logical reasoning questions were more or less logical based and required less or no calculations. LR questions were based on set of conditions, Logical arguments, puzzles and Venn diagrams.

AN OUTLINE OF THE SECTIONS

Verbal Ability and Reading Comprehension

Verbal ability is the ability to comprehend and reason using concepts expressed through words. It is a vital component of management entrance exams like CAT.

The questions in this section broadly test abilities in word power, analogies, sentence correction and verbal reasoning. This means that it demands a good vocabulary and a strong command of English.

> Verbal Ability test questions are designed to measure your ability to quickly process verbal information and to make accurate decisions.

The VARC section of CAT is the section to be attempted first in the exam. It needs to be handled very carefully and calmly, so that you remain in good mood for the rest of the test. Similar to other sections, it is also a one hour test. You should be prepared to face questions of both the direct and the inferential type questions. The second part i.e. the Reading Comprehension covers the major part of VARC.

To make the syllabus clearer to you, we have compiled f questions from each topic asked in previous years CAT and have also made an outline of the format of the questions that may come in the test. Please note that this exhaustive analysis is just a prediction by our experts, such varieties of questions may or may not come in the main test.

Part-1: Verbal Ability

- Share of Verbal Ability (VA) questions in VARC section of CAT: **30%**
- Total VA based questions: 10
- Topics on which VA questions are based
    - ✓ Essence of short paragraph/Para summary - (3-4 questions);
    - ✓ Jumbled Paragraphs (3-4 questions)
    - ✓ Jumbled paragraphs with out of context sentence (2-3)
- *Type of Questions:* There will be both the MCQs and the TITA questions.
- *Marking scheme:* For MCQs, there is three marks for every correct choice and 1 marks deduction for each wrong answer. For Non-MCQs, the marks allotted are three but there is no negative marking involved in this type of questions.
- ✓ The out of context sentence has to be picked out.
- Format of the questions which can be asked: Until three years ago, following type of questions also formed the part of CAT syllabus. Since these topics are still the part of syllabus for CAT, it is possible you may see these questions again in CAT 2018:
    - ✓ English Usage
    - ✓ Sentence Correction
    - Fill in the blanks
    - ✓ Paragraph Completion
    - ✓ Paragraph Jumble
    - ✓ Vocabulary-Usage in context
    - ✓ Synonyms/Antonyms/Homophones/Homograms/Homo-graphs (Vocabulary Based)

Part-2: Reading Comprehension

Our analysis comprehended that the share of Reading Comprehension in VARC section of CAT is **70%**

- Format of questions:
    - ✓ Essence of paragraph questions are based on around 5-6 sentences;
    - ✓ Questions on Jumbled paragraphs and out of context

jumbled paragraphs have 4 -5 jumbled sentences which are to be placed in a coherent manner. A total of 5 Reading Comprehension passages are usually asked in the test, same can be expected in 2018 test. Usually the RC passages are based on:

✓ Current Affairs;
✓ Social and Economic issues;
✓ Literature;
✓ Science & Culture;
✓ Abstract topics;
✓ History; and
✓ Fiction

Our analysis comprehended that the share of Reading Comprehension in VARC section of CAT is **70%**

An overview of the VARC questions in CAT 2017

Sectional difficulty was moderate
Total Questions: 34

- 24 questions on Reading comprehension in 5 passages MCQ type
- 10 questions in Verbal Ability out of which 7 were non-MCQ type

Analysis of the questions

- There were 3 MCQs and 7 Non-MCQs in the section

Topics and Question type

Topic	Number of Questions	Question Types	Difficulty Level
Out of the context	3	TITA	Easy to Moderate
Paragraph Jumbles	4	TITA	Easy to Moderate
Paragraph Summary	3	MCQs	Easy to Moderate

- Jumbled Paragraphs: 4 questions each comprising 5 Jumbled Sentences
- Odd Sentence Out: 3 questions with jumbled sentences out of which one sentence in each question has to be picked as 'Odd sentence out'
- Para Summary: 3 questions were on choosing the correct sentence summarizing the short paragraph.
- It is to be noted that each question was from different topic.

If we consider the previous year paper, the questions in Verbal Ability were dominated by Verbal Logic and did not carry any negative marking, though they needed prior practice to aim for a high percentile. The summary questions were easy.

The Para-jumble section was tough. Even the odd one out questions had close options. Subjective Parajumbles should have been attempted without wasting a lot of time. All the four questions were difficult. There were many ambiguous sentences, too.

Hence, students should train themselves to be careful in time management, to face any such situation in the coming year as these types of questions could lead to wastage of time. It is estimated that the four questions should have been attempted in around 6 minutes with two correct answers.

Reading Comprehension (24 Questions)

- Number of RC passages: 5 (2 short, 3 long)
- Format of RC based questions: MCQs with 1/3 negative marking
- Short RC passage followed by 3 questions each
- Long RC passage followed by 6 questions each
- There were total 5 passages - three passages of 450-650 words in length and two passages of 300 words each. The three passages had 6 questions each and the other two had 3 questions each. Only one passage was difficult to read. The options were really close. They were very easy.
- The Reading Comprehensions were from familiar area like Economics and Environmental Studies
- There were many logical structured questions. The options were extremely tricky. RCs were majorly factual, not being inordinately lengthy or abstract in nature.
- RC passages were based on the topics like:
  - ✓ Loss of Jobs due to closing of small shops (stores) but compensated by Malls
  - ✓ North India getting preferred to East India in past few hundred years
  - ✓ How Gutenberg Press brought revolution and changed the world with printing of books, pamphlets, literature and helped the people become free from traditions imposed by clerics
  - ✓ Other topics were also based on:
  - o Modernization,
  - o Geographical Diversification of Maps, etc

These topics are suggested by the experts only on the basis of analysis of past few years and should not be considered as an exhaustive list. As there is no clear cut definition of RC topics in CAT syllabus, RC passage on any topic can come in CAT 2018.

- Division of questions: 6 questions based on each long passage and 3 questions based on each shorter passage
- Length of RC passages: CAT has 3 longer RC passages of around 600-900 words; shorter passages are of around 300-600 words in CAT syllabus as reflected in the last 3 years.
- Format of the questions which can be asked:
  - ✓ Questions based on information in RC passage;
  - ✓ Explanation of the words & phrases as used in the passage;

✓ In context of the passage - True/false statements;
✓ Author's view on various issues raised in the RC passage;
✓ Inference from the passage;
✓ Main idea of RC passage;
✓ Purpose of the RC passage
- Past trends of topics:
  ✓ Education System;
  ✓ Sustainable Economic Development;
  ✓ Anthropology /Excruciating Rituals & Reasons;
  ✓ Government Definition of Poverty
  ✓ Treatment of Household work

With a moderate level of paper many students ended up attempting a lot of questions from RC passages and all questions from Verbal Logic. Overall, the CAT 2017 witnessed a moderate level of difficulty and the VARC sections were manageable and easy in nature.

Vocabulary Based

EXAMPLE: The word given below is used in sentences in four different ways. Choose the option in which the usage of the word is incorrect or inappropriate. (2012)

HIT

(a) In his new book he hits off the American temperament with amazing insight.
(b) What will happen when the story hits the front page?
(c) This course will hit the high spots of ancient history.
(d) Critics hit off at the administration's new energy policy.

Word Usage

EXAMPLE: In each question, there are five sentences. Each sentence has pairs of words/phrases that are italicized and highlighted. From the italicized and highlighted word(s)/phrase(s), select the most appropriate word(s)/phrase (s) to from correct sentences.

(2016)

(i) While evacuating people from the flood ravaged areas *precedence* (A) / *precedent* (B) was given to women and children.
(ii) The best was to reach the summit is by trekking up the hill, *alternately* (A) / *alternatively* (B) you can go on horse back
(iii) His impeccable manners perfectly *complimented* (A) / *complemented* (B) his polished looks and fashionable attire.
(iv) There has been a *noticeable* (A) / *notable* (B) improvement in Tarun's academic performance lately.
(v) You must be *discreet* (A) / *discrete* (B) about your plans

(a) AABAB   (b) ABBBB
(c) BABAA   (d) ABBAA

Sentence Completion

EXAMPLE: There are two gaps in the sentence/paragraph given below. From the pairs of words given, choose the one that fills the gaps most appropriately.

For Septimius Severus stood as a ___________ reminder of what Libya had once been: a Mediterranean region of immense cultural and economic wealth, anything but ___________ from the world beyond the sea. **(2013)**

(a)   constant, analogous
(b)   wistful, isolated
(c)   steady, different
(d)   nostalgic, indistinguishable

Parajumbles

EXAMPLE: The sentences given below, when properly sequenced, form a coherent paragraph. Each sentence is labelled with a letter. Choose the most logical order of sentences from among the given choices.

A. On the whole, we have not arrived at any general consensus over the nature and causes of fascism in our time.

B. Historians, sociologists, social psychologists, and political theorists have been debating this question since Mussolini's seizure of power in 1922.

C. However, with limited success.

D. What is the 'true' nature of fascism?

E. Is it something radically new to political experience, a unique creation of the 20th century; or is it merely old tyranny possessed of new, more efficient techniques for gaining and holding power? **(2012)**

(a)   ABCDE   (b)   DEABC
(c)   DEBCA   (d)   ADEBC

Sentence Correction

EXAMPLE: Given below are five sentences that form a paragraph. Identify the sentence(s) or part(s) of sentence(s) that is/are correct in terms of grammar and usage (including spelling, punctuation and logical consistency). Then, choose the most appropriate option.

A. A tarot is one of the most wonderful of human inventions.

B. Despite all the outcry of philosophers, this pack of pictures,

C. in whom destiny is reflected as in a mirror with multiple facets,

D. remains so vital and exercises so irresistible an attraction on

E. imaginative minds that it is hardly possible that it could ever be abolished. **(2012)**

(a)   A only   (b)   A and B
(c)   D and E   (d)   D only

EXAMPLE: In the question, four different ways of presenting an idea are given. Choose the one that conforms most closely to Standard English usage **(2016)**

(i) The inflexibility of the laws, which prevent them from being adapted for emergencies, may in certain cases render them Pernicious and thereby cause the ruin of the state in a time of crisis.

(ii) The inflexibility of the laws, which prevents them from being adapted for emergencies may in certain cases render them Pernicious, thereby cause the ruin of the state in a time of crisis.

(iii) The inflexibility of the laws, which prevents them from being adapted for emergencies may in certain cases render them Pernicious, and thereby cause the ruin of the state in a time of crisis.

(iv) The inflexibility of the laws, which prevents them from being adapted for emergencies may in certain cases render them Pernicious and thereby causing the ruin of the state in a time of crisis.

(a) (i)   (b) (ii)
(c) (iii)   (d) (iv)

Paragraph Completion

EXAMPLE: Each of the following questions has a paragraph from which the last sentence has been deleted. From the given options, choose the one that completes the paragraph in the most appropriate way. **(2016)**

Jawaharlal Nehru seemed an unlikely candidate to lead India towards its vision. Under the cotton Khadi he wore in deference to the dictates of Congress, he remained the quintessential English gentleman. In a land of mysteries, he was a cool rationalist. The mind that had exulted in the discovery of science at Cambridge never ceased to be appalled by his fellow Indians who refused to stir from their homes on days proclaimed inauspicious by their favourite astrologers. He was a publicly declared agnostic in the most intensely spiritual area in the world, and he never ceased to proclaim the horror the word 'religion' inspired in him. Nehru despised India's priests, her sadhus, her chanting monks and pious 'skerkhs'.

(a) And yet, the India of those sadhus and the superstition haunted masses had accepted Nehru.

(b) They had only served, he felt, to impede her progress.

(c) The Mahatma had made it clear that it was on his shoulders that he wished his mantle to fall.

(d) Nehru's heart told him to follow the Mahatma and his heart, he would later admit, had beed right.

Reading Comprehension

EXAMPLE: The passage below is accompanied by a set of questions. Choose the best answer to each question. (2017)

I used a smartphone GPS to find my way through the cobblestoned maze of Geneva's Old Town, in search of a handmade machine that changed the world more than any other invention. Near a 13th–Century cathedral in this Swiss city on the shores of a lovely lake, I found what I was looking for: a Gutenberg printing press. "This was the Internet of its day – at least as influential as the iphone," said Gabriel de Montmollin, the director of the Museum of the Reformation, toying with the replica of Johann Gutenberg's great invention.

[Before the invention of the printing press] it used to take four monks…up to a year to produce a single book. With the advance in movable type in 15th-Century Europe, one press could crank out 3,000 pages a day. Before long, average people could travel to places that used to be unknown to them – with maps! Medical information passed more freely and quickly, diminishing the sway of quacks… The printing press offered the prospect that tyrants would never be able to kill a book or suppress an idea. Gutenberg's brainchild broke the monopoly that clerics had on scripture. And later, stirred by pamphlets from a version of that same press, the American colonies rose up against a king and gave birth to a nation.

So, a question in the summer of this 10th anniversary of the iPhone: has the device that is perhaps the most revolutionary of all time given us a single magnificent idea? Nearly every advancement of the written word through new technology has also advanced humankind. Sure, you can say the iPhone changed everything. By putting the world's recorded knowledge in the palm of a hand, it revolutionized work, dining, travel and socializing. It made us more narcissistic – here's more of me doing cool stuff ! – and it unleashed an army of awful trolls. We no longer have the patience to sit through a baseball game without that reach to the pocket. And one more casualty of Apple selling more than a billion phones in a decade's time: daydreaming has become a lost art.

For all of that, I'm Still waiting to see if the Iphone can do what the printing press did for religion and democracy… the Geneva museum makes a strong case that the printing press opened more minds than anything else…. It's hard to imagine the French or American revolutions without those enlightened voices in pirnt….

Not long after Steve Jobs introduced his iPhone, he said the bound book was probably headed for history's attic. Not so fast. After a period of rapid growth in e-books, something closer to the medium for Chaucer's volumes has made a great comeback.

The hope of the iPhone, and the Internet in general, was that it would free people in closed societies. But the failure of the Arab Spring, and the continued suppression of ideas in North Korea, China and Iran, has not borne that out…. The iPhone is still young. It has certainly been

"One of the most important, world–changing and successful products in history," as Apple C.E.O. Tim Cook said, But I'm not sure if the world changed for the better with the iPhone– as it did with the printing press–or merely changed.

1. The printing press has been likened to the Internet for which one of the following reasons?
    (a) It enabled rapid access to new information and the sharing of new ideas.
    (b) It represented new and revolutionary technology compared to the past.
    (c) It encouraged reading among people by giving them access to thousands of books.
    (d) It gave people access to pamphlets and literature in several languages.

2. According to the passage, the invention of the printing press did all of the following EXCEPT
    (a) Promoted the spread of enlightened political views across countries.
    (b) Gave people direct access to authentic medical information and religious texts.
    (c) Shortened the time taken to produce books and pamphlets.
    (d) Enabled people to perform various tasks simultaneously.

3. Steve Jobs predicted which one of the following with the introduction of the iPhone?
    (a) People would switch from reading on the Internet to reading on their iPhones.
    (b) People would lose interest in historical and traditional classics.
    (c) Reading printed books would become a thing of the past.
    (d) The production of e-books would eventually fall.

Paragraph Summary

EXAMPLE: The passage given above is followed by four summaries. Choose the option that best captures the author's position.

(2017)

For each of the past three years, temperatures have hit peaks not seen since the birth of meteorology, and probably not for more than 110,000 years. The amount of carbon dioxide in the air is at its highest level in 4 million years. This does not cause storms like Harvey- there have always been storms and hurricanes along the Gulf of Mexico- but it makes them wetter and more powerful. As the seas warm, they evaporate more easily and provide energy to storm fronts. As the air above them warms, it holds more water vapour. For every half a degree Celsius in warming, there is about a 3% increases in atmospheric moisture content. Scientists call this the Clausius-Clapeyron equation. This means the skies fill more quickly and have more to dump. The storm surge was greater because sea levels have risen 20 cm as a result of more than 100 years of humanstorm surge was greater because sea levels have risen 20 cm as a result of more than 100 years of human–related global warming which has melted glaciers and thermally expanded the volume of seawater.

(a) The storm Harvey is one of the regular, annual ones from the Gulf of Mexico; global warming and Harvey are unrelated phenomena.

(b) Global warming does not breed storms but makes them more destructive,; the Clausius-Clapeyron equation, though it predicts potential increase in atmospheric moisture content, cannot predict the scale of damage storms might wreck.

(c) Global warming melts glaciers, resulting in seawater volume expansion; this enables more water vapour to fill the air above faster. Thus, modern storms contain more destructive energy.

(d) It is naive to think that rising sea levels and the force of tropical storms are unrelated; Harvey was destructive as global warming has armed it with more moisture content, but this may not be true of all storms.

Odd one Out

EXAMPLE: Five sentences related to a topic are given below. Four of them can be put together to form a meaningful and coherent short paragraph. Identify the odd one out. **(2017)**

(a) Neuroscientists have just begun studying exercise's impact within brain cells-on the genes themselves.

(b) Even there, in the roots of our biology, they've found signs of the body's influence on the mind.

(c) It turns out that moving our muscles produces proteins that travel through the bloodstream and into the brain, where they play pivotal roles in the mechanisms of our highest thought processes.

(d) In today's technology-driven, plasma-screened-in world, it's easy to forget that we are born movers– animals, in fact– because we've engineered movement right out of our lives.

(e) It's only in the past few years that neuroscientists have begun to describe these factors and how they work, and each new discovery adds awe-inspiring depth to the picture.

Coherent Paragraph

EXAMPLE: The five sentences (labelled A, B, C, D, E) given in this question, when properly sequenced, form a coherent paragraph. Each sentence is labelled with a number. Decide on the proper order for the sentences and key in this sequence of five numbers as your answer. **(2017)**

(A) This visual turn in social media has merely accentuated this announcing instinct of ours, enabling us with easy-to-create, easy-to-share, easy-to-store and easy-to-consume platforms, gadgets and apps.

(B) There is absolutely nothing new about us framing the vision of who we are or what we want, visually or otherwise, in our Facebook page, for example.

(C) Turning the pages of most family albums, which belong to a period well before the digital dissemination of self-created and self-curated moments and images, would reconfirm the basic instinct of documenting our presence in a particular space, on a significant occasion, with others who matter.

(D) We are empowered to book our faces and act as celebrities within the confinement of our respective friend lists, and communicate our activities, companionship and locations with minimal clicks and touches.

(E) What is unprecedented is not the desire to put out newsfeeds related to the self, but the ease with which this broadcast operation can now be executed, often provoking (un) anticipated responses from beyond one's immediate location.

FIJ's

EXAMPLE: The following question has a set of five sequentially ordered statements. Each statement can be classified as one of the following.

Facts, which deal with pieces of information that one has heard, seen or read, and which are open to discovery or verification (the answer option indicates such a statement with an 'F').

Inferences, which are conclusions drawn about the unknown, on the basis of the known (the answer option indicates such a statement with an 'I').

Judgments, which are opinions that imply approval or disapproval of persons, objects, situations and occurrences in the past, the present or the future (the answer option indicates such a statement with a 'J').

Select the answer option that best describes the set of statements.

(2016)

(A) The renewed corporate interest in power is welcome, given the huge investment backlog in the vexed sector and the routine revenue leakages.

(B) Reportedly, industrial houses like Reliance Industries and the Aditya Birla Group are keen to foray into power equipment manufacture.

(C) In tandem, we need proactive policy to wipe out continuing losses of state power utilities, and regular disclosure of SEB finances.

(D) Of late, the tendency has been to clamp up on the huge annual losses of power utilizes – the latest Economic Survey like the previous one is mum on losses, subsidies and plain theft of power; instead we have some pious intentions to gather 'baseline data' and use information technology application for accounting and auditing power distribution.

(E) We do need to step up IT for meter reading, billing and collections, of course, but in parallel, what is essential indeed vital, is improved governance in power delivery and follow through.

(a) JFIFJ   (b) IJFJJ

(c) FJJIF   (d) JFJIJ

Data Interpretation and Logical Reasoning

The Data Interpretation and Logical Reasoning (DILR) section was re-originated as a separate section in CAT 4 years back. During this period, the DILR questions were clubbed to Quant and Verbal Ability sections respectively.

The DILR section was re-introduced as a separate 3rd section by IIM Ahmedabad, the then convening IIM in CAT 2015. In 2016 IIM Bangalore and in 2017 IIM Lucknow also followed the pattern. And from the past 3 years there are three sections in CAT namely VARC, DILR and QA.

From a review of the past years' papers of CAT for DILR we found that there are 24 MCQs and 8 Non- MCQs in DILR section of CAT.

Key features of CAT for DILR

CAT Syllabus for DILR section in CAT 2018 is divided in 2 parts – Data Interpretation and Logical Reasoning. The 1st part of CAT 2018 syllabus covers questions based on Data Interpretation (DI) and the 2nd part is based on questions on different topics on Logical Reasoning.

Part-1: Data Interpretation (DI)

In this section it is tested that how candidates can interpret the given data and answer questions based on it.

- Share of DI questions in DILR section of CAT: **50%**
- Total DI questions: 16
- Number of MCQs: 12
- Number of Non MCQs: 4
- Topics on which DI questions are based:
  - ✓ Data Tables,
  - ✓ Data charts,
  - ✓ Bar diagrams,
  - ✓ Pie charts, Graphs,
  - ✓ Data analysis and
  - ✓ comparison among others

- Questions are in the set of 4 questions. Questions on interpretation and analysis of data based on
    - ✓ text,
    - ✓ tables,
    - ✓ graphs (line, area),
    - ✓ charts (column, bar, pie),
    - ✓ Venn diagram

    Data could be given in form of tables, charts or graphs.
- Past trend of topics: Table (Student Pass percentages over 5 years; Comprehension – Marks in Two sections of papers; Films, Launch, Completion, Release and Profits; Table on Consumption of Veg and Non-Veg Protein; Happiness Index: 4 questions based on Table; Kids Learning in Rural Areas: Data table based 4 questions; Flight operation
- It is to be remembered that the topics are only indicative and not exhaustive.

Part-2: Logical Reasoning (LR)

- Share of LR questions in DILR section of CAT: 50%
- Total LR questions expected in 2018 exam: 16
- Number of MCQs: 12
- Number of Non MCQs: 4
- Topics covered in CAT test syllabus 2018 on which LR questions are based:
    - ✓ Clocks,
    - ✓ Calendars,
    - ✓ Binary Logic,
    - ✓ Seating Arrangement,
    - ✓ Blood Relations,
    - ✓ Logical Sequence,
    - ✓ Assumption, Premise and Conclusion,
    - ✓ Linear and matrix arrangement

CAT entrance exam syllabus defines that questions in LR section can be individual or can be in the set of 4 questions.

Past trend of topics in CAT Syllabus: Distribution/Arrangement; Venn Diagrams; Arrangement of files in folders; Students using various Trains and the fares for the same; Seating Arrangement; Direction sense for Cars; Ordering items; Burgers/Fries/ Ice Cream

An analysis of DILR Section of CAT 2017

Total Questions: 32
- All questions in sets of 4 questions each
- 16 Questions on DI
- 16 on LR
- 8 Non MCQs

The sectional difficulty was high thus was considered to be the make or break section for entry into the top B-schools.
The questions were lengthy and calculation intensive.

Analysis of Type and Content of questions

I. Data Interpretation (DI)

Format of questions: 12 MCQs and 4 Non-MCQs
- Number of problems: Each of the 4 Problems was followed by a set of 4 Questions
- Topics of DI problems:
  - ✓ Happiness Index: 4 questions based on Table
  - ✓ Kids Learning in Rural Areas: Data table based 4 questions.
  - ✓ Flight operation
  - ✓ 1 question set had inherent data on which 4 questions each was based

II. Logical Reasoning (LR)

Format of questions: 12 MCQs and 4 Non-MCQs
- Number of problems: 4
- Each problem was followed by a set of 4 questions
- Topics of LR problems: Question sets were based on:
  - ✓ Seating Arrangement
  - ✓ Direction sense for Cars
  - ✓ Ordering items- Burgers/Fries/ Ice Cream

Examples of Questions from Past Papers
Table Based

EXAMPLE: Answer the questions on the basis of the information given below.

The table given below shows the data related to a few key financial indicators for fourteen European countries in the FY 2011-12.

Cyprus	2.2	4.6	61.1	5.7
Denmark	2.2	3	46.6	4.6
Estonia	2.4	5.7	7.7	1.7
Finland	1.1	3.1	45.4	3.4
France	1.5	3.3	83.5	8
Germany	1.9	2.9	74.8	4.5
Italy	1.4	4.6	118	5.1
Latvia	1.2	7.5	48	8.6
Malta	1.7	4.4	72	3.8
Netherlands	1.1	3.1	64.6	5.6
Poland	2.4	5.9	53.9	7.3
Portugal	1.1	6.5	83.2	7.3

(2013)

1. If the Fiscal-deficit of France was x Euros, which was 50% more than that of Belgium, then what was the Debt (in Euros) of Belgium in FY 2011-12?
    (a)   13x   (b)   7x
    (c)   14x   (d)   6.5x

2. The countries with the Long-term interest rate less than 4% per annum, Debt to GDP ratio less than 60% and Fiscal-deficit not more than 4.6% were given a AAA rating. The number of countries rated AAA among the fourteen in FY 2011-12 was
    (a)   0   (b)   1
    (c)   2   (d)   None of these

3. If the GDP (in Euros) of Finland was 50% more than that of Italy, then by what percent was the Fiscaldeficit (in Euros) of Italy more/less than that of Finland in FY 2011-12?
    (a)   0   (b)   1.5
    (c)   0.5   (d)   Cannot be determined

Line Graph

EXAMPLE: These questions are based on the figure given below.

Mid-year Prices of Essential Commodities

1. During 1996-2002, the number of commodities that exhibited a net overall increase and a net overall decrease, respectively, were **(2003)**

    (a)   3 and   (b)   2 and 4
    (c)   4 and 2   (d)   5 and 1

2. The number of commodities that experienced a price decline for two or more consecutive years is   **(2003)**

    (a)   2   (b)   3
    (c)   4   (d)   5

3. For which commodities did a price increase immediately follow a price decline only once in this period?   **(2003)**

    (a)   Rice, Edible oil & Dal (b)   Egg and Dal
    (c)   Onion only   (d)   Egg and Onion

Combination of Graphs

EXAMPLE: Answer the questions on the basis of the information given below.

The following pie chart gives the distribution of the total loans disbursed by ADB in 2012 among eleven Asian countries.
Total amount of loans disbursed = Rs. 7200 cr

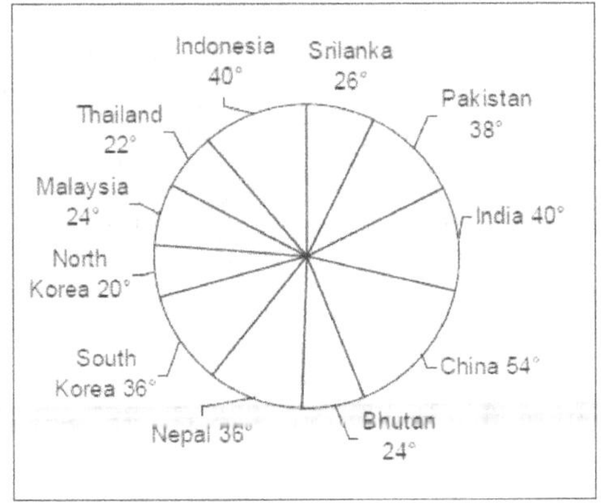

The following line graph gives the percentage contribution of loan from ADB in the total investment made in different sectors in the same year by India and China.

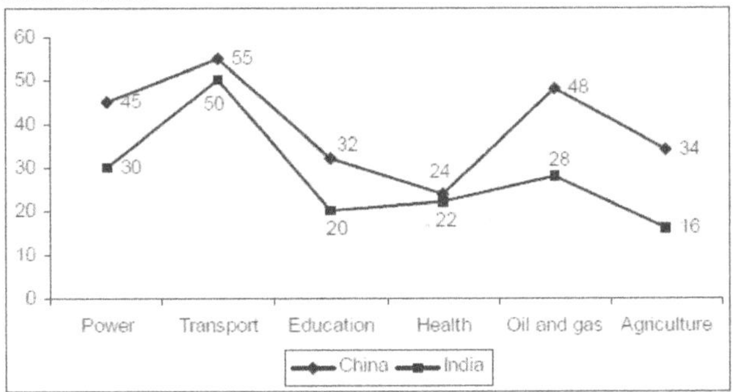

For both China and India, the loan received from ADB was utilized in the given sectors only. **(2015)**

1. If the total investment in Education sector in China was 60% higher than that in India, then what is the ratio of A and B, where

    A : The percentage of loan from ADB invested in Education sector by China

    B : The percentage of loan from ADB invested in Education sector by India

    (a) 256 : 135
    (b) 256 : 189
    (c) 256 : 225
    (d) Cannot be determined

2. The amount of loan invested in Transport sector by China was equal to 60% of the total loan given by ADB to Malaysia. The amount of loan invested in Transport sector by India was equal to 60% of the total loan given by ADB to North Korea. The total investment made in Transport sector by India was approximately what percent of that made by china?

(a) 75.76   (b) 91.67
(c) 80.80   (d) 81.81

3. If the total investments made in Education, Health and Agriculture sectors in India in 2012 was Rs. 150 cr., Rs. 120 cr and Rs. 400 cr. respectively, then the amount of ADB loan invested by India in these three sectors constitute what percentage of the total loan granted to India by ADB?

(a) 15.05%   (b) 18.85%
(c) 12.33%   (d) 16.66%

4. The total loan invested in Power, Transport and Education sectors by India was 500 cr. What was the maximum possible investment (in Rs. crore) in these three sectors made by India? [The loan amount invested in all of these three sectors is a multiple of 30 cr]

(a) 2000   (b) 2100
(c) 2360   (d) 2400

Caselets

EXAMPLE: Read the information given below and answer the questions that follow :

There are three different cable channels namely Ahead, Luck and Bang. In a survey it was found that 85% of viewers respond to Bang, 20 % to Luck, and 30% to Ahead. 20% of viewers respond to exactly two channels and 5% to none.

1. What percentage of the viewers responded to all three ? **(2007)**
(a) 10   (b) 12
(c) 14   (d) None of these

2. Assuming 20% respond to Ahead and Bang and 16% respond to Bang and Luck, what is the percentage of viewers who watch only Luck ? **(2007)**
(a) 20   (b) 10
(c) 16   (d) None of these

Arrangements

EXAMPLE: Answer the questions on the basis of the information given below.

H1, H2, H3 and H4 are four horses that participated in each of the four different races – Race-I, Race-II, Race-III and Race-IV – during an annual horse-racing event in Goa. Each horse is owned by a different owner among Rahul, Dharma, Dablu and Ritesh, in no particular order. None of the four horses finished at the same position in more than two of the four races. In each race the four horses were given ranks 1, 2, 3 and 4 according to the positions at which they finished in the race. It is also known that: **(2009)**

(i)   In Race-I, H2 finished third and Ritesh's horse finished first. Interestingly, in Race-II, H2 finished first and Ritesh's horse finished third.
(ii) In Race-IV, H2 finished third and H3 finished fourth.
(iii) Dablu's horse finished at the same position in Race-I and Race-II, and also in Race-III and Race-IV.
(iv) In Race-IV, H1 and H3 interchanged the positions at which they had finished in Race-II.
(v)   In Race-III, H3 finished fourth and H4 finished second.
(vi) Rahul's horse did not finish first in any of the four races.

1.   Who are the owners of H3 and H4 respectively?
     (a) Ritesh and Rahul   (b) Dablu and Ritesh
     (c) Rahul and Dablu   (d) Cannot be determined
2.   Whose horse finished third in Race-III?
     (a) Rahul   (b) Ritesh
     (c) Dharma   (d) Either Rahul or Dablu
3.   If the horse with the lowest sum of ranks in the four races won a Jackpot of ₹1 crore, which horse won the Jackpot?
     (a) H1   (b) H2
     (c) H3   (d) H4

Rankings

EXAMPLE: Answer the questions on the basis of the information given below.

In a given season of F1 racing, 9 races are to be held. There are 8 teams with two drivers in each team and the points are awarded to the drivers in each race as per to the following table.

Rank	1st	2nd	3rd	4th	5th	6th	7th	8th	9th to 16th
Points	10	8	6	5	4	3	2	1	0

Two championships viz. 'Driver's Championship' and 'Constructor's Championship' take place simultaneously.

'Driver's Championship' is given to the player who has the maximum number of points at the end of the season.

'Constructor's Championship' is given to the team for which the sum of the points of two its drivers is the maximum. A driver is said to get the podium finish only when he is among the top 3 rankers in a race. After the first 6 races, the point standings of the 16 drivers is as follows: **(2015)**

Driver	Team	Points
Alonso	Renault	54
Schumacher	Ferrari	39
Kimi	Mclaren	29
Fisichella	Renault	27
Montoya	Mclaren	22
Massa	Ferrari	22
Button	Honda	21
Barichello	Honda	10
Villeneuve	Red Bull	4
Webber	Williams	3
Roseberg	Williams	2
Coulthard	BMW Soubers	1
Heidfeld	Red Bull	0
Klien	BMW Soubers	0
Liuzzi	Toro Rosso	0
Scott Speed	Toro Rosso	0

1. If Alonso got the podium finish in each of the first 6 races, then what was the maximum number of races in which he had 2nd rank?
   (a) 4
   (b) 3
   (c) 2
   (d) 1

2. Apart from the first six races, Alonso got the podium finish in the 7th race as well. However, he was not allowed to participate in the subsequent races due to mechanical failure. At the end of the season, if Schumacher won the 'Driver's Championship', then which of the following could have been his lowest rank in any of the last three races?
   (a) 5th
   (b) 6th
   (c) 7th
   (d) 4th

3. Which of the following statements CANNOT be true?
   (a) Renault and Ferrari had a tie for the 'Constructor's Championship'.
   (b) Alonso got the podium finish in each of the first 6 races out of which he did not have rank 1st in the 6th race.
   (c) Fisichella got the podium finish in the 9th race and Honda won the 'Constructor's Championship'.
   (d) Barichello got the podium finish in the 3rd race but he did not score any point in the 1st race.

4. If Schumacher ranked 9th in one of the first six races, then which of the following CANNOT be the points scored by him in any one of the first six races?

(a) 3

(b) 2

(c) 1

(d) 0

Quantitative Aptitude

It is suggested that you should start preparing for Quant with the topics which frequently appear in CAT in Arithmetic, Numbers and Geometry etc. and understand all the basic concepts, question types and applications for the same. Since childhood, we have heard that mathematics and numbers are just a game of regular practice. And this section requires the same approach.

After going through the details below, you will be able to decide the further action plan. After a bit of research, you will able to prepare a study which will answer the following questions:

- What are the areas in which you need more practice?
- Which are the sections requiring an expert's guidance? and
- Which are the sections you are most comfortable with?

Just be regular and try to solve the maximum number of questions of each type. And, be very cautious as even a very silly mistake can cost you a year.

Important Topics of CAT syllabus of QA

The majority of questions in Quant can come from:

- Arithmetic (10 questions) on
  - ✓ Percentage,
  - ✓ Profit & loss,
  - ✓ Speed-distance,
  - ✓ Time & Work (increase in manpower reduction in days of work to complete the project),
  - ✓ Ratio and others
- Geometry (3 problems based on Concepts)
- Higher Math
- Probability
- Number System
- Permutation and Combination
- Integers
- Algebra

These topics are suggested by the experts only on the basis of analysis of past few years and should not be considered as an exhaustive list. As there is no clear cut definition CAT syllabus, any type of question can come in CAT 2018.

An Analysis of CAT 2017

Overall Analysis

Total Questions: 34

- More questions on Arithmetic
- 11 Questions were Non-MCQ type
- Sectional difficulty level was easy

Slot 1

Analysis of Type and Content of questions

- Arithmetic (10 questions) on Percentage, Profit & loss, Speed-distance, Time &

Work (increase in manpower reduction in days of work to complete the project); Ratio and others
- Geometry (3 problems based on Concepts)
- Higher Math
- Probability (Bayes Theorem)
- Number System, Permutation and Combination
- Integers
- Algebra

Slot 2

Analysis of Type and Content of questions in Quant:
- Arithmetic (9 questions) on Speed-distance, Time & Work; Ratio; Percentage, Profit & loss, Interest, time and distance
- Geometry (4 problems)
- Series and sequence- 3 questions
- Mensuration-2 questions
- Log & Inequality-1 question
- Modulas-2 questions
- Number system & PnC-3 questions
- Algebra-4 questions

Examples of questions from past papers:

Mixtures

EXAMPLE: The ratio of alcohol to water in an alcohol-water solution is 9 : 1. The rate of evaporation per hour of alcohol and water on boiling is 20% and 5% respectively. The minimum number of hours for which the solution needs to be boiled so as it contains at least 18% of water?

(2013)

(a) 3   (b) 4
(c) 3.5   (d) 4.5

Progressions

EXAMPLE: If the square of the 7th term of an arithmetic progression with positive common difference equals the product of the 3rd and 17th terms, then the ratio of the first term to the common difference is

(a) 2 : 3   (b) 3 : 2
(c) 3 : 4   (d) 4 : 3

Average

EXAMPLE: A class consists of 20 boys and 30 girls. In the mid-semester examination, the average score of the girls was 5 higher than that of the boys. In the final exam, however, the average score of the girls dropped by 3 while the average score of the entire class increased by 2. The increase in the average score of the boys is

(a) 9.5   (b) 10
(c) 4.5   (d) 6

Triangles

EXAMPLE: From a triangle ABC with sides of lengths 40 ft, 25 ft and 35 ft, a triangular portion GBC is cut off where G is the centroid of ABC. The area, in sq ft, of the remaining portion of triangle ABC is

(a) $225\sqrt{3}$ (b) $\dfrac{500}{\sqrt{3}}$
(c) $\dfrac{275}{\sqrt{3}}$ (d) $\dfrac{250}{\sqrt{3}}$

Equations

EXAMPLE: If $x + 1 = x^2$ and $x > 0$, then $2x^4$ is

(a) $6 + 4\sqrt{5}$

(b) $3 + 5\sqrt{5}$

(c) $5 + 3\sqrt{5}$

(d) $7 + 3\sqrt{5}$

HCF & LCM

EXAMPLE: How many ordered triplets (a, b, c) exist such that LCM (a, b) = 1000, LCM (b, c) = 2000, LCM (c, a) = 2000 and HCF (a, b) = k × 125?

(2015)

(a) 32

(b) 28

(c) 24

(d) 20

Time, Speed & Distance

EXAMPLE: A man leaves his home and walks at a speed of 12 km per hour, reaching the railway station 10 minutes after the train had departed. If instead he had walked at a speed of 15 km per hour, he would have reached the station 10 minutes before the train's departure. The distance (in km) from his home to the railway station is **(2017)**

EXAMPLE: A man travels by a motor boat down a river to his office and back. With the speed of the river unchanged, if he doubles the speed of his motor boat, then his total travel time gets reduced by 75%. The ratio of the original speed of the motor boat to the speed of the river is

(2017)

(a) $\sqrt{6} : \sqrt{2}$

(b) $\sqrt{7} : 2$

(c) $2\sqrt{5} : 3$

(d) $3 : 2$

EXAMPLE: A person can complete a job in 120 days. He works alone on Day 1. On Day 2, he is joined by another person who also can complete the job in exactly 120 days. On Day 3, they are joined by another person of equal efficiency. Like this, everyday a new person with the same efficiency joins the work. How many days are required to complete the job? **(2017)**

Lines

EXAMPLE: The area of the closed region bounded by the equation $|x| + |y| = 2$ in the two-dimensional plane is **(2017)**

(a) 4π

(b) 4

(c) 8

(d) 2π

Percentage

EXAMPLE: Ravi invests 50% of his monthly savings in fixed deposits. Thirty percent of the rest of his savings is invested in stocks and the rest goes into Ravi's savings bank account. If the total amount deposited by him in the bank (for savings account and fixed deposits) is ₹59500, then Ravi's total monthly savings (in ₹) is

(2017)

Profit & Loss

EXAMPLE: If a seller gives a discount of 15% on retail price, She still makes a profit of 2%. Which of the following ensures that she makes a profit of 20%?

(2017)

(a) Give a discount of 5% on retail price.

(b) Give a discount of 2% on retail price.

(c) Increase the retail price by 2%.

(d) Sell at retail price.

Logarithm

EXAMPLE: Suppose, $\log_3 x = \log_{12} y = a$, where x, y are positive numbers. If G is the geometric mean of x and y, and $\log_6 G$ is equal to

(2017)

(a) $\sqrt{a}$

(b) 2a

(c) a/2

(d) a

Area & Volume

EXAMPLE: A conical vessel, with a circular base, is filled with water to two-thirds of its volume. The pointed end of the cone is snipped off and replaced with a lid. The lid is kept open for 10 hours

every day during which some water evaporates. The volume of the water that evaporates on a day is directly proportional to the area of the water surface at the beginning of the day. The volume of the water left in the container after evaporation on the 1st day is half the volume of the original cone. If V is the volume of the original cone, then what is the volume of the water that evaporates on the 2nd day?

(2011)

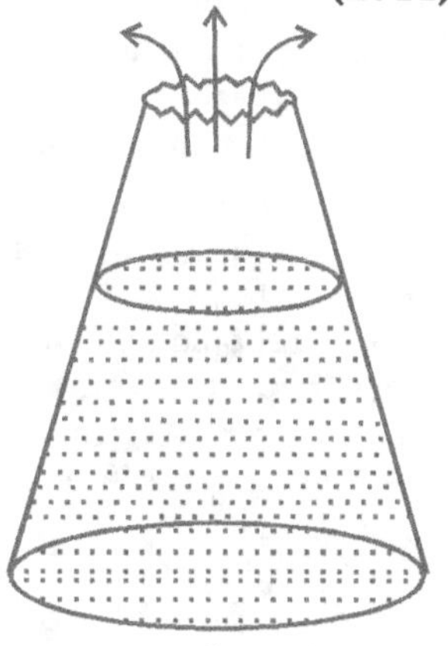

(a) $\dfrac{V}{6}\left(\dfrac{3}{2}\right)^{\frac{3}{2}}$

(b) $\dfrac{V}{4}$

(c) $\dfrac{V}{6}\left(\dfrac{3}{2}\right)^{\frac{2}{3}}$

(d) $\dfrac{V}{4}\left(\dfrac{3}{2}\right)^{\frac{3}{4}}$

Strategy to crack CAT

CAT is considered as a fairly simple exam that tests a student's basic numerical and verbal abilities. It looks tough because it is application intensive unlike the school or college exams!

To begin with the preparation for CAT, you need to know the answer of a couple of very important questions which include: i) Where are you right now with regard to the preparation? ii) Where do you aspire to be after a few months?

The answers to the questions above would come from your

- ✓ Educational background,
- ✓ Overall profile,
- ✓ Aspirations, and
- ✓ Hold over aptitude tests

Also, you should remember these three important things while preparing for CAT, that are:

1. Getting your fundamentals strong
2. Doing the grind to gain speed and automaticity
3. Tackling tough questions and getting exam ready

The admission to IIMs is possible only through high scores in CAT, a highly competitive Management exam. And as you are aware that CAT is a computer based test, start getting habitual of working on a computer.

If you have never taken CAT before, you might want to understand the pattern, topics and syllabus in detail. The best way to do it is by taking a mock/ any previous year CAT paper. Once you do this activity and compare your knowledge against what is required for all the topics that come under the expected category, you can start tackling it individually.

As, we all know that only a strong foundation can support a building firmly, the preliminary or initial stage becomes a very important and crucial time. So, start constructing your dream of a successful career and life ahead with utmost attention. To understand the strategy or the action plan to be followed, read and understand the points we have discussed below.

Approach needed for dealing with the three sections

CAT is not just about giving a fixed set of hours. It's about practising something daily and consistently. Let's consider the strategy to be followed for the different sections:

1. Verbal Ability and Reading Comprehension

Divided into two halves RC and VA, this section comprises of 34 questions (24 in RC and 10 in VA). The RC questions have negative marking while the VA section doesn't have negative markings.

As summarized by our experts, RC's are all about elimination. You eliminate the three choices and get the correct one. Make sure you practise variety of passages and at least 5 passages daily. VA

Section, it is non-negative, but that is the catch. People get lured by it and end up wasting a lot of time and energy.

Verbal Ability is a tricky portion in CAT. It requires you to have an understanding of the types of questions asked in CAT, the level of grammar and CAT vocabulary question types, coupled with various forms of reasoning and in-depth understanding of comprehensions. But the evaluation does not stop at the questions itself.

The exam actually wants you to adopt a holistic approach for the exam, and pay sufficient attention to the three parts that constitute any language:

✓ Reading
✓ Grammar
✓ Vocabulary

Come up with an action plan for each of these and pay individual attention to these sections.

Remember, one of the most central aspects of your preparation revolves around reading and so simply work on your reading skills.

2. Quantitative Aptitude

This section depends 100% on your conceptual clarity. Be sure to clear and make your basic fundamentals strong for the subject. Also, make sure you practise tests in a phased manner, progressing from easy to difficult problems.

The more you practise, less are your chances of committing silly mistakes, as you will catch the areas where you make errors.

Also, more practice means you will be acquainted with the different varieties of questions from a particular topic which can come in the final test.

3. Data Interpretation and Logical Reasoning

DI and Reasoning skills can be developed over a period of time. CAT Data Interpretation requires good calculation skills, ability to interpret and analyze data and identify traps in the question. Many a time the solution is very easy but is presented in a twisted manner that makes it appear as a typical one.

Close inspection of the data given is required, coupled with the fact that you should have adequate practice of the various question types. This will help you understand the problems better. So, make sure you practise different types of sets and expose yourself to as much variety as possible.

For Logical Reasoning, you should start by solving puzzles. These help establish a certain familiarity with reasoning problems, and also provide you the different kinds of approaches and tricks used by question setters in the actual exam. Similar to Data Interpretation, Logical Reasoning can be improved by regular practice.

Action plan

A few basic things that you have to do to better your chances of getting into a top level B-school:

1. Solve all previous year CAT papers
2. A mock test every 10 days for 3-4 months and then at least once a week for 3 months that will make a total of at least 25-30 tests, which will give you a clear idea of where to focus at the time of revision.
3. Solving questions from all the sections from the material you compiled / preparation through social media groups/forums/ etc. You must solve 10-15 questions a day on an average.
4. Also, be focused on the non-material preparation which involves reading blogs, editorials, novels, etc.
5. Do remember that a high score in one section does not guarantee a high score in another one; all three evaluate three distinct sets of knowledge and skills. So, keep a balance and keep moving devoting proper time to each one depending on your proficiency in each topic of the section and the level of difficulty of the questions asked in the exam from the topics.

Preparation Milestones

Now considering that you have solved more than 3000 questions in total, it's a decent score. And it would take around 1-2 hours a day on an average on non-mock days and around 4-5 hours on mock days (which can be accommodated during the weekends).

Your preparation milestones might look somewhat like this:

- You should ideally finish off the CAT papers and basics of preparation (all the important concepts, formulas and question types) within 3 months time, so that you are in fine shape once the mock season starts.
- Post that, it will be more of an identify-error-and-work-on-it exercise and you should be mending the major gaps in your preparation.
- By the time the CAT notification comes out (end of July), you should be operating at least 80-85% of your capacity. Post that, the focus would shift to your strategy (considering the changes in pattern, interface etc.)
- Minor additions to your knowledge base can be made till mid-end October after which, you would spend more time revising and analyzing your previous mocks.
- Be cautious not to be guided by any new material or book towards the zenith of your target that is the last month before the test. It is wise to revise.

CHAPTER 3

PREPARING FOR CAT: AN OVERVIEW

As generally believed, CAT (Common Admission Test) is one of the toughest exams to crack. CAT toppers find their way to get into top IIMs with their consistent efforts deployed in the right direction.

It's the proper strategy that matters the most; spending lots of time with the books doesn't guarantee a positive result. But researching and understanding the right approach, charting the perfect plan and a proper schedule that has a balanced outlook is something required; it will empower you to reach your target.

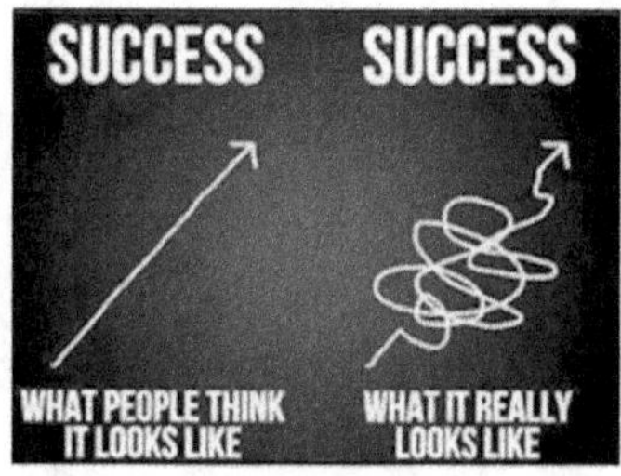

As generally perceived, reaching such a target is not an easy task, you have to spend lots of time, energy and efforts; but it's worth it. Just keep your spirits up!!!

It is to be noted that the questions in competitive exams are 'not difficult' but they are just a bit 'different'.

Remember that winners don't do different things; they do things differently.

Similarly, you should also try to focus your attention not only on hard work but also on smart work. Smart work involves

a whole set of skills and features, which we will discuss in detail in this chapter. Preparation for CAT requires a lot of hard work and one has to go through many sleepless nights to finish the syllabus. If a proper strategy is not followed, then a wrong way will consume lots of time and energy.

Wherever smart people work, doors are unlocked.
- Steve Wozniak

Also, one will have to constantly motivate himself/herself to keep working hard. Try to give positive inputs to your mind; keep repeating to yourself to keep learning.

Most importantly, prepare and consider all the parts in all the 3 sections of CAT equally important if you wish to get shortlisted by top IIMs.

If you score 100 percentile in one section and 65 percentile in another section in CAT, some experts say it is as good as scoring 'zero' percentile in CAT since most of the IIMs won't shortlist you.

The Ds you need to succeed

To be successful, you need to develop certain skills. It's not that those who are too brilliant or gifted will only achieve the target, but anyone who is clear and dedicated towards the desired goal can excel.

The process starts with a desire in heart and then taking the decision and planning the strategy in mind.

Experts have listed some Ds essential for gaining success, whether in exam, job or if we talk in totality, in life. They are:

Desire

A desire to achieve your final goal is the first thing you need to drive yourself to take action. You should be craving to attain the success that you dream of, enough to be willing to make necessary sacrifices to achieve it.

Now, you have taken the first step as you desired to do an MBA, and that to from a premier college of repute and hence your decision of preparing for CAT.

Dedication

Make the decision right now to always be willing to do whatever is necessary, to pay any price, and go to any distance to achieve your final goal. Many people suggest that for some time you should stay away from all the things you love and enjoy, as they will be a distraction, and get involved only in studies. But this is not a rule; it all depends on person to person. You should just be honest to yourself and your work.

Determination

Next, what you should do is to be determined and focused in your

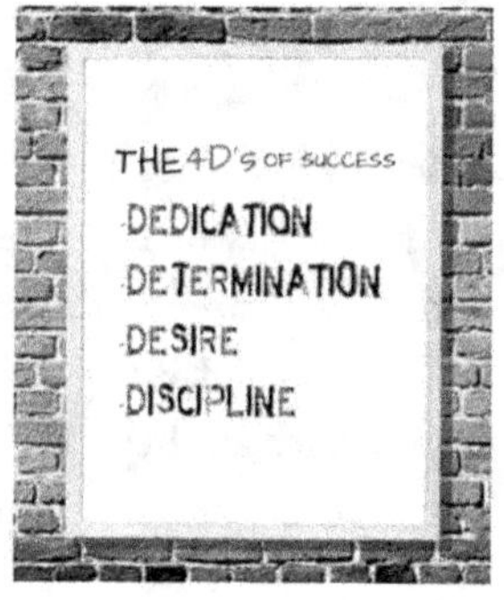

efforts. People often say I tried doing my best, but try not to repeat that. Don't just try, exert yourself, and be so involved in the preparation that not only you but other people also agree and they say - YESSS!!! You did your BEST!!!

There will be many obstacles between you and your final goal. Determination is what will help push you forward and stay persevered despite setbacks and challenging circumstances.

Discipline

Self-discipline is often considered, to some extent, a substitute for motivation. Unless and until you are disciplined your target is unachievable. Planning of going miles won't take you anywhere. But, moving just even a few steps can accelerate your journey. And, this is what is required and expected of you. Be consistent!!!

There are others who list these 6 Ds as prerequisite for succeeding in life, they include:

Desire, **D**etermination, **D**iscipline, **D**evotion, **D**edication and **D**estiny

The sixth D is not in our hands, but as it is said that luck favours only those, who are willing to take risks and make sincere efforts. And this is only in your hands. Start early and keep going. All the best for a good start!!

THE MAKEUP

As mentioned earlier, CAT (Common Admission Test) is one of the toughest exams to crack. CAT toppers find their way to get into top IIMs with their consistent efforts deployed in the right direction. It's that proper strategy that matters the most. Spending lots of time with the books doesn't guarantee a positive result. But researching and understanding the right approach, charting the perfect plan and a proper schedule that has a balanced outlook is something required; it will impact and empower you.

An MBA will not only make you learn the concepts and applications of management, but apart from the subject knowledge, you have to learn lots of other things that will shape up your personality.

Values for success

We will now discuss some of those traits that will eventually help you to be ready to make your mark in the ever developing professional world.

Attitude

It is one of the most important traits required to be successful in any competitive examinations. It is important how serious you are about your studies and the forthcoming examinations. Keep reading toppers' remarks, their success stories that will help in motivating you throughout and in developing a positive attitude.

Keep believing that there is nothing like being 'impossible'. Forget 'I can't' erase this word from your dictionary and put your sincere efforts in your work.

Be determined and there is nothing in this world that can stop you from achieving your goals. Accept every challenge with a smile and put it down with your efforts.

Keep Moving

Always remember that there are many people who have their hopes and expectations attached to you and your result is the only way of paying back all they have done for you. Work hard to reach where you and your loved ones want to you to see. There are many if's, buts', fears, apprehensions; just forget all and just focus.

It is necessary to have a clear goal and work with single-minded dedication towards it. One must have a firm grasp over all topics and should be aware of the previous years' questions. Also, never lose faith in yourself as that is of utmost importance.

We should always keep on moving, may be sometimes we are slow and at times fast, some times in the direction of the flow, another time against it, what is required is putting in hard work and not staying still, just continuing your efforts.

Resolve to stop only when you have achieved success

The most common difficulty in studying is the simple failure to get down to regular concentrated work. It is hard to make a start.

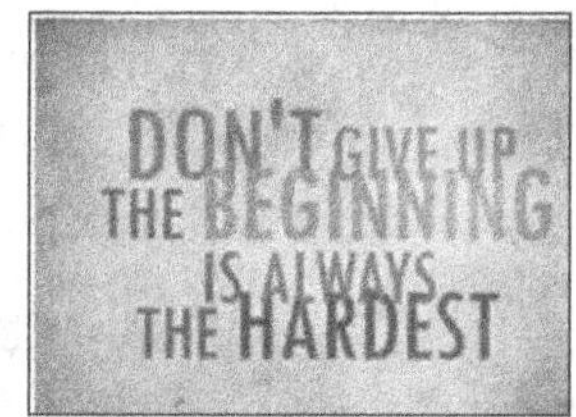

Your internal and external motives should impel you to start and complete the work. Take it up as a challenge. Prove to yourself and others that once you have started preparing for an examination, you have the determination to succeed in it.

Be regular and attentive

In order to work regularly and continuously all throughout the year, try to make studies your habit.

> *I find the great thing in this world is not so much where we stand, as in what direction we are moving... we must sail sometimes with the wind and sometimes against it... but we must sail and not drift nor lie at anchor.*
>
> *— Oliver Wendell Holmes*

To get into the habit of studying make sure that you experience satisfaction in the beginning of your preparation. So, start with your favourite subject and topic.

When you find weariness approaching, rouse yourself and remember that 'if you give up all that you have done has been done in vain...'

Create and relate with your interest

When you find a subject interesting and enjoyable, you desire to learn more. The more you learn about a subject, the easier it becomes. Your interest and enjoyment of the subject increases if you focus upon its relevance in your everyday life.

Do not restrict yourself to just learning the subject for an hour or so every day, but try and relate it to your life as whole.

Have self-confidence and motivation

Researchers say that in the success of candidate self-confidence and motivation plays a more important role than even subject knowledge. Studies further state that attitude and other soft skills (which include concentration, self-confidence, inner strength etc.) contribute up to 70 to 80% to success. This means that soft skills are much more important than subject knowledge but unfortunately very few students give importance to these skills.

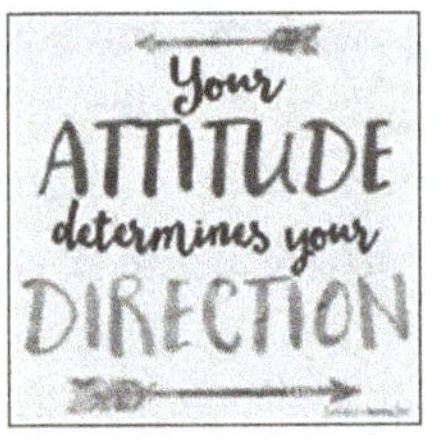

Most of the students are functionally very strong and behaviourally very weak and often their reason for failure is not lack of knowledge or hard work but lack of motivation and positive attitude.

So, the first and the most important step is to build positive attitude towards your preparation. And to have positive attitude towards your preparation, it is very important to answer the following question-

"Why am I studying?"

Every task should have a sense of purpose or motive behind it. Your motive will define the motivation level to achieve the task which ultimately will build up your attitude and move you towards your goal.

Failure is the opportunity to begin again more intelligently. - Henry Ford

Belief —affects→ Conscious state of mind —affects→ Attitude —affects→ Action —results in→ Achievement —results in→ Further strengthening of belief —results in→ SUCCESS

The Basics: Input, Output and the Feedback

There are 4 stages of information processing and it is a repeated cycle of events. This is the process involving your whole preparation to test cycle.

Decision-making>Input>
<Feedback> Output

The first stage of this process is the input. You gain information from various sources you collect and compile them, and then come the next stage. The second stage of this process is the decision-making. In this decision-making phase, you must decide the future action plan. You will have to decide which books and sources you need to consult? What should be your timetable? What should be the approach? What are the sections where extra care should be taken? etc.

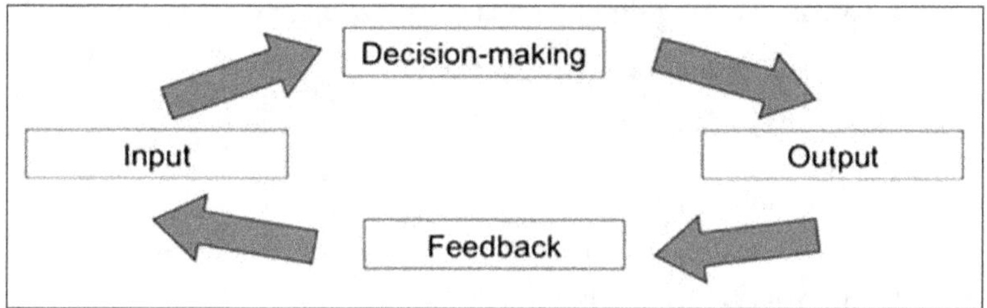

The third stage of this process is the output. The action is performed; you have given the mocks and solved the practice papers. Now is the time to reflect and analyze your preparation and your abilities.

The last stage of this process is the feedback. It is the evaluation of your output i.e. the test of the knowledge and information you have gathered from different sources such as books, coaching institutes' study material and the internet. Now, you need to focus and understand whether to repeat i.e. study in the same manner or to make few changes; it will depend on the success rate or the score you attained in the tests.

Importance of Input, Output and the Feedback in your preparation

The right approach is to first of all understand, what all is expected of you? And, what all should you put in? It will include the following concerns: what should be the inputs to get the desired output? How will you prepare a systematic plan? And also to decide the strategy to be followed. This should be done after understanding your target and taking into account the feedback.

A candidate targeting 95 percentile or say A++ institute will have a different approach than one willing to just get an MBA degree from any college in the list. The harder your target, the more toiling required.

We will now discuss the basic process in detail for it; we will first list the inputs and outputs involved in the whole cycle.

Inputs

> **Understanding the exam pattern:** First and foremost, search and research on the pattern of the exam - an exhaustive study of it, which should include - the weightage and the important sections, and then compare those with your weak areas and accordingly prepare a schedule, organize a plan.

> **Devising a strategy or a plan:**
  - day wise,
  - wise
  - month wise

Setting targets and preparing to-do-lists helps a lot in regularizing and monitoring your progress. Keep a journal and pen down on a daily basis. Try to give yourself the deadline for each topic. Be your own teacher and monitor.

> **Learning and mastering the concepts:** This is of utmost importance, as a building with a strong foundation only stands firm.

If you won't understand the basics, it is impossible for you to find a solution. Be very observant and focused in your approach.

The foundation stones for a balanced success are honesty, character, integrity, faith, love and loyalty - Zig Ziglar

> **Reading newspapers, books and journals regularly:** This habit should be nurtured from childhood, but better late than never. Read, read and read as often as you can. Make it a ritual to start the day with a newspaper.

- **Choosing the right material:** We all know that nowadays there are lots and lots of information available online, and a bunch of institutes have crept in every nook and corner of the city. But, just getting anything advertised as worthy enough to read will not solve your purpose, study and collect lots of material and pick out what all is relevant and useful for you.
- **Practising an ample amount of questions:** The more you practise the better prepared you are. This will make you confident to face any type of question, as you will be acquainted with most of them.
- **Solving previous years' papers:** This habit will help you in understanding the pattern and levels of difficulty of the questions asked.
- **Practising a lot of mock tests:** Doing so will sharpen your knowledge and make you familiar with the exam and acquainted with the exam pattern. The mocks prepared by the experts will also give you an idea of the type of questions expected in the test.
- **Getting comfortable with computers:** It is an important point to keep in mind that this is a computer based test. May be you have excelled in every practise paper and are thorough with all the notes; but if are not familiar with the system and the windows, your hard work will be a waste, time and efforts will go in drain.

Outputs

- **Clarity of concepts:** After your extensive preparation, you should be clear with the concepts so that you can work on various types of problems related to them.
- **Proper application of the concepts learned:** Learning is considered only half knowledge. It's not complete until you know how to apply it properly, that will make your attempts and efforts worthwhile.

There are various aspects of learning which will help you in the exam and even in life after that. You should just be aware of when and how to apply it.

> **Smart understanding of problems:** After spending time and observing and solving different varieties of problems, you will gain a better understanding of the problems. And will be smart enough to tackle even the unknown and complex ones.

> With time and consistent efforts, You will have a better
> - reading speed
> - comprehension speed
> - vocabulary
> - grammatical skills

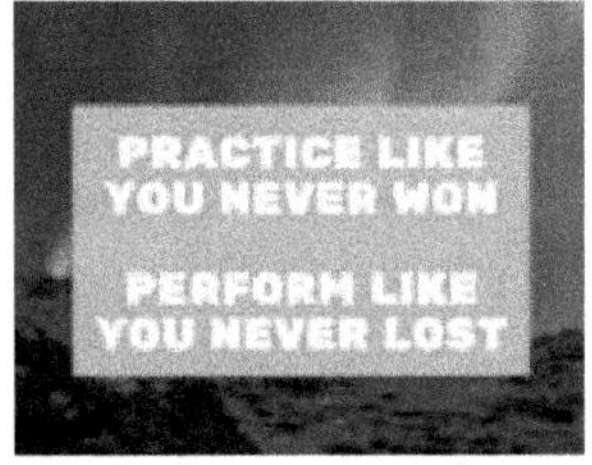

You all must have heard *'Practice makes a man perfect'*, thus after your repeated efforts and labour, you will be much better in English reading and writing.

Your verbal skills will be improved and your personality will be more impressive.

LEARNING FIRST

Since most of the questions in the competitions are based on fundamentals and their applications so the first step is to establish a solid base, by mastering the fundamentals. For being proficient with the fundamentals you have to be very focused and determined. Be clear about your aim and then resolve to put in your best efforts.

As you are well aware that this is a tough exam hence just qualifying won't do the job. The percentiles are booming high and the number of aspirants is also increasing with each passing year.

Taking exams is stressful, but you can make it easier by improving the way you study.

Tips to follow

Learning requires a lot of practice. So, it is advised that

- Do your first practice as soon as possible. This is best step after you have just finished reading and understanding the concept, or after your class (if you have joined one).
- Paying attention in your class will help you immensely

once exam time comes. Don't be in a wrong impression, thinking you'll just "absorb" knowledge; be an active learner. Start with the aim to be a step ahead from the day before. Keep progressing!!

- It is believed that you remember more just after waking up and before sleeping at night. Try to use this time for focusing on important and challenging topics. During this time, our brain creates the neurological connections that enable us to retain the information. So, try to have a quick review of the whole day's study and do another practice before the end of the day.

- After a few days, do your third practice. In this practice you might be going over the whole week's lectures or your compiled study material.

- Look for interesting and interactive ways to remember things. To test if you've really learned the material, ask yourself questions or make flashcards. Fix a day say Sunday, for group discussion with your friends. It happens many a time that certain concepts get clearer when we are discussing and explaining it to other people.

- Go over your notes and convert them into a study guide, and then read over the guide many times until you feel confident. You could organize the content into a proper format with suitable headings.

- Making your own notes helps in a great deal. You decide the various sections, reframe the sentences for easy and quick review, this is also going to improve your English language skills. Furthermore, while writing down you are done with one round of the revision.

Try to stretch out your practice sessions as you go, forcing yourself to remember the key points for longer and longer periods. After every session put different marks on the topics according to your ability in it. This approach will be very beneficial in the future revisions.

- Soon you will note that you have several consecutive ticks beside many topics, and there may be some that you are finding hard to remember. These problem topics probably are unclear to you, and you should do what you need to clarify the topic or section. Perhaps you can consult the internet or ask your senior or fellow mates for more memorable information or clarification.

- Once you have several consecutive ticks for each item, you've got it all learned! One more review before the exam will probably be sufficient.

- Don't use too many courses or books. Most of the students end up buying 3 to 4 books for one subject.

> **Winners see the gain, losers see the pain - Shiv Khera**

- Remember that more than 80 to 90% problems in most of the books are same so what you are doing is just repetition of same problems.

- The best option is that just buy 1 or 2 books to master the fundamentals and then go for different question banks to do more and more practice. Decide about the course and books after discussing with your seniors and friends and then stick to them.

Five Simple Steps of Effective Study

Studying for your exams effectively and efficiently will keep you from feeling unprepared, and it will set you up for success!

If you follow the proper step by step schedule, it will surely increase your chances of qualifying the test.

> *There is more learning in the question itself*
> *than the answer - Andrew Weremy*

For your convenience, we have compiled a procedure to be followed; it comprises of:

- **Learning the concepts:** If you won't know the 'abc' of something, it's very obvious you won't be able to form words. And if anyhow, by hit and trail will anyone be able to do that, it won't make the meaning clear. So the first thing to do is to clear the concepts of the subject. It is two step processes:
  - Get an overview
  - Determine key ideas
- **Practicing the concepts and its application:** As we have already discussed that if you don't know the application of what all you have learned and summarized, nothing will make sense. So, its' of utmost importance to understand the correct application: where

and how it is to be used to get maximum benefit out of the knowledge acquired.

- ➢ **Recalling, revising & memorizing:** It is a proven fact that human mind is constantly working and there is an ample amount of information stored in it. Until and unless, you keep on repeating the data that is of importance, it may get lost in the pack. Just keep on repeating, revising and memorizing whatever you learn. Move the stuff from short term to long term memory areas.

- ➢ **Test your understanding:** An important aspect of the process of preparing for an exam or learning is doing self evaluation to know your progress. Doing this way you will get to know about the areas which need extra attention. And what all can be ignored for a while. Being aware of your ability and the level of difficulty will save much of your precious time and labour.

- ➢ **Analyzing your performance and taking corrective measures:** Just knowing those details is not going to help in any way; you must analyze your errors, your strengths and your

weak areas and accordingly alter and reframe a workable time table.

Remember the process of learning; new things can be an exciting adventure

THE GRIND

By now, you are aware of all that is necessary to qualify - the pattern, the syllabus, the weightage and the level of questions asked. You must have finished reading almost all the sections at least once. Here comes the time to repeat and repeat the lessons, the true meaning of 'grind'.

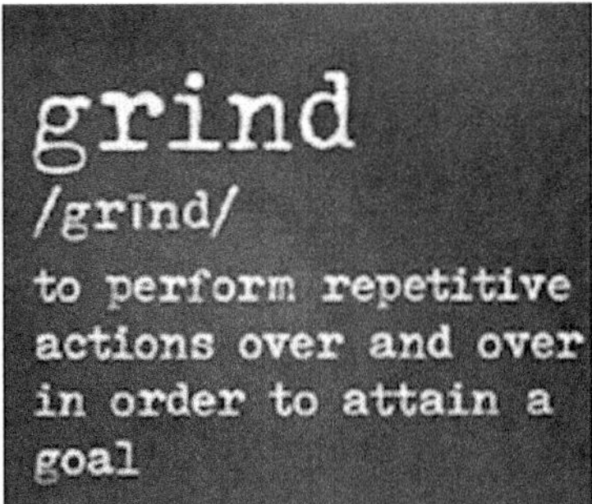

It is often said to be the acronym of **G**et **R**eady **I**t's a **N**ew **D**ay. From this, we can infer that what is required is to go through the preparation. As you daily repeat the process of getting up, doing the daily chores, studying and then sleeping; similarly should go through what all you have learned till that day.

Opportunity won't always knock if you don't first build the door.

Rise and Grind! Keep in mind, the efforts you put in and your level of dedication should be inversely proportional to the time left for the test. Remember what controls your attention controls your life. It is believed - where your attention goes, energy flows and so goes your life.

Keep giving positive inputs to yourself. Set realistic targets and try to achieve maximum, but don't lose heart on the days when you are few steps behind your set goal of the day. Give auto suggestion to yourself: I may not be there yet, but am one step closer than where I was yesterday.

May be till now, what you were doing was enough for that time, but by each passing day you need to work harder and harder. Perform in a way such that you don't have time to think about any distractions and have no regrets.

➢ **Look out for the shortcuts and dwell on them:** CAT is time bound! You can ace CAT if you can master the art of Time Optimization. During your revisions, you know how to work out that problem, but is there a better shortcut? If Yes! Dwell on that shortcut technique. It will save lots of your time.

➢ **Have only 3 targets :** It is your personal choice as to when and how do you want to study and when to relax. It is also up to you to decide what all do you want to keep in your schedule but, some experts believe that for a few months, you should try to keep all other things at bay and only be having 3 targets which are:

> **Be calculative:** Now is the time to be conscious of each and every thing you do. You should prepare a time table and follow it diligently. Keep record of the time you are spending in different sections as well as the time spent in recreation. Even the times when you are away from your books, try recalling the formulae and calculations inside your mind.

> **Make yourself extremely good with numbers:** Calculate manually on every

occasion you have, whether adding up your grocery bills to calculation of taxes at hotel bills to random numbers addition. Make yourself extremely good with numbers. Keep yourself surrounded by the numbers and mathematical signs

> **Try developing puzzle solving as a hobby:** This hobby is going to only have dual but multiple purposes; that include an exercise of

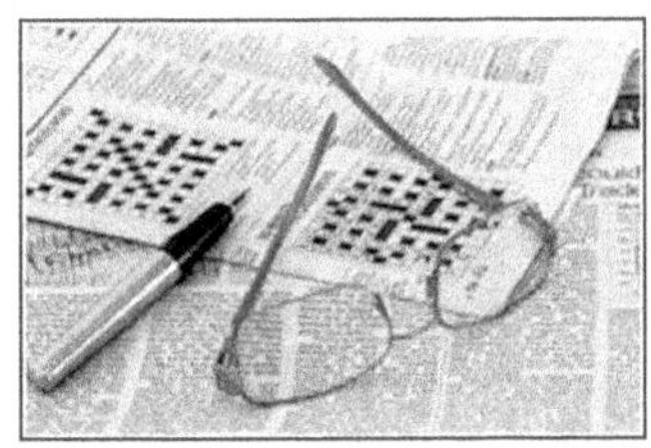

the mind, pleasure from doing something interesting and creative, also competition spirit as you can play a timed game with your friends or siblings.

> **Be a collector and a reader** : Try to collect pieces of information from various sources; newspapers, magazines, books and

the internet. Analyze the authenticity of what you read and pick accordingly. Reading will give you contentment, knowledge as well as an improved English language reading and grammatical skills.

Do remember:

> CAT is not about knowing everything and attempting everything. CAT is about attempting what you know and having accuracy greater than 80% in whatever selective you attempt.

> CAT is touted to be very difficult without practice. Achieving your goal requires a sound understanding of your challenge, and careful planning to overcome it.
> For your progress, follow the process of stopping, thinking, acting and then reflecting on your situation
> CAT is known to test your proficiency in time management and problem solving ability under stress along with knowledge.

CULMINATION

The most important point that decides the fate is the final stage - the climax. Be it in any novel, movie or your journey to land at a management institute of your choice, this is a very decisive time. By this time, you would be in your final leg towards your CAT journey.

In less than a month, you will be back to your original self, those family times, weekend parties, Television shows, lazy Sundays, social networking, etc. all will be back in action! (At least temporarily, for some time you can!! until you begin your PI/GD preparations).

We all can guess how exhausting this final phase can be, but only the person who stands there, can measure the actual depth of it. You almost want to give up, but you know that you have done too much to give up right now.

Here is a checklist before you hit the "3 weeks before CAT" mark. Remember final leg is not a phase where you push yourself/be too harsh on yourself; but the phase where you should be very calm, composed and confident because you have come this far with CAT preparations! Don't panic watching the ticking clock; just be confident about your abilities. Here, we have prepared the checklist, go through it:

➢ **Have only one vision RE vision:** By now, you have learnt whatever you need to learn; there is no point trying to push in that chapter you left out, now. Do not waste your time and energy on stuff that you do not know, instead dive deeper into whatever that you know well. *"CAT is not about knowing everything; it is about the depth of what you know."*

This is the time, when you should have only one vision RE VISION, which means going through all what you have already done.

> *I will always choose a lazy person to do a difficult job because a lazy person will find an easy way to do it -Bill Gates*

"Revise, re-revise, re-re revise..." all your mock papers and solution. Keep writing it down as you revise as at times even your hands have a memory that might surprise you during CAT.

➢ **Say 'yes' to healthy food and mild workouts:** You have worked hard and come this far! Imagine how brutal it would be if you were to fall sick on the day of CAT!? Eat healthy and stay fit!

It will keep you more energetic and fresh. You have literally sat through your entire CAT preparations that you can do mild workouts or yoga.

➢ **Stop thinking about the outcome:** Do not go into the details of the expected number of questions you will solve and get a rough estimate of your CAT score. Many people do that. Stop that! Avoid it strictly. CAT is relative, and you do not want to end up false hopes as the batch strength and type varies each year. Your only mantra should be "ANSWER AS MUCH AS WHAT YOU KNOW VERY WELL".

**Don't Stress.
Do Your Best.
Forget the Rest.**

Don't get lured into setting false targets for yourself. Also, if you are eating, concentrate on how yummy the food is; if you are going to bed think about happy times and how proud you are of yourself instead of having thoughts like "what will happen if I flunk CAT? Will I get IIM calls etc?"

You can reach your target when you start early and remain positive throughout the process.

However hard the time may seem, you should be dedicated and honest with your efforts.

➢ **6-8 hours of sleep:** You have compromised enough on your sleep till now. You need to be wide awake during your 3 hours of CAT with the highest level of concentration.

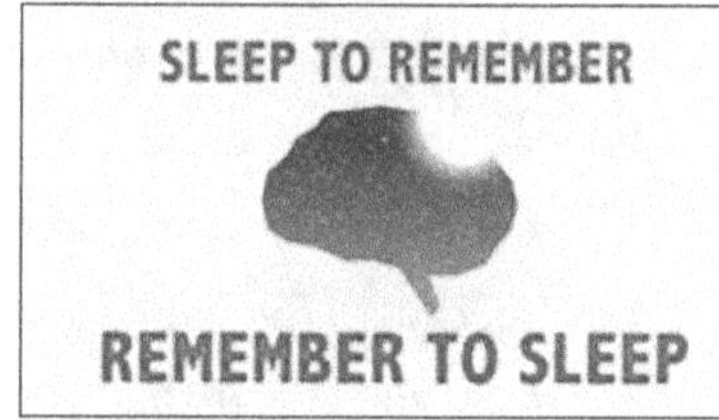

So, for that it is necessary to have good six to eight hours of sleep. Remember not to sleep more than that as your body would start looking for more sleep and you might end up feeling sleepy for the rest of the day.

➢ **Don't cling to things, vent out your worries and move on:** You are scared and you are worried and you feel stuck. Try to ignore any dispute or matter than can affect your peace of mind. Go to your parents, coaching guide, friends, grandparents, anyone you feel relaxed with, discuss and move on. You have better things to do right now rather than worrying.

➢ **Treat yourself, You are the BEST!:** You want to grab that candy bar and watch 2 episodes of your favourite serial, for a break log on hotstar or Netflix, whatever pleases you! GO AHEAD! But just keep a check on the time you spend, it is not wrong to take a refreshing break. It is never wrong to treat yourself, now! Because when you treat yourself, you know that you have done something to deserve it.

> *To discover your mission and put it into action - instead of worrying on the sidelines - is to find peace of mind and a heart full of love. Scilla Elworthy*

When you know you have done something to deserve it, you know you have done that well. When you know you have done that well, you become confident of yourself. When you become confident you can conquer the entire world!

To sum up, we can say that:

➢ Correct strategy & time schedule is the key to crack the exam.

➢ Prepare a proper time table according to your daily schedule and manage your time equally for all the subjects.

➢ Gather all the details about the syllabus and cover every single topic in your preparation.

➢ Find out the best books and study materials for CAT preparations.

➢ Practice from previous year question papers it will help you to know more about the exam pattern.

> Take healthy & nutritious diet and do exercise & yoga it will help you to remain physically fit.

Follow all this, hope and work for the best!! All the very best for your exams and a successful life ahead.

IT'S NOT OVER YET

Qualifying the CAT written test had put you in a different section of qualifiers, but a lot is still to be worked upon. There are stages of your screening, only after you

have climbed each step carefully, will you be able to reach an IIM or one such prestigious institute. We can say that you've just won a battle, the war is not over yet.

After CAT Written test, you will have to appear in the Group Discussion (GD), the Personal Interview (PI) and the Written Ability Test (WAT).

Once CAT results are out, the shortlisted candidates will have to appear for Group Discussion (GD), Personal Interview (PI) and Written Ability Test (WAT). Based on a candidate's performance in these, various MBA colleges select deserving students. Preparing for GD PI is not something that can be done in a day or two, thus candidates must start preparing for the same well in advance.

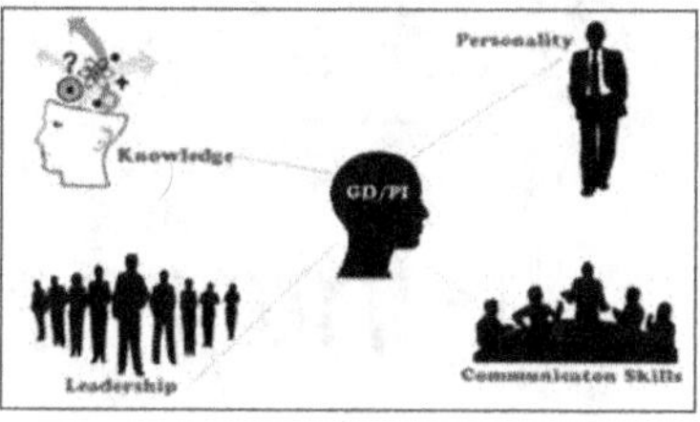

Now, IIMs are giving more importance to WAT-PI performance and profile with each passing year. The GD and PI focus on various aspects; they test the knowledge, the leadership skills, the communication skills as well as the overall personality of the candidate.

Those who don't take WAT-PI seriously thinking that they have good communication skills and the CAT percentile is good enough to take them to IIMs are making a big mistake. Don't move with this mindset; work even harder after 'clearing' (i.e. scoring decent percentile) in the CAT.

Few useful tips:

> **Start keeping a record of the last dates of submissions of the college form.** Make a diary noting down all the important dates and the events approaching. Many aspirants make a mistake of focusing only on studies till CAT and they think will focus on the colleges later on, the outcome is they miss one of the best colleges. Be careful that you don't repeat this mistake and regret later.

> **Focus on improving your interpersonal skills.** The GD and PI round of any big B-school is a whole new struggle. Start preparing for it from very beginning only. These will be of help throughout your life; even organizations select candidates with good interpersonal skills in the campus recruitment.

> **Prepare few lines or one page about the trending terms.** Start a habit of writing on any topic daily. Start with topics you are comfortable with, of areas of your interest, slowly moving to trending terms, which will keep you updated and informed. For example, rethinking Union Budget, Increasing brand participation in messaging platforms, Effects of Demonetization, changes in economy after GST, AI, Twitter, Bitcoin, etc.

> **Keep a track of Current Affairs.** This habit is going to help you in all spheres, be it your preparations for the exams or on a larger platform; it helps in preparing for your job interviews. This will present you as a learned and smart individual who is well conversant and hence will get you an overall enhanced personality.

> **Expand your network.** Join some forums and start

connecting with people all around who will be joining the same batch as you; it would be beneficial to both. A larger number of minds means more queries, more solutions and hence more knowledge.

It happens many a time that an aspirant feels shy in asking to the tutor or senior but is more comfortable putting up his/her point in front of friends and batch mates.

Depending on your marks and if you fulfill the other criteria, you can be shortlisted for WAT, GD and PI. From that process the final shortlist for the class is declared. IIMs have started declaring their criteria have a look at them once.

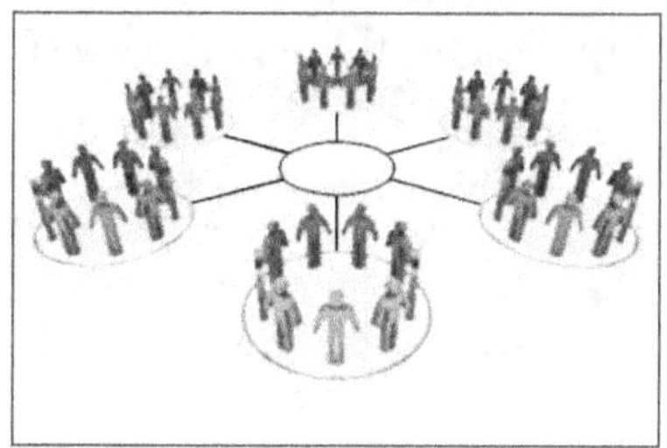

One of the most important decisions that will affect the rest of the aspirant's educational journey will be college selection. If one gets selected in any of the IIMs, there can certainly be nothing better than that, but what if this does not happen? The next step would be to look for a top B-school other than IIM.

Few institutes like MDI, NITIE, FMS, IMT-G and XIMB as well use CAT score for their selection procedure. Other institute follow the same procedure but there criteria varies, for more info you can check college individual sites or last year cutoff to get an idea.

It's always said that one should 'hope for the best and be prepared for the worst.' That's why it is advisable to keep other options open. You should keep yourself abreast with the updates of other exams like IIFT, SNAP, MICA, XAT, TISS, X-GMAT and NMAT as well. Keep yourself informed about the latest happenings in the field and the institutes.

SELF-STUDY VS. COACHING INSTITUTES

One question that every student probably asks themselves is - should I join a coaching class or rely on myself i.e. doing self-study. Some experts suggest that instead of going for coaching classes, go for online resources. As in this era of Internet revolution, it is very easy for everyone to access the internet, and you have vast amounts of credible resources to support your preparation goals.

You will find some great sites to

help you with your preparation goals and that too in the most affordable way. There are some sites that even have tailor-made video library for each of the separate MBA exam that you would probably wish to write. And, CAT being the most prestigious amongst the lot, will give you lots of useful stuff there. On top of that, they also prepare you for the GD & PI. You just need to have a strong determination and put in lots of hard work to excel.

However, according to some alumni, joining a coaching institute helps a great deal as it provides an environment and a proper guidance which is very essential to crack such an unpredictable test.

Coaching Centres

The major thing that distinguishes coaching centres from internet or your friends is Discipline. They might be taking heavy amount of money, but they provide few things in return which are of utmost importance, like you get to know of some useful techniques. A competition spirit develops between peers, which is a positive motivation to push you forward.

Coaching centres are not for understanding the concepts. In this era you can do it from

internet listening to lectures in online classes and watching videos on YouTube much more easily. But what the classes provide is unmatchable; you have teachers and mentors who help in problem solving as well as providing valuable tips.

A regular schedule is what is required in the preparation of any exam, and this is provided by the coaching; a proper time table that how much time needs to be allotted to which section; furthermore, the tests every week are a boon.

A coaching also gives you an exposure of the test environment that helps to understand the level of difficulty of the questions, the sections which are more significant, what can be the pattern of exam the coming year, etc. The success stories you hear by the alumni and seniors helps to motivate in times of distress. Without browsing on the internet for long and referring to a number of books you get quality material at one place at the institute.

If you are seriously following what your mentors tell you to do, the enormous task of covering whole syllabus becomes very structured and feasible. Whereas, when you are studying by yourself, chances are that you might get confused midway or get panic- stricken.

But there is a large percentage of people criticising the coaching centres, the major factors for this aversion include: the hefty amount of money they charge, freshers and ad hoc faculties are generally hired as they will ask for lesser salary, but the problem is they can't provide much guidance, as they are less experienced.

Also, nowadays coaching is not considered as a temple - place of study to learn but a mere business. They fill an ample number of aspirants in each batch and then it really becomes impossible for the faculty to focus on the need of each individual.

Let's now look at the other mode i.e. self-study, and then try to prepare a proper strategy for an entry into the management world.

Self-study

There is no alternative to self-study in the preparation of CAT which requires no formal coaching unless you really need it. Experts recommend that you should start your preparation with self-study. Later you can make it a mix with the help from coaching to avoid wastage of time.

To start with, first of all start reading newspapers; this will help in improving your English and reading skills. In addition to it, it will also prepare you for WAT and GD which is the next step to climb after the written test. You should start with reading any national daily like TOI or HT, then move to Hindu Editorials. In some time, raise your standards by moving to Economic Times and alike later on.

The experts' advice - Read, read and read! It helps a lot in Reading Comprehension. The area which will test you the most is Logical Reasoning and Data Interpretation. So it is better not to waste any time, and start as soon as you decide to attempt the test.

Make sure to work on your profile and maintain a good percentage CGPA if you are still in college. Your overall profile matters a lot in the final analysis.

As far as timings are concerned you should dedicate a minimum of 3–4 hours per day in weekdays and in weekends try to spend 10–

12 hours. The reason being every person is different from each other and you can't blindly follow what somebody else does.

Plan of action for CAT Preparation

Self-preparation is the best preparation strategy for CAT, however, you should have enough time on your disposal. If a candidate gets stuck on some question due to his/her lack of conceptual clarity, the time is wasted and depression begins to set in. No matter whether it is a small Quant formula, LR logic, or Verbal usage clarity, they need a simple push to come out of the shallow waters. This help can be provided by the experts online or offline depending upon your preference.

Most of the candidates coming from Engineering or other technical background find it easy to get along well with Quant, DI and LR but when it comes to Verbal Ability and Reading Comprehension, they find the section too difficult. It is where they need an expert guidance.

Preparation of CAT needs improvement in your speed and accuracy as the time to solve per question is reduced now. Till 2013, the test taker had 2.32 minutes per question to solve but since 2014 the time has been reduced to 1.8 minute per question to solve. Ironically, it will not be sufficient to score overall high in CAT for the year 2018. Your section-wise score should also be high to become eligible for getting shortlisted at IIMs.

With lots of reasoning and arguments in Quant, DI and LR to be absorbed which you might not find interesting, you need to have a few tried and tested study methods and motivational techniques to fall back on that will reinvigorate you and make the process of studying a little more enjoyable.

Here we give you a few ideas to help you bring back the joy of preparing CAT and succeed even in your least favourite subjects.

1. **Set your notes to music:** Music can be used in lots of different ways to help you study. You're probably good at remembering lyrics to songs, because the melody and rhymes help cement the words in your mind; you can use the same principle in your studies. If you're struggling to remember formulae, facts

or figures, try setting them to music. It may feel a little cheesy, but picking a tune and substituting the lyrics is a great way to remember those facts that just won't stick.

2. **Use interactive learning materials:** With plenty of online material and other web resources, you're sure to be able to find some fun in interactive learning software for the subject you're trying to tackle.

Such software makes use of multimedia information to help you absorb information more easily, and may include audio, videos and quizzes in addition to straightforward text to read. It also makes the process more enjoyable by breaking up the monotony of studying from books.

3. **Use flashcards:** Flashcards are a really useful revision resource to make your study more enjoyable. Try condensing the topic into as few words as you can; it's quite challenging. Also, design them in such a way that they are visually memorable.

Adding colourful drawings to each card to illustrate each topic means that when you're struggling to remember something, perhaps in class, you can recall what you drew on the card. The chances are that the rest will come back to you when you remember the visual cue.

4. **Create posters:** Summarizing concepts on posters gives you something different to do, and also allows you to be a bit creative with your designs, injecting some fun into your studying in the process. Let's say you're learning about Data Interpretation question. You could design a poster showing the sales of books in various branches

of a publishing company that illustrates what is the ratio of total sales of that particular branch for various years to the total sales of the whole company.

5. **Make up some mnemonics:** It is a great memory tool, a shortcut technique of linking typical things to others. It refers to when you translate information into a form in which you can more easily remember it. For example, many people use the mnemonic "My Very Eager Mother Just Served Us Noodles" for the planets.

> **Mnemonics**
>
> • A weird word that means "memory tool". Mnemonics are methods for remembering information that is otherwise difficult to recall. Mnemonics use as many of the best functions of your brain as possible to store information.

6. **A change of place of study:** Changing your environment can be a great way of regaining your enthusiasm for studying. However, it shouldn't bring with it too many distractions. This is a simple means of making studying more enjoyable. This could mean studying in the library rather than at home, moving your desk to the windows so that you can enjoy the view each time you look up from your books.

7. **Study in small bursts on each topic:** Anything becomes dull if you spend too much time on it, so keep the fun element by stopping before you reach that point. Don't try to spend an entire day studying a single topic; you'll soon get bored of it! Instead, map out a timetable allocating no more than an hour per topic, breaking bigger ones down if necessary. This means that you'll have a varied day and be better able to retain interest and enthusiasm for individual subjects.

8. **Treat yourself:** Rewarding yourself for your efforts is an important part of making studying more enjoyable, as well as motivating yourself. Keep some healthy snacks with you while you're studying, such as sliced fresh fruit, dried fruit or nuts.

9. **Study with a friend:** It can be difficult to motivate one when studying alone.

Working with friends is a great way to boost creativity by exchanging ideas. It's enormously beneficial to those given to procrastination – particularly when you can help each other understand concepts you're struggling with. Engage in some academic discussions and debates. Give each other little mini lectures, complete with presentations – this helps you learn the subjects as well as giving you valuable practice at presenting.

Following these tips should help avoid boredom when you're studying and keep your productivity levels high. Even the subjects you think are dull can be made interesting and enjoyable if you take the right approach, and maintaining this positive attitude is sure to do wonders for your grades!

THE COMMON DO'S AND DON'TS

It is of utmost importance to keep in mind the things you need to do while preparing and attempting CAT. We should keep in mind, that knowing what all should be avoided is equally important for getting success in the exam.

For your convenience, we have prepared a list of both- the do's and the don'ts. Take a look and be alert as being aware of both the facets of the coin makes you better prepared and confident to perform.

Before the exam

Do's

➤ Keep a notepad and record every difficult word you come across. It may be while reading newspapers, articles or even watching a movie. Remember to note down its meaning there and then. Go through all words every time you open the notepad.

➤ Go through all your class notes and practice work, do ensure that you clarify any kind of doubts you may have. Do not delay or keep it for later.

➤ Discuss your performance in mocks and online tests with

mentors and seek feedback from them. While working on those sections, again be attentive so that you don't repeat the previous mistakes.

➢ Revise all formulas or theorems before the exam, especially when it comes to Quantitative sections.

➢ As we already discussed, CAT is not as much about hard work as about smart work. Make your own acronyms; associate them with your life.

➢ Fill in your CAT form much before the deadline. It is always considered advantageous, more so in getting the desired location or test centre.

➢ Be very careful with your details as any misinformation may lead to rejection of your application.

Don'ts

➢ Don't forget the basic concepts you learned in the beginning. Some questions just may be the twisted ones involving the core knowledge.

➢ Don't spend too much time on any particular question, so as you are left with very less time for others which you could have cracked.

➢ If you feel like you are just about to find the solution and need only a clue, for the time being skip it instead of spending ample amount in one go.

➢ Keep reminding yourself that it's time bound and there is negative marking in the test.

➢ It's human to forget something, don't spoil your mood feeling guilty.

➢ Do not stress in the last few days of preparation. Stay with a cool mind as stress will only kill your precious time with no productive results.

➢ Do not feel demotivated in case your mock performances are not good enough. It is not the final indicator of your CAT score as there are several other factors to consider. What you do on the final day cannot be pre-decided whatsoever.

➢ Do not forget to download your admit card and get it printed well before the D-day. It is not advisable to take any chances.

➢ Do not forget to keep all the belongings (photographs, identity proofs, etc.) required at one place well before time.

- Never stay awake a night before the test, as lack of sleep has proven to be a bane for several students who could have performed better. State of mind and freshness are important considerations for a better performance.

During the exam:

Do's

- Keep in mind your strengths and weaknesses and accordingly devote your time on the various topics.

- Stay extremely calm in the examination hall. Jittering and panicking will only make you lose concentration.

- In case of any query, never hesitate to put them forward. Always contact the concerned authority to clarify the same.

- Follow the instructions carefully. Any inconsistency is totally unacceptable as the authorities are very strict relating to the conduct of the examination.

- Make sure that your test has been completed and is properly accepted.

Don'ts

- Do not try to use any unfair means as it is only inviting trouble. The centres have well equipped means of detecting it along with non-negotiable penalties.

- In case of technical glitches, do not panic. Follow the required protocol and it will be satisfyingly dealt.

- Do not hurry in the end and ensure the final acceptance, as it is a CBT (computer based test).

CHAPTER 4

TIP & TECHNIQUES TO CRACK VARC

IMPORTANCE OF VARC BY CAT GURU GAJENDRA KUMAR

VA-RC is a very important portion not only for CAT but also for any kind of competitive examinations.

Since CAT has sectional weightage of 34 marks, it makes the section equally important as quantitative ability section. So, it is equally important to focus on and crack the VA-RC section to add on to a good overall percentile.

The aspirants must frame appropriate strategy for the section as each topic requires different techniques to learn. One cannot follow the traditional method to answer the RC passage, as in CAT exam, RC contains 16 questions i.e. 4-5 RC passages. So it is very important for an aspirant to grasp the technicality of passage. One should increase the reading speed and the understanding as well. To achieve this one must go through English newspapers like, Economic Times and The Hindu etc. One should also read non fiction novels.

Another portion of this section is VA i.e. English usage which includes sentence correction, grammar, critical reasoning, deductive logics, paragraph completion, jumbled paragraph and the total weightage of this portion is 18 marks.

Students often ask me the question that should we practice VA as much as Quant. My answer is yes; but not resembling the way you practice quant. Rather, you have to read a great deal to increase your proficiency level on Reading ability, as CAT lays emphasis on testing reading ability of the candidate. You can see that as much as full 1/3 of the section is Reading Comprehension. In a nut-shell the examiner desires to evaluate how well a candidate can relate to the ideas presented in the passage.

So, to crack the exam i.e. to achieve 99+ percentile, this section will help to boost your marks.

Let see the CAT-2017's Topic breakup which will help us to understand the strategies we should frame and work upon it.

Topic	No. of Questions	Level
Reading Comprehension	24	Easy-Moderate
Para-jumble	4	Difficult
Summary(MCQ based)	3	Easy
Para-jumble (odd sentence out)	3	Moderate to Difficult.

Thus, for achieving good score or percentile in CAT exam one must know the technicality of solving RC passage due to its high marks weightage which ultimately affects the overall percentile to get increased.

PARAJUMBLES

Parajumble questions in CAT are designed to check your understanding of the language and whether you are able to logically co-relate different parts of a paragraph. The sentences given in each question, when properly sequenced, form a coherent paragraph. Each sentence is labelled with an alphabetic letter. The test taker has to choose the most logical order of sentences from among the given choices to construct a coherent paragraph.

How to Crack Parajumbles

The trick is to Identify the **First Sentence**, how we are able to follow the clues to identify the First Sentence is important , hence these are the Clues :

➢ First sentence can be a Noun
➢ It can never be a Pronoun
➢ Articles both Definite or Indefinite can be the First Sentence
➢ **But , So, Now** will never be the First Sentence
➢ **'Hence, Finally** and **Therefore'** will always be the **Last Sentence**

OR

➢ First Sentence – Noun
➢ Then Spot the " Central Theme "
➢ Followed by " Activity, Talking or Analysis ", what happens when
➢ Special Word – Connectives
➢ Followed by " Articles, Pronoun and Adjectives "

Example 1:

Duryodhana was a wicked prince.

P.   One day Bhima made Duryodhana fall from a tree from which Duryodhana was stealing fruits.

Q.   He did not like that Pandavas should be loved and respected by the people of Hastinapur.

R.   Duryodhana specially hated Bhima.

S.   Among the Pandavas, Bhima was extraordinarily strong and powerful.

T.   This enraged Duryodhana so much that he began to think of removing Bhima from his way.

OPTIONS:

(a)   PSQTR   (b)   QTPRS   (c)   QSRPT   (d)   PSRQT

Explanation to Solution:

To arrange the above example, firstly we have to find the clues that will help us to locate the qualifier. Here the clue is 'he' as it the pronoun used for Duryodhana. So this means Q is the qualifier of sentence 1 and our answer will begin with Q. So with this, we can eliminate options (a) and (d).

Now, we are left with two choices (b) and (c). We have to decide by sequence that which sentence should come first.

The option (b) states that T will be the second sentence. Now read T sentence. It does not seem to be an independent sentence as it starts from 'this', representing something that has occurred before this sentence.

So the only option left is OPTION (c), which is the correct answer.

Few Other Clues :

➢   Transition Words
➢   Identify the Personal Pronoun
➢   Demonstrative Pronoun
➢   Combining with Logic
➢   Acronym Approach
➢   Time Sequence
➢   Theory Approach
➢   Article Approach
➢   Noun Pronoun Adjective
➢   Identifying the Opening and Closing Sentence
➢   Key words Approach (in some sentences, few key words get repeated in the Subsequent sentences, too)
➢   Structured Approach, where one tries to find out what the Author tries to convey in a structured way.
➢   Indicating words can also help in unravelling Parajumble

We can also decipher a Parajumble by the following :

1. Qualifier is a sentence that tells us about other sentences.
2. Try to Locate the Qualifier, it will help us to identify the First sentence or Sentence which takes the passage forward.
3. Try to build the Flow of the narration.
4. Try to eliminate wrong sentences as Qualifier, like any sentence gives us a feel of End or Closing of a paragraph.
5. Identify the Mandatory Pairs, this helps in building sequence and certain set of sentences come as pair, those will never be the opening sentences or Qualifiers.
6. Transaction words will never be qualifier like **Again, Also, Besides, As well,** etc. connects a sentence.
7. Identify Pronoun Anecdotes/ Personal Pronouns.
8. Look for short Form or abbreviation or Acronym, they can never be Qualifiers.
9. The Opening and Closing Sequence (OCS).
10. The TIME Sequences Approach

Support Signal Words: Look for the words or phrases supporting a given sentence. Sentences containing these words will generally not be the opening sentence. These sentences will follow immediately the sentence supported. Some examples of such words are:

Furthermore	additionally	also	and
indeed	besides	as well	too
likewise	moreover		

Example 2:

The digital-storytelling movement started in the early 1990s with performance artists such as San Francisco-based Atchley. But the technique is just beginning to take hold in the world of e-business. At last fall`s national Digital Storytelling Festival in Crested Butte, Colo., nearly half of the people signed up represented corporations. "The stories that people are telling on the Web around corporate brands are astounding" says Atchley. "Knowledge is best shared and remembered through a good story, and companies are just starting to catch on to all that this can mean ______________________

(a) If so, digital storytelling will see that computer prices continue to plummet in near future.

(b) If so, digital storytelling will link high-speed data lines and more people to the Web.

(c) If so, digital storytelling will help companies to know more than what they already know.

(d)   If so, digital storytelling will become more popular.

(e)   if so, Digital story telling will be less popular

Analysis :

(a)   **Incorrect – Change of Scope** - as Computer prices were beyond the Scope hence out of Context

(b)   **Incorrect – Change of Scope** -as High-speed data and Web not discussed hence out of context.

(c)   **Incorrect – Change of Scope**-The focus of the paragraph is on digital storytelling not on how it will help the companies.

(d)   **Correct – On account of scope and continuity –** The focus is on digital storytelling, and also takes forward the impact of interest of companies- more popularity.

(e)   **Incorrect- Change of Tone-** The paragraph only spoke about the popularity of Digital Platform , hence this sentence is not correct.

Fact Inference Judgement (FIJ)

FACTS deal with pieces of information that one has heard, seen or read, and which are open to discovery or verification. Facts are those statements which involve dates, natural phenomena, events etc. **INFERENCES** are conclusions drawn about the unknown on the basis of the known. Inferences check your ability to read between the lines. **JUDGEMENTS** are opinions that imply approval or disapproval of persons, objects situations and occurrences in the past, present or future. Judgement can be identified from statements that Imply approval or disapproval, Impose compulsion or Predict using will or shall.

Facts

➢   Information which can be desirable

➢   Could be Universal Truth or some Relevant action

➢   Anything that is Seen, Heard or Read is a Fact but it should not be a Perception

➢   Any Other opinion can be seen as Fact, whereas one's own opinion is taken as Inference or Judgement

➢   Figures, Stats or Data are Facts or Tools of Facts, but should be a complete Fact not Partial or Slice of Fact

➢   Tends to Bring People in unison or Agreement

The Salient Feature of Facts

1. Facts are based on Cold Data

➢   Repetitive Nature of Action is a fact, not One of incident

- ➤ Facts should be bare, not tilted towards any opinion or provocation
- ➤ Facts should not be misconstrued or Skewed
- ➤ Facts should have many layers or dimensions Not just Unidirectional

Example: If we are Reading Batting Record of any Batsman then

- ➤ We should be able to know how much portion or percentage of Runs he scored in India and Abroad
- ➤ Runs scored in various Batting positions
- ➤ Runs scored in First innings and in Second Innings
- ➤ Runs scored under various Captains
- ➤ Runs scored against various Nations

Thus just knowing The batting Record is not a Complete Fact , it's a fact but not a Comprehensive and Exhaustive as one would like to

2. Facts should be based on Cold Data in a period of Time, which means it should not be

- ➤ Seasonal in nature
- ➤ It may not be One of Events in a Year
- ➤ It should not be based on ACTS of God like Tsunami, Earth quake or Landslide

3. Facts should be always be

- ➤ Comprehensive, Exhaustive
- ➤ Not Partial, Fragmented , Subjective, Portion or Slice of Main Data cannot be ever taken as a fact, Statistically may be Correct but can be misleading from the point of inference or Judgement

Example : Development during early Post Independence, Development in Pre Internet Age, Development Post Internet Age, are all slice of Data of Indian Development in last 70 yrs, but in itself they are misleading or Not comprehensive or Exhaustive.

FACTS in itself is Hard and Cold, NEVER Misleading

Inference:

We can try to find out or justify our inference by using 6Ws
Who, When, Where, What, Which, Why & How

This question if we ask on the Facts or stats which is presented to us, will give us the Logical flow and relevance of

Why it's important? What for its being discussed?

Similarly we can put it in Test against all the above mentioned Parameters and get the Factual Inference rather than biased or prejudiced.

1. It is like a Conclusion drawn from the Data.

Example – If our imports are more than our export, it proves we are yet to be self-sufficient in our industrial growth or trade, now if we import more of consumer durable products than capital goods, then we can infer that our industrial growth is in very poor shape as we are importing what we should manufacture. Also, it proves our cost of production is higher than imports.

When 1992 the markets were opened under PM Mr. PV Narsimha Rao, the craze for foreign goods and utilities went down drastically from Import point of view, we got in the habit of Levis, Lee Nike, Adidas effortlessly.

2.   Inference is also by-product of our Experiential Learning too.

Example: When we see anyone wearing their religious symbol on them in person, we tend to believe that that person is a hardliner or very pious, someone who can be more inflexible than most, we have many prominent examples around us, regarding this, hence not anyone is named.

3.   Our Inferences are coloured by views of people close to us.

Example : The household, neighbourhood or society creates or colours our views, like the person close to us, has impact on our liking or disliking some person, party, ideology or faith. Like People who do badly in School are taken as failures or no good, but many out of them in later years become very successful hence we tend to get influenced by opinions and influencers.

4.   We tend to align our thought process with facts to build an inference, like people with Left leaning will only talk about Concentration of wealth in the hands of few. But will never talk about skill and responsibility and Business acumen all these. 1 % people have which majority may not have, majority might have an idea or skill sets to run small set-ups not such massive or huge units.

Judgement

> Facts or Inference are there to help us to come to conclusion hence Judgement.

> We do not want to take decision on Pre-conceived notions; hence, we need data and try to come to Logical inference.

> Sometimes mistakes can be taken as Act done on purpose; thus, one needs to dissect the Action from the Person.

> Opinions Changes with Time and perspective, depending on which side of the table one is at, receiving end or giving end.

> Opinions can be based on Approval or Disapproval of the Subject matter, but as discussed its time and situation bound.

> Judgements are arguable and contestable they are definite but not perfect; they can be based on Perceptions too.

Examples:

'JUDGMENT' STATEMENTS:

1) So much of our day-to-day focus seems to be on getting things done, trudging our way through the tasks of living- it can feel like a treadmill that gets you nowhere; where is the childlike joy?

2) We are not doing things that make us happy; that which brings us joy; the things that we cannot wait to do because we enjoy them so much.

3) This is the stuff that joyful living is made of- identifying your calling and committing yourself wholeheartedly to it.

4) When this happens, each moment becomes a celebration of you; there is a rush of energy that comes with feeling completely immersed in doing what you love most.

5) Given the poor quality of service in the public service, the HIV/AIDS affected should be switching to private initiatives that supply anti-retroviral drugs (ARVs) at a low cost.

6) But how ironic it is that we should face a perennial shortage of drugs when India is one of the world's largest suppliers of generic drugs to the developing world.

7) The Mid-day Meal scheme has been a significant incentive for the poor to send their little ones to school, thus establishing the vital link between healthy bodies and healthy minds.

8) The goal of universalisation of elementary education has to be a pre-requisite for the evolution and development of our country.

9) We should not be hopelessly addicted to an erroneous belief that corruption in India is caused by the crookedness of Indians.

10) Red tape leads to corruption and distorts people's character.

11) Inequitable distribution of all kinds of resources is certainly one of the strongest and most sinister sources of conflict.

12) Extensive disarmament is the only insurance for our future; imagine the amount of resources that can be released and redeployed.

Word Usage

This chapter will help you to avoid making some of the most common mistakes of usage. Do you worry about the correct use of affect and effect or flaunt and flout? Are you uncertain about whether to say different from or different than or if you should say 'a historic event' or 'an historic event'?

We can Use same word in different sentences and meaning remains the same; though treatment remains different, not usage.

Example: Similar

➢ On being told that she was white and that one of the servants was black, she concluded that all who occupied a **similar** menial position were of the same hue; and whenever I asked her the colour of a servant she would say "black."

➢ She opened her eyes to find all three gazing at her with **similar** guarded looks.

➢ She reached the top of the stairs and stared at a **similar** scene leading past the Arch and all the way up the park toward the city.

➢ She straightened and very carefully folded the sweater before placing it with **similar** care into the bag.

➢ The sensations were similar to her bond with Jule: sweet and warm.

Similar Usage to Some important words

1. Seam - noun

a line where two pieces of fabric are sewn together in a garment or other article.

Synonyms : join, stitching, joint, closure, line, suture

an underground layer of a mineral such as coal or gold.

"the buried forests became seams of coal"

Synonyms : layer, stratum, vein, lode, deposit

Seam - verb

join with a seam.

"it can be used for seaming garments"

make a long, narrow indentation in.

"men in middle age have seamed faces"

Usage of Seam in similar Sentences

➢ The lignite in this region also warms the ranchman's cabin, being easily mined where a **seam** is exposed in the walls of a ravine or on the side of a hill.

➢ Megan stepped forward and the heel of her sandal sank into a **seam** in the walkway.

➢ Rich strips of alluvial soil, however, **seam** a cold clay-marl, needing intensive cultivation to become highly productive.

➢ In the oldest form of this class of working, where the size of the pillar is equal to the width of the stall or excavation, about 4 of the whole **seam** will be removed, the remainder being left in the pillars.

➢ I was 40 fathoms in depth, we multiply the depth by the rate of inclination, 40 X 8 = 320 fathoms, which gives the point at which the coal **seam** A should reach the surface.

> Number and nature of the coal seams in new ground, or the position of the particular **seam** or seams which it is proposed to work in extensions of known coalfields.

> At Monceaux les Mines, in France, a **seam** 40 ft.

> A coal **seam** with a soft pavement and a hard roof is the most subject to a " creep."

> The name is from a word meaning "to roast till puckered" or "drawn up," in reference, it is suggested, to a peculiar **seam** in their mocassins, though other explanations have been proposed.

> but immediately on crossing the dislocation seen in the figure it is changed and the deeper **seam** D is found.

> With careful packing it is estimated that the surface subsidence will not exceed 40% of the thickness of the **seam** removed, and will usually be considerably less.

Usage of Plebian in Sentences

> But the Kabuki-za and its yakusha (actors) remained always a **plebeian** institution.

> In theory, the twelve **plebeian** centuries were open to all freeborn youths of the age of seventeen, although in practice preference was given to the members of the older families.

> Its utterances (plebiscite) had the full force of law; it elected the tribunes of the plebs and the **plebeian** aediles, and it pronounced judgment on the penalties which they proposed.

> GAIUS MARIUS (155-86 B.C.), Roman general, of **plebeian** descent, the son of a small farmer of Cereatae

> MARCUS FULVIUS NOBILIOR, Roman general, a member of one of the most important families of the **plebeian** Fulvian gens.

> Enamoured of the beautiful daughter of the **plebeian** centurion Virginius, Claudius attempted to seize her by an abuse of justice.

> If so, there would be no place in Athens for those great **plebeian** houses, once patrician in some other commonwealth, out of which the later Roman nobilitas was so largely formed.

> The agricultural **plebeian** of old Rome and the feudal noble of contemporary Europe were both of them at Venice impossible characters.

> GAIUS FLAMINIUS, Roman statesman and general, of **plebeian** family.

Usage of Rebuff in Sentences

- Since your offer does not benefit me, I will have to **rebuff** it and walk away empty-handed.
- The pretty woman's **rebuff** was so kind that Jack did not feel bad when she turned down his offer to dance.
- Because the position does not pay well, Kelly decided to **rebuff** her supervisor's offer of a promotion.
- The unattractive girl was shocked when the star of the football team did not **rebuff** her invitation to the dance.
- Does anybody understand why the poor woman chose to **rebuff** her million-dollar inheritance?
- When my wife is angry with me, she will **rebuff** my attempts to get back in her favour.
- Since Alice is married to Jeff, she is going to **rebuff** Bill's lunch invitation.

Usage of Resonance in Sentences

- The two piano keys played together provided a good example of resonance.
- The length of the pipe may be varied by pouring in water, and this is done until we get maximum resonance of the pipe to the fork.
- The neon tube glowed when it was in resonance with the wireless telegraph antenna.
- Standing as usual in the middle of the hall and choosing the place where the resonance was best, Natasha began to sing her mother's favourite song.
- The effects of resonance were studied by the music students.
- "Now, Sonya!" she said, going to the very middle of the room, where she considered the resonance was best.

Usage of Prodigal in Sentences

- They live frugally, and are only **prodigal** in powder and human life.
- Every **prodigal**, therefore, is a public enemy; every frugal man a public benefactor.
- His eldest brother being a **prodigal** he succeeded to the paternal estate, but threw the will into the fire on his brother's promising to reform.
- The subjects of the "**Prodigal** Son" and "St Jerome in the Wilderness" he on the other hand treats in an almost purely northern spirit.
- Henry was the most **prodigal** of lovers, and gave her all rights over the duchy of Valentinois.

- Why vicarious suffering is needed, or why the God who is the loving Father does not simply forgive, as in the parable of the **prodigal** son, is not asked.
- To his fellow workers he was uniformly generous, free from jealousy, and **prodigal** of praise.

Usage of Ostentation in Sentences

- His library of 70,000 volumes was one of his forms of **ostentation**, and so was his gallery of pictures.
- At the most important crisis of his life in 1783, he almost made an **ostentation** of disorder and of indifference not only to appearances, but even to decency.
- This prelate was related to the English king, Edward II., and after a life spent in strife and **ostentation**, he died on the 24th of September 1333.
- Against these may be set the vices of pride, **ostentation**, love of bloodshed, contempt of inferiors, and loose manners.

Usage of Morbid in Sentences

- His early studies were directed chiefly to **morbid** anatomy.
- She would seem to have been from the first of a **morbid** and unhealthy temperament.
- The cells met with in **morbid** parts which are in a state of active vitality are built up of the same components as those Structure of found in normal tissues.

Usage of Mundane in Sentences

- The way he described her, I don't think she paid much attention to the **mundane** things in life.
- Only looking up at the sky did Pierre cease to feel how sordid and humiliating were all **mundane** things compared with the heights to which his soul had just been raised.
- Books on **mundane** subjects, not at all conducive to the spiritual edification of the faithful, were read by the tsar's counsellors, and a theatre had been erected, in which the tsar often witnessed very unedifying dramas and ballets.
- The distinction between the poor teachings of **mundane** science and our sacred all-embracing teaching is clear to me.
- The Armenians also make use of the **mundane** era of Constantinople, and sometimes conjoin both methods of computation in the same documents.

Usage of Ostracism in Sentences

➤ The conflict between the two leaders ended in the **ostracism** of Aristides, at a date variously given between 485 and 482.

➤ It is an extraordinary fact that, if **ostracism** was introduced in 598 B.C. for the purpose of expelling Hipparchus it was not till twenty years later that he was condemned.

➤ The whites who were responsible for the conduct of the blacks were warned or driven away by social and business **ostracism** or by violence.

➤ Aristotle, admitting its usefulness, rightly describes **ostracism** as in theory tyrannical; Montesquieu (Esprit des lois, xii.).

Usage of Deja vu in sentences

➤ He instantly realized that he was having a **deja vu** once he started feeling dizzy after stepping into the new house.

➤ Experiencing **deja vu** for the first time can be a weird feeling. It can make your doubt your own reality.

➤ Having a **deja vu** can be a happy as well as a shocking experience, depending on the stimuli that may have been fed into your subconscious over a period of time.

➤ Why is this movie causing me a **deja vu**? Have I seen a movie with a similar storyline before?

➤ The company was gradually failing because all their new products were giving their customers a sense of **deja vu**.

➤ Even after the restaurant was refurbished, it gave patrons a strong **deja vu** of the older decor.

➤ The **deja vu** my father had when I was being felicitated was so overwhelming, that he almost fainted.

➤ I don't mind getting a **deja vu** of my dream, but I don't want to experience my nightmare again.

Usage of Altruist in Sentences

➤ To overlook the Cyrenaic recognition of social obligation and the hedonistic value of **altruistic** emotion is a very common expedient of those who are opposed to all hedonistic theories of life.

➤ In accordance with my theory of the brain, each corresponds with one of our three **altruistic** instincts - veneration, attachment and benevolence."

➤ We would restrict our **altruistic** activity to weekends and possibly an evening or two a week by phone, if it worked.

- ➢ And so in the ideal state everyone will derive egoistic pleasure from doing such **altruistic** acts as may still be needed.
- ➢ How do we know it is not our own selfish desires disguised by the unconscious into seemingly **altruistic** motives?
- ➢ **Altruistic** donations of eggs should be allowed.

Usage of Anachronism in Sentences

- ➢ Since there were not laptop computers during the Civil War, the presence of a portable computer in the history film is a definite **anachronism**.
- ➢ These days the habit of introducing yourself to a new neighbour with a welcome gift has become an **anachronism**.
- ➢ Soon physical books will be completely replaced by e-books and will represent nothing more than an **anachronism**.
- ➢ In today's computer world, a floppy disk is an **anachronism**.
- ➢ When I saw the ancient typewriter in the technology store, I knew I was looking at an **anachronism**.
- ➢ It is always fun to go to my grandmother's house and watch her **anachronism**, her large black and white television.

Usage of Cabal in Sentences

Hundreds of workers formed a **cabal** to demonstrate their dissatisfaction with the firm's healthcare plan.

Because the billionaire is paranoid, he believes his children have formed a **cabal** to steal his money.

A number of board members were part of the **cabal** that sought to remove the company founder from his position as chairman.

During the past few months, independent rebels have formed a united **cabal** in order to displace the dictator.

As a **cabal**, the women were able to apply enough pressure to gain voting rights.

Usage of Chalet in Sentences

- ➢ The proper name for these nuts is Sennhiitten or **chalets**, but the latter term is incorrectly applied also to houses in the village below.
- ➢ The appearance of the houses is precisely that of Swiss **chalets**, picturesque and comfortable - the only drawback being a want of chimneys, which the Bhutias do not know how to construct.

Usage of Enigmatic in Sentences

- ➢ These **enigmatic** speeches were all that the multitudes got, but the disciples in private were taught their lesson of hope.

- Her skin was golden from the sun, which brought out the **enigmatic** eyes, and made them glow with the otherworldly beauty displayed by her and the one called Evelyn.
- When the idea, itself indefinite, gets no further than a struggle and endeavour for its appropriate expression, we have the symbolic, which is the Oriental, form of art, which seeks to compensate its imperfect expression by colossal and **enigmatic** structures.
- This **enigmatic** personage appeared in Islay, and rather had his pretences thrust on him than assumed them; he was half-witted.
- These outbursts, very terse and **enigmatic**, are charged with religious emotion, and turn often on some subtle point of Arahatship, that is, of the Buddhist ideal of life.
- He'd never met the **enigmatic** deity, but he'd heard past-Death go off about this man after every interaction.
- The position was complicated by the somewhat **enigmatic** attitude of Russia; for the Neapolitan Liberals, with many of whom Count Capo d'Istria, the Russian minister of foreign affairs, had been on friendly terms, proclaimed that they had the " moral support " of the tsar.
- Almost every sentence in it is **enigmatic**. As now published, there are always subjoined to it certain appendixes, which are ascribed to Confucius himself.
- 3-13 we have another Jewish fragment of a very **enigmatic** character.
- His doctrinal position is explained in his letters to his patron Eusebius, bishop of the imperial city of Nicomedia, and to Alexander of Alexandria, and in the fragments of the poem in which he set forth his dogmas, which bears the **enigmatic** title of " Thalia " (06XECa), used in Homer, in the sense of " a goodly banquet," most unjustly ridiculed by Athanasius as an imitation of the licentious style of the drinking-songs of the Egyptian Sotades (270 B.C.).
- In this lady he had found a sitter whose face and smile possessed in a singular degree the haunting, **enigmatic** charm in which he delighted.

Amos still has frequent visions cf a more or less **enigmatic** character, as Micaiah had, but there is little trace of this in the great prophets after him.

Usage of Halitosis in Sentences

Then, people could start reporting all their medical issues—headaches, halitosis, heart disease—and we will begin to see commonalities between genes and conditions we do not generally regard as genetic.

Usage of Low Brow in Sentences

- In this enjoyable, disposable, by-the-numbers comedy lark, there's a constant stream of **lowbrow** gags and pratfalls.
- Despite the crackdowns, **lowbrow** theatre seems set to stay in Pakistan.
- Some art curators would consider late AC/DC singer Bon Scott too **lowbrow** a subject on which to base an exhibition.
- His agenda takes in the highbrow and **lowbrow**, from David Beckham and Britney Spears to French film theory, Patrick White

Usage of Actuary in sentences

- Graduating at Harvard in 1825, he was a teacher till 1835, was an **actuary** in 1835-1845, and then became assistant at the Washington observatory.
- He was also frequently employed as consulting **actuary**, a business in which his mathematical powers, combined with sound judgment and business-like habits, fitted him to take the highest place.
- Appointed in 1862 **actuary** to the United States sanitary commission, he issued in 1869 an important volume of Military and Anthropological Statistics.
- There, however, he remained only six months, for certain views on slavery, strongly held and injudiciously expressed, entailed unpleasant consequences, and necessitated his return to England, where he obtained in 1844 the post of **actuary** to the Legal and Equitable Life Assurance Company.

Usage of Prevaricate in Sentences

- In order to get his bill passed, the politician went out of his way to **prevaricate** about the release of the environmental study.
- Because my sister Sarah does not take bad news well, I always **prevaricate** when telling her something she does not want to hear.
- In hopes of avoiding questions about his recent car accident, the actor tried to **prevaricate** during his interview.
- When you **prevaricate**, you only make a complicated situation worse than it already is.
- Even after she had been sworn in for her testimony, the witness continued to **prevaricate** about her relationship with the defendant.
- Miles has a tendency to **prevaricate** when he believes things are not going his way.

HOMONYM/ HOMOPHONE/HOMOGRAPH

Homonym

A homonym is a word that is said or spelled the same way as another word but has a different meaning. "Write" and "right" is a good example of a pair of homonyms. Homonym traces back to the Greek words homos, meaning "same," and onuma, meaning "name." So a homonym is sort of like two people who have the same name: called the same thing but different. A homonym can be a word that sounds the same as something else — like by ("near") and buy ("purchase") — or it can be spelled exactly the same way and pronounced differently — like minute (unit of time) and minute ("tiny").

Examples of Homonyms

Here are a few more examples of homonym pairs:
- address (to speak to)/address (location)
- air (oxygen)/air (a lilting tune)
- band (a musical group)/band (a ring)
- bark (a tree's out layer)/bark (the sound a dog makes)
- current (up to date)/current (flow of water)
- die (to cease living)/die (a cube marked with numbers one through six)
- fair (equitable)/fair (beautiful)
- kind (type)/kind (caring)
- lie (to recline)/lie (to tell a falsehood)
- match (to pair like items)/match (a stick for making a flame)
- mean (average)/mean (not nice)
- Pole (a person from Poland)/pole (a piece of metal that holds a flag)
- pound (unit of weight)/pound (to beat)
- ream (a pile of paper)/ream (to juice a citrus fruit)
- rose (to have gotten up)/rose (a flower)
- spring (a season)/spring (coiled metal)
- tender (gentle)/tender (to pay money)
- tire (to grow fatigued)/tire (part of a wheel)

Homophone

A homophone is a word that sounds the same as another word but has a different meaning and/or spelling. "Flower" and "flour" are homophones because they are pronounced the same but you certainly can't bake a cake using daffodils. Other common homophones are write and right, meet and meat, peace and piece. You have to listen to the context to know which word someone means if they're spoken aloud.

If they say they like your jeans (genes?), they're probably talking about your pants and not your height and eye color — but you'd have to figure it out from the situation!

Examples of Homophone

- ad, add
- ail, ale
- air, heir
- aisle, I'll, isle
- all, awl
- allowed, aloud
- alms, arms
- altar, alter
- arc, ark
- aren't, aunt
- ate, eight
- auger, augur
- auk, orc
- aural, oral
- away, aweigh
- **awe, oar, or, ore**
- axel, axle
- **aye, eye, I**
- bail, bale
- bait, bate
- baize, bays
- bald, bawled
- ball, bawl
- band, banned
- bard, barred
- bare, bear
- bark, barque
- baron, barren
- base, bass
- bay, bey
- bazaar, bizarre
- be, bee
- beach, beech
- bean, been
- beat, beet
- beau, bow
- beer, bier
- **bel, bell, belle**
- berry, bury
- berth, birth
- **bight, bite, byte**
- billed, build
- bitten, bittern
- blew, blue
- bloc, block
- boar, bore
- board, bored
- boarder, border
- bold, bowled
- boos, booze
- born, borne
- bough, bow
- boy, buoy
- brae, bray

Homograph

Homograph talk about two words that are spelled the same but have different meanings and are pronounced differently — like "sow," meaning female pig, and "sow," to plant seeds. The word homograph merges homos, the Greek word for "same," with graph, "to write." If two words are written identically but don't share a meaning, they are homographs. Some examples are close ("to shut") and close ("nearby"); and bass ("deep") and bass ("the fish"). Homographs are confusing at first glance, but once you read them in the context of a sentence or hear them spoken aloud, you'll easily figure out which word is intended.

Examples of Homograph

agape – with mouth open OR love

bass – type of fish OR low, deep voice

bat - piece of sports equipment OR an animal

bow – type of knot OR to incline

down – a lower place OR soft fluff on a bird

entrance – the way in OR to delight

evening – smoothing out OR after sunset

fine – of good quality OR a levy

learned – past tense of learn OR knowledgeable

minute – tiny OR unit of time

moped – was gloomy OR motorcyle

number – more numb OR numerical value

row – line OR argument OR propel a boat

sewer – drain OR person who sews

wave – move the hand in greeting OR sea water coming into shore

wound – past tense of wind OR to injure

10 FIGURES OF SPEECH YOU MUST KNOW

A figure of speech is an expression that has a meaning other than the literal meaning. It is designed to portray an idea more clearly or more interestingly. The most common types of figures of speech are metaphors, similes, idioms, personification, hyperbole, and euphemisms. If you analyze the past years papers you will notice that there have been direct questions on Figures of Speech in some of the management aptitude tests like CAT, XAT. Further, you must know them as they often form a part of Critical Reasoning, Reading Comprehension, Passage Completion, etc.

1. Metaphor

A metaphor affirms that one thing is something that it literally is not.
Examples: This house is a prison. He's a real gannet. She listened with a stone face. Would you like to have any dinosaurs in here?

2. Simile

A simile equates one thing to another (often with the use of the word like or as).

Examples: He eats like a horse. He is as big as an elephant. The child is as thin as a rake. She wore the dress that fits like a glove.

3. Personification

Personification is when non-human objects are given human traits.

Examples: She wandered into the jungle lonely as a cloud. Time flew and it was time for me to go back to my hometown. Her old Mercedes tends to give up on long hills.

4. Hyperbole

Hyperbole is an exaggeration or extravagant statement used for effect.

Example: She had a million dollar question. They won a tonne of cash. She is dying to shop for new Agatha Christie novel that just came into the market.

5. Synecdoche

In Synecdoche, a part is used to represent the whole.

Examples: (ABC s for alphabet or the whole for a part) - India won the World Cup in 1983.

6. ALITERATION

Alliteration draws attention to the phrase and is often used for emphasis. The initial consonant sound is usually repeated in two neighbouring words although sometimes the repetition occurs also in words that are not neighbours.

Examples: Catherina's cat clawed her couch, creating chaos. Kat's kids kept calling. Tom took tons of tools to make toys for tots.

7. Allusion

Allusion relies on the reader being able to understand the allusion and being familiar with the meaning hidden behind the words.

Example: Bob acts like a real Romeo with the ladies. (Romeo, the lead character in Shakespeare's play, Romeo and Juliet, is regarded as a true romantic hero who won over Juliet against her family's wishes).

8. IRONY

Irony is a figure of speech in which there is a contradiction of expectation between what is said what is really meant. There are three types of irony: verbal, dramatic and situational.

Example: A plumber works on leaky faucets all day and comes home to find there is no water in his home. Looking at his son's report card, Father says, "Wow, you could win an award for your grades!"

9. UNDERSTATEMENT

It is a figure of speech used by speaker to deliberately make a situation seem less important or serious than it really is.

Examples: She got the highest grades in class. An understatement could be: "She did OK on that test." (Modest), You just hit the biggest lottery of all time! An understatement could be: "I'm kind of excited." (Modest)

10. EUPHEMISM

Euphemism is used to express a mild, indirect, or vague term to substitute for a harsh, blunt, or offensive term. Some euphemisms intend to amuse, while others intend to give positive appearances to negative events or even mislead entirely.

Examples: Passed away instead of died; Correctional facility instead of jail; Collateral damage instead of accidental deaths; Pregnancy termination instead of abortion; On the streets instead of homeless.

Common Errors in English

A number of students face lot of problems while solving the questions based on common errors or sentence correction because most of the time, they are unaware of the rules of grammar which leads to committing very common mistakes.

To enhance your grammar knowledge and help you overcome committing common mistakes, below are given some examples along with explanations that will be very helpful and handy to you.

- ➤ Only I and my friend were at the concert. (WRONG)

  Only my friend and I were at the concert. (RIGHT)

  (Pronouns order – **I** and **me** come last when more than one pronoun is used in a phrase, **you** comes next to last, and **third-person** pronoun comes first.)

- ➤ Everybody will get their share. (WRONG)
  Everybody will get **his** share.   (RIGHT)

  ('Everybody' may sound like 'a lot of people', but it is a singular noun and takes a singular verb.)

- ➤ Everybody will get their share. (WRONG)
  Everybody will get **his** share.   (RIGHT)

  ('Everybody' may sound like 'a lot of people', but it is a singular noun and takes a singular verb.)

- ➤ They realized where their weak points were and how to get rid of them.   (WRONG)

They realized where their weak points were and how **they could** get rid of them (RIGHT)

(A fragment with a missing subject; hence, an appropriate subject to form an independent clause should be included.)

➤ While doing the work, there are obstacles ahead. (WRONG)
While doing the work, **they met with** obstacles. (RIGHT)

(Needs to revise a dangling modifier by naming the appropriate doer of the action as the subject of the main clause.)

➤ Andamans are a group of islands. (WRONG)
The Andamans are a group of islands. (RIGHT)

('The' is used with the places consisting many islands; for example – The Bahamas, The Maldives, The Philippines and The West Indies etc.)

➤ She neither speaks English nor French. (WRONG)
She speaks neither English nor French. (RIGHT)

(Here, 'neither' modifies the verb 'speak' whereas, it should modify the language 'English'.)

➤ I saw him to play. (WRONG)
I saw **him play**.   (RIGHT)

(Here, use of the preposition 'to' is inappropriate. There are two patterns of this kind of sentences: 1) I saw him play = I saw him play throughout the game. 2) I saw him playing = I saw him on the field but I don't know whether he actually finished the action.)

➤ I didn't see him too.   (WRONG)
I didn't see him either. (RIGHT)

('Either' is used in negative sentences to add an agreeing thought: Tom doesn't speak French. Sam doesn't speak French either.)

➤ Nobody is bound to suffering. (WRONG)
Nobody is **bound to suffer**.   (RIGHT)

('Bound' after verb + 'to' infinitive means certain or extremely likely to happen like, you're bound to forget people's name often.)

➤ She rarely goes to theatre.   (WRONG)
She rarely goes **to the theatre**. (RIGHT)

('The', the definite article is used because you're talking about something 'definite'.)

TIPS AND TECHNIQUES IN COMMON ERRORS

➢ Read the sentence all the way through. Even if you think the error is in part B, make sure to read the entire sentence as this will help prevent you from falling into traps.

➢ Always check for subject-verb agreement. The verb needs to take a form that matches the subject.

➢ You are not done only by picking the error because it sounds weird or because it's not the word you would use. You should be able to explain to yourself what error the answer you picked contains. If you can't do so, it's probably not the right choice.

➢ Lastly, read English newspapers and articles etc. as much as you can so that you get accustomed to English language. Reading habits, many times, help you pick the errors just by having a glance over the sentence.

TIPS AND TECHNIQUES FOR VOCABULARY

➢ Read regularly from a variety of sources like newspapers, magazines and blogs etc. as this habit will help you learn new words as well usages of words in different contexts.

➢ Make a target of learning a new word daily. This technique is used by many people and they have successfully enhanced their vocabulary.

➢ You should play word games like – Crossword puzzles, Anagrams, Word jumbles and Scrabbles etc. This method will help you discover new words.

➢ Engage yourself in talking with people in English whenever you get an opportunity so that you may practice the words that you have learnt. Apart from this, it will also help you learn new words during the conversation and in addition help you enhance your fluency in spoken English.

Reading comprehension

Reading comprehension is the most favoured section in English because it doesn't require prior knowledge to solve RCs (Reading Comprehensions). Greater chances of VARC high accuracy in it act as a game changer in clearing the cut off in English section.

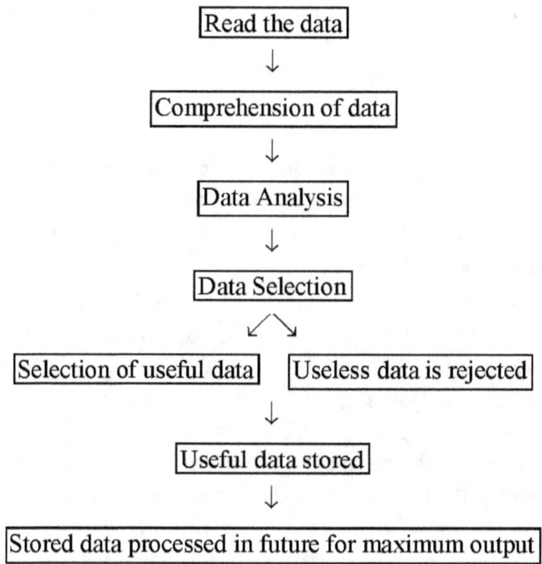

Here are some tips and techniques to easily approach RCs with high accuracy.

➢ You need to have ample RCs practice on computer to pass this section with flying colours because while attempting RCs online, you can't underline important points and mark different areas in the passage and therefore, you need to hone your skills by practising regularly.

➢ Quickly skim through the passage before you read the passage thoroughly or attempt the questions.

➢ Before you start reading the passage, go through the questions that need to be answered. This will give you a fair idea about what the passage talks about. Once you start reading the passage, you can start locating the answers to questions.

➢ It is very important to make inferences while reading the passage because most of the questions are not asked directly. Your understanding of the passage and its theme is of utmost importance as it helps you to eliminate the wrong options and pick the right one.

➢ Before reading the entire passage, first, read the first and last paragraph of the RC to have an idea what the author is saying in the paragraph. This will help you in having an overview of the whole passage.

> When you are attempting a question based on phrase, just read the two-three lines above and below that phrase to have an idea what is implicit from that phrase.

Examples:

DIRECTIONS (QS. 1 - 5): Read the following passage carefully and answer the questions given below it. Certain words/ phrases have been printed in bold to help you locate them while answering some of the questions.

The Indian education sector is one of the largest sunrise sectors contributing to the country's economic and social growth. The Indian education system, considered as one of the largest in the world, is divided into two major segments of core and non-core businesses. While, schools and higher education form the core group, the non-core business consists of pre-schools, vocational training and coaching classes. The education sector in India is evolving, led by the **emergence** of new niche sectors like vocational training, finishing schools, child-skill enhancement and e-learning. India has emerged as a strong potential market for investments in training and education sector, due to its favourable demographics (young population) and being a services-driven economy. Indian education sector's market size in Financial Year, 2012-13 estimated to be USD 71.2 billion is expected to increase to USD 109.8 billion by Financial Year 2015-2016 due to the expected strong demand for quality education. The market grew at a CAGR of 16.5% during Financial Year 2015-2016.

Education has been made an important and integral part of the national development efforts. The tremendous increase in the number of students and of educational institutions has given rise to the term 'education explosion'. No doubt, this has resulted in serious problems such as inadequacy of financial resources and infrastructure and **dilution** of personal attention to the education and character-formation of the students. Also, there is the unwanted side-effect of enormous increase in the number of educated unemployed. However, we cannot overlook the advantages of education explosion in India. Mere increase in the percentage of literate people does not indicate a qualitative change in the educational standards of the people and a substantial improvement in manpower resources of India. Unemployment problem in India cannot be blamed on the availability of large masses of educated people in India. Uncertainty and vacillation have marked the government's policy regarding the medium of education in India. While the government policy in this respect has not changed, a significant increase in the number of schools-primary and secondary-imparting education through the English medium is a significant development. Thousands of nursery schools that have mushroomed since the last decade **purport** to impart education to infants through English. This is an unwanted development which has been **deprecated** by educationalists and political leaders. Regarding the medium of instruction in colleges and universities, many State Governments have already decided, in principle, to switch over to the regional language. However, the implementation in this respect has remained very slow.

Today, virtually, every university in India is offering correspondence courses for different degrees and diplomas. In fact, correspondence education has opened new vistas for the educational system which could not successfully meet the challenging problem of providing infrastructure for multitudes of new entrants into the portals of higher education. The public demand for higher education was initially met through evening colleges; now correspondence education has come to the rescue of the worried education administrators.

1. Which of the following facts is not true regarding the Indian education sector as per the passage?

    (a) It is still in the process of development.

    (b) It is one of the contributors to India's growth.

    (c) There has been a recent trend towards the adoption of regional languages as the medium of instruction.

    (d) Mushrooming of schools imparting English education has been appreciated.

    (e) The number of educated unemployed has increased.

2. As per the passage, India's education system has been able to attract investments because of

    A. The demographic factor.
    B. The Indian economy being service-driven.
    C. Indian democratic governance being an attractive issue.

    (a) Only A   (b) Only B
    (c) Only C   (d) Both A and B
    (e) Both B and C

3. As per the passage, which of the following explains the term 'education explosion'?

    A. Huge investment in the education sector.

    B. Pro-active government policy towards the education sector.

C. Spurt in the number of students and educational institutions.
(a) Both A and B   (b) Only C
(c) Both B and C   (d) Only B
(e) All of the above statements are correct

4. Which of the following can be inferred from the passage?
   A. Increase in literacy level signifies a qualitative increase in educational attainment of people.
   B. Literacy levels are closely related to improvement in manpower resources.
   C. The existence of educated people does not necessarily contribute to the problem of unemployment.
   (a) Only A   (b) Only B
   (c) Only C   (d) Both A and B
   (e) All A, B and C

5. According to the passage, which of the following statement(s) is/are correct?
   (a) Increase in English medium schools is a welcome sign for the Indian education sector.
   (b) Increase in English medium schools in India is an insignificant, though wanted development.
   (c) Correspondence education has proved to be a panacea in terms of educating people without proper infrastructure.
   (d) The implementation of regional languages as medium of instruction has been quite fast.
   (e) The prospects for future growth of India's education sector look bleak.

FILL IN THE BLANKS

Sentence completion or fill in the blanks is a type of test in which a word or two are removed and you are to select the most appropriate word(s) from the given options so that the sentence remains grammatically and contextually correct. This section tests your vocabulary skills and reading practice. Your abilities to understand the main idea of the sentence and the logical structure of the sentence are also tested.

Examples of the latest pattern of questions

DIRECTION (1-5): In question given below there are two statements, each statement consists of two blanks. You have to choose the option which provides the correct set of words that fits both the blanks in both the statements appropriately and in the same order making them meaningful and grammatically correct.

1. (A) Consumers in India are already beginning to feel the _______ as petrol and diesel prices have _______ multi-year highs.
   (B) It was her hard _______ that saved his life as he was about to get _______ by the fast moving truck.
   (a) tweak, grown   (b) pinch, hit
   (c) squeeze, knocked   (d) burden, buffeted
   (e) cramp, bumped

2. (A) The _______ of actors at the _______ concert was nothing new.
   (B) At the _______, the thieves made their _______ plan to execute in the very next day.
   (a) get-together, plummet
   (b) meeting, grisly
   (c) tryst, appalling
   (d) amour, grotesque
   (e) rendezvous, nocturnal

3. (A) His tough _______ with the dealer made sure that he was very concerned about the proper _______ of his family in the new city.
   (B) In the current state of Brexit _______, a spirit of reasonable _______ could well define the future.
   (a) dealings, settlement
   (b) arguments, compliance
   (c) negotiations, accommodation
   (d) talks, conniption
   (e) dispute, leniency

4. (A) The _______, which are generally conducted between January and March, had a late start this year, and were less _______ than were seen in recent years.
   (B) The military _______ administered by the Indian army showed _______ use of indigenously built fighter jets.
   (a) manoeuvre, extensive
   (b) tactic, stunning
   (c) exercise, capacious
   (d) activity, amorphous
   (e) cessation, huge

5. (A) His love for cars never _______ because even in his old age, he used to _______ short his spending to buy the latest one in the market.

   (B) Indian gold demand ______ as jewellers expected import tax ______ in budget.

(a) diminished, slit

(b) dwindled, rip

(c) waned, cut

(d) drooped, chip

(e) decreased, praise

IMPORTANT TIPS AND TECHNIQUES TO SOLVE SENTENCE COMPLETION

- It is advised not to look at the options straightaway. At first, read the sentence and think of a word that fits in the blank appropriately. This strategy will help you find the missing word easily because when you read the sentence, you catch the theme, tone and context of the sentence.

- When you look at the options, make sure you find the option that best replaces the word that you had thought of initially. Ensure that the meaning of the sentence is intact. Once you have placed the likely option, do check that the sentence gives out a plausible meaning.

- Concentrate on eliminating the options rather than finding the correct one. In sentence completion test, your knowledge and understanding of vocabulary and common idioms-phrases of English language is tested. You must consider all of the choices before you confirm your answer, even if your predicted answer is among the choices. The difference between the best answer and the second best answer is sometimes very subtle. When you think that you have the correct answer, read the entire sentence to yourself, using your best choice.

- Keeping a close eye on grammar rules can sometimes help you find the correct word easily. For instance, if the article 'an' comes before the blank then you can immediately go for the option that begins with a vowel or a word the pronunciation of which sounds like a vowel.

- You should look for indicators in the sentence; if any. Indicators tell you what is coming up. They indicate that the part of the sentence is either drawing a contrast with something stated previously or supporting something stated previously. Examples of some contrast indicators are – But, Despite, Although, However, Nevertheless and Yet etc. Examples of some support indicators are – And, For, Likewise, Also, Furthermore, Moreover and In addition, etc. Examples of cause and effect indicators are – Thus, Therefore, Hence, Because, If...then, etc.

- Lastly, read English newspapers and magazines regularly as this will enhance your grammatical understanding and you will also come to see how various words are used in different contexts. Reading habits, at times, help you get the correct word just by having a quick glance at the options.

PASSAGE COMPLETION

Passage completion is a test in which a paragraph is given with an omitted line and you have to find this omitted line from the given options.

For example:

1. Women's boxing is yet to be recognized as an Olympic support, _________. If that happens, the dream of most of the tough girls may come true.
    - (A) The International Boxing Association has been campaigning to include it as an event in the 2008 Beijing Olympics.
    - (B) Though boxing is a very tough sport many women are seen willing to take up professional boxing now-a-days.
    - (C) Even some state governments are now willing to employ the women pugilists.
    - (a) Only A
    - (b) Only B
    - (c) Both A and C
    - (d) Both B and C
    - (e) All A, B and C

2. The audiences for crosswords and Sudoku, understandably, overlap greatly, but there are differences, too. A crossword attracts a more literary person, while Sudoku appeals to a keenly logical mind.

Some crossword enthusiasts turn up their noses at Sudoku because they feel it lacks depth. A good crossword requires vocabulary, knowledge, mental flexibility and sometimes even a sense of humour to complete. It touches numerous areas of life and provides an 'Aha!' or two along the way. ____________

(a) Sudoku, on the other hand, is just a logical exercise, each one similar to the last.

(b) Sudoku, incidentally, is growing faster in popularity than crosswords, even among the literati.

(c) Sudoku, on the other hand, can be attempted and enjoyed even by children.

(d) Sudoku, however, is not exciting in any sense of the term.

(e) Sudoku, whereas, gives better enthusiasm.

TIPS AND TECHNIQUES TO SOLVE PASSAGE COMPLETION

> It is very important to read the passage without missing any line to understand the inherent message/view/opinion the author wants to convey. This also helps you out in drawing the topic or the central idea of the passage which is vital while choosing the correct option.

> After reading the passage carefully, have a glance on the options and try to find the correct sentence by matching the subject-matter/topic of the passage with that of the given options.

> The options which appear to be irrelevant or out of context should be ignored instantly.

> After eliminating the mismatch options, you will be left with two or may be three options to choose from. Now, you need to judge which of the left options matches with the tone of the author and correctly fits the blank.

> Try to find the selected options one by one at the missing space and judge it on the basis of tone, context, logic, sequence and symmetry. The option which qualifies these criteria will be the right one and should be chosen.

> After finding the correct option, read the passage for the last time to finally conclude that after filling the blank with your selected option, the passage reflects a complete picture/meaning.

ODD ONE OUT

Let us now move to the various techniques to solve different kinds of Odd One Out/Sentence Exclusion questions which are an integral part of the Verbal ability section of CAT. .... an analysis of the Verbal Ability section in the exams and some strategies to solve it. There are also some basic examples of Odd One Out. Hence this section on Odd One Out will help you raise your score based on strong concepts and not guesswork.

1. Odd One Out (Sentences)

It is only a renewed (and I'd say much easier) way of testing the old concept of solving Para-jumbles. Here, we are going to list some tips and strategies that will help you solve these questions in no time at all!

Step 1: Read the Directions

You need to be absolutely certain of exactly on what basis you are being asked to pick out the odd sentence. So do not ignore the directions before the question, even though it may seem repetitive. For example, you may have been asked to pick out the odd sentence based on the varieties of activities being spoken of in them, but you assume that you were asked to pick out the one that defies the logical sequence without reading the instructions for the question. This is potentially fatal.

Step 2: Understand the central theme

This is the key to solving such questions. Read each of the sentences and you will be able to identify the logical sequence or the scheme of events being followed in the question. There will however be that one sentence that does not fit into the scheme. Once you have grasped the common concept in all of the sentences, it gives you a head start into identifying your 'odd' sentence.

Step 3: Identify the opening sentence

This is going to be a relatively general sentence, one that introduces a place, person or a concept. Once you have grasped the general theme, it should be relatively easy to identify the introductory statement that initiates the scheme of events.

Step 4: Track the sequence

Try and place each of the sentences into a logical scheme of events. Establish a connecting link between the sentences and check for coherence between them. The sentence that does not logically fit into the established sequence is the odd sentence here.

Step 5: The logic matters; not the subject matter

The potentially added sentence might have very similar subject matter as the other sentences. However, what matters is whether the sentence fits into the logical pattern of the other sentences, in the established sequence more than the content of the sentence.

Example:

A. Legislating laws to prohibit marriage between races hurt the couples involved

B. and Often couples who had lived together for years had to separate

C. These laws prohibited intermarriage between people of different races

D. Which caused loneliness and bitterness because of ignorance and a desire to see themselves as better than people of other races?

E. Up to the 1960s, miscegenation laws were still enforced in some parts of the United States

1. ABCD (E)   2. EDCA (B)   3. ADEB (C)   4.ECBA (D)

II. Odd one Out (Word)

Sometimes, there may come some questions for picking an odd word from a list of four words. You need to analyze the common factor in three words, it may be semantic or from a field or category. At, times it may be a bit tricky, stay calm and focus then. Your study of vocabulary section will be of help then.

1. Identify the odd word from the every set:

   (a)   Quell   (b)   Ruffle
   (c)   Allay   (d)   Control

PARAGRAPH SUMMARY

Paragraph summary means making a paragraph of 15-16 lines concise and writing it in two to three lines. Summarizing a paragraph involves the knowledge of reading comprehension, one word substitution and also of synonyms.

How to Approach

➢ Read to grasp the essence of the text. Put yourself in the shoes of the author and think what he is trying to convey.

➢ Sometimes the paragraph may be on a complete abstract topic. In such a case, read it carefully two times, if you don't get the meaning out of it in the first read.

➢ Identifying the central theme will mean you have almost won the battle cause the choices provided mostly have the theme as an option.

➢ is to understand flow of key ideas in the passage.

Tips to follow

Ideal time: CAT 2017 3 questions on summarizing the paragraph. All were MCQ based single correct type questions. There is no right sure shot way to this, just make sure you develop habit of summarizing maximum number of paragraph, keeping an eye on the time you spend on each.

Practice Schedule: You should practice 4–5 passages daily in the beginning of your preparation, preferably from different genres. You can increase it later on to 6–8 whatever you feel like. Initially you can be liberal on yourself but practice time bound at a later stage.

Total command: There is nothing called total command in CAT, as you already know there is no fixed syllabus. Practice variety of paragraphs. All you can hope is to increase your current level so as to bring the best in you. Only yardstick is your performance before vs. your performance now.

Reading speed: Your reading speed is the number of words you can read and understand per minute. Remember, if you don't understand because you're reading very fast, it is of no use.

Calculate your reading speed. In this way you will be able to supervise your improvement.

To understand the types of questions asked in CAT, try to find solution of the examples given below.

Example

The passage given below is followed by four summaries. choose the option that best captures the author's position.

1. To me, a "classic" means precisely the opposite of what my predecessors understood: a work is classical by reason of its resistance to contemporaneity and supposed universality, by reason of its capacity to indicate human particularity and difference in that past epoch. The classic is not what tells me about shared humanity–or, more truthfully put, what lets me recognize myself as already present in the past, what nourishes in me the illusion that everything has been like me and has existed only to prepare the way for me. Instead, the classic is what gives access to radically different forms of human consciousness for any given generation of readers, and thereby expands for them the range of possibilities of what it means to be a human being.

   (a) A classic is able to focus on the contemporary human condition and a unified experience of human consciousness.

   (b) A classic is a work seeks to resist particularity and temporal difference even as it focuses on a common humanity.

   (c) A classic is a work exploring the new, going beyond the universal, the contemporary, and the notion of a unified human consciousness.

   (d) A classic is a work that provides access to a universal experience of the human race as opposed to radically different forms of human consciousness.

   The passage below is followed by four summaries. Choose the option that best captures the author's position.

CHAPTER 5

TIPS & TECHNIQUE TO CRACK DILR

IMPORTANCE OF DILR FOR CAT BY CAT BY GURU GAJENDRA KUMAR

We know that the since present pattern of CAT examination has changed since 2015. These are three sections now:-

- Quantitative Ability
- Data Interpretation and Logical Reasoning
- Verbal Ability and Reading Comprehension

The following table will help you to understand the CAT 2017's actual pattern in DILR.

Section	No of Questions	No of MCQ Questions	No of Non-MCQ Questions	Difficulty level
Logical Reasoning and Data Interpretation	32	24	8	Difficult

The section "DILR" is the most scoring section, if one has clear concept of the topics and has prepared it well.

Data interpretation is all about various data in the form of graphs i.e. line graph, bar graph, pie chart, etc.

Basically, it is all about the data or we can say it is the numerical representation of theoretical facts. For example, how many mopeds are manufactured in consecutive years by the TVS automobile company?

The graphs are prepared in either very simple or very confusing manner; sometimes it needs a lot of quick calculations. So, it is suggested that in this portion of the section one should follow quick calculation techniques. This is how you can beat the time consuming problems.

Basically, to excel yourself in this section, you need to clear the concept and go through the difficulty level of the question from previous year papers.

Tips & Technique to Crack DILR

For strategic preparation one must follow the Topic breakup of previous year's papers and plan and practice more to the important topics, for example CAT-2017's topic breakup as follows-

Data Interpretation

Topics	Number of Questions	Types of Questions
Data Table	8	MCQ
Bar Graph	8	MCQ
Pie Chart	4	Non-MCQ
Line Graph	4	MCQ

Logical Reasoning

Topics	Numbers of Questions	Types of Questions
Team Formulation	4	Non-MCQ
Family par	4	MCQ

On the other hand, LR does not have any mathematical calculations but requires general logic. CAT questions are not as easy as compared to the topics belonging to other competitive examinations; they are at times very difficult as well as time-consuming.

The best way to solve the LR portion is to write down all the necessary points and use it as required. For example, if someone is solving a linear arrangement problem, he/she must know how to eliminate the unnecessary possibilities and follow the step by step information to solve the problems.

One must practice the various concepts under LR and follow the methodical way to solve the problem, so that candidates can save time during the examination.

As we can see that last year this particular section was a bit difficult. However, do not be disheartened because if the section was difficult for you, then it was difficult for the rest of the candidates too. Thus, the number of questions attempted plunges and the correct attempt up to 10-12 questions will fetch you enough percentile to justify your score and a call from the IIMs.

DATA INTERPRETATION

The Data Interpretation section of CAT is divided into two parts. It consists of graphs, charts and tables from which you have to analyze data.

Aspirants before the official exam, should be familiar not only with the question types they will see on the exam, but also with the different ways the exam may present data:

- Line graphs
- Bar graphs
- Pie charts
- Scatter plots
- Tables
- Multiple data sources

Aspirants should have good knowledge as well as comfort level with this concepts. These consist primarily (but not exclusively) of the following:

- Percentage
- Average
- Ratio
- Proportion
- Data comparison

Tips to Crack Data Interpretation

- **Read the Questions Carefully:**
  In Data Interpretation, questions will consist of statistics, numbers & diagrams that might look difficult but are actually not at all difficult to solve. The scarier a DI set,the easier it is to solve. So don't loose heart and loose your confidence. Don't start finding the easier-set.

- **Improve your Calculation Speed:**
  The Date Interpretation section needs much calculation. Such calculations can waste your time. So learn shortcuts and strategies. Vedic Maths is the best technique which can be used to save time in complex calculations.So it is good to learn Vedic Maths Techniques which makes Data Interpretation more easy and fun-loving.

- **Know all types of Data Interpretation questions:**
  When you will start practicing DI questions for a while, you'll notice that there are different types or formats of questions in this section. There will be bar charts, tables, pie charts etc. There will also be questions where a lot of text/information will be provided in 1 long paragraph.Start reading newspapers which have data interpretation, bar graphs,line graphs etc.
- **Day-to-day preparation**
  It is necessary to practice Data Interpretation questions at least once a day. Follow one strategy to solve at least one question of Data Interpretation, it will be enough to crack Data Interpretation in CAT.

Types of Graphs:

(1) Line Graph

In line graph type questions information of a variable is given with respect to the other variable. This information is given on Cartesian co-ordinate plane that has two axes namely X axis and Y axis.

Consider an example where marks of 3 students A, B, C is given for their 4 semester.

	Sem 1	Sem 2	Sem 3	Sem 4
A	60	65	80	75
B	70	75	80	85
C	75	65	70	80

The same information can be given by line graph where it is easier to compare the rate of increase or decrease.

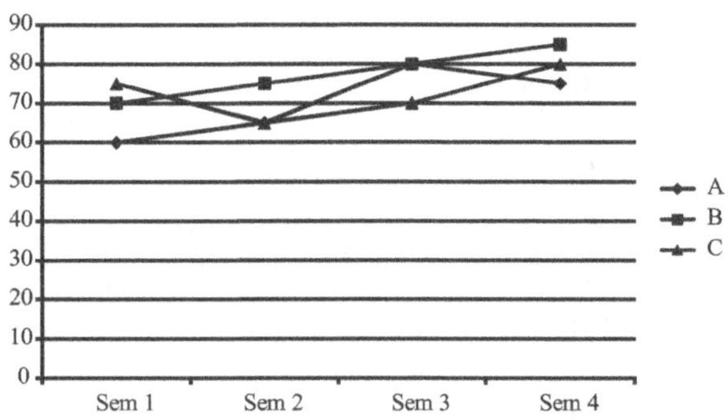

Line graph questions comes in the examinations from data interpretation are generally based on various types –

1. **Single line graph :** graphs representing single line which shows changes in a single variable over a certain period of time.
2. **More than one line graph:** in this type of graphs two or more dependent variable are represented.
3. **Mixed variables :** in the same graph, when two continuous variables having different units of measurement.

The above mentioned types are most frequently asked graphs in different types of examinations e.g banking, any govt. jobs , CAT, MAT, IBPS etc.

Line graphs are very useful for visual representa-tions from time series, categorical data, frequency distributions etc.

Example 1:

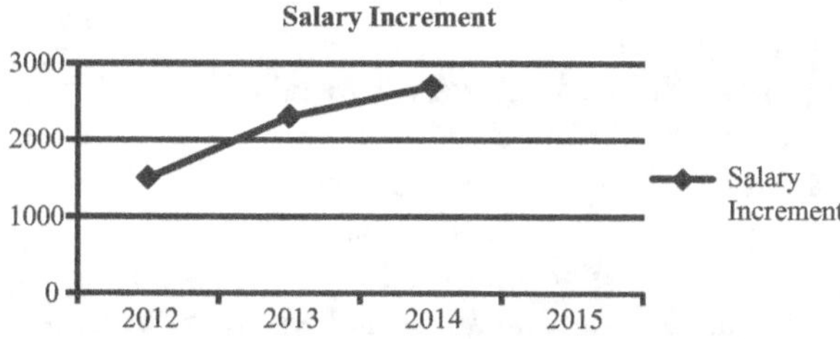

Above graph is showing Annual salary increment of Radhekishan. Answer the following questions carefully:

1. What is the percentage increment in 2013(approx)?
    (a)   53 %   (b)   54%
    (c)   56%   (d)   58%

Sol.(a) Salary of Radhekishan in 2012 : ₹1500 in 2013 salary is : ₹2300.

$$\text{Percentage} = \frac{2300-1500}{1500} \times 100 = 53.33\%$$

So, increment in the salary is 53.33%.

Example 2: Study the given graph carefully to answer the questions that follow:

Number of days taken by three carpenters to finish making one piece each of four different items of furniture

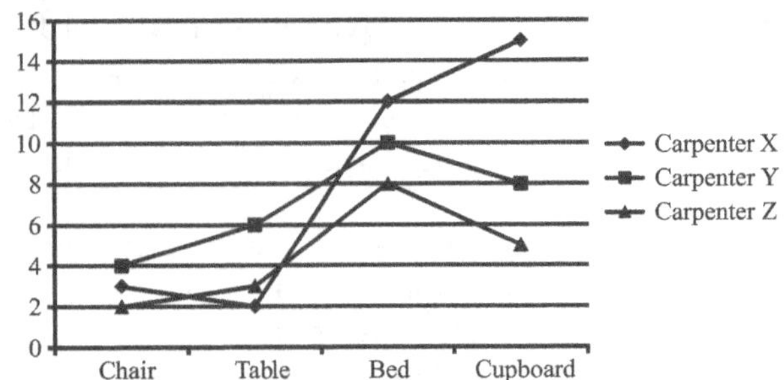

1. If carpenter X and carpenter Y were to make a chair together how many days would they take?

    (a) 1 day
    (b) 4 days
    (c) 12/7 days
    (d) 2 days

Sol.(c) Carpenter X takes 3 days to make a chair and carpenter Y takes 4 days to make a chair. $\dfrac{1}{3}+\dfrac{1}{4}=\dfrac{7}{12}$ = i.e., $\dfrac{12}{7}$ days to make a chair together.

2. If carpenter X, Y and Z were to make a table together how many days would they take?

    (a) 4 days
    (b) 3 days
    (c) 1 day
    (d) 2 days

Sol.(c) X takes 2 days to make a table, Y takes 6 days to make a table and Z takes 3 days to make a chair. Together they take $\dfrac{1}{2}+\dfrac{1}{6}+\dfrac{1}{3}=\dfrac{6}{6}=1$ day to make a table

3. What is the total number of days that Carpenter Z will take to make one piece each of all the four items together?

    (a) 32 days
    (b) 23 days
    (c) 11/59 days
    (d) 11/32 days

Sol.(b) Z will take 2 + 3 + 8 + 10 = 23 days to make each piece.

Rate of Increase or Decrease

Rate of increase or decrease can be determine just by observation of line graph. Rate of increase is more for line graph whose slope (Or inclination) with respect to horizon or X-axis is more.

Consider two graphs A and B and observe the pattern and determine rate of increase of which variable is more. Consider business done by two corporate houses from January to April.

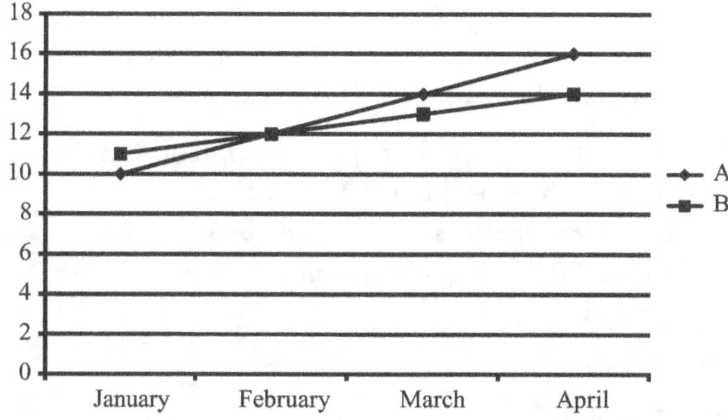

From the graph we can observe that the slope of A is more than that of B or in other words we can say that increment of business done by corporate House A is more than increment done by B.

Similarly we can observe that average business done by corporate house A is more than that done by B.

Data Table

DATA TABLE is one of the frequently ask questions. Tables are one of the most versatile methods of systematic presentation of quantitative data. It is very easier than other graphs to extract information from the tables.

Usually questions are asked on Single data type and multiple data type questions.

Example 1: The following table shows the bus fare from different places of one way bus fare from one place to another. Answer the following questions from the table.

BUS FARE chart of Route no 06

Places	Garia	Tollygunj	Anwar Shah	Rash Bihari	Hazra
Garia	-	7	10	10	15
Tollygunj	7	-	5	7	10
Anwar Shah	10	5	-	7	10
Rash Bihari	10	7	7	-	5
Hazra	15	10	10	5	-

1. What is the Minimum fare of the BUS running on the route no 06?

(a)   15   (b) 10   (c)   7   (d) 5

Sol.(d) As it is very clear from the table that the minimum bus fare is 5. Hence option (d) is the answer.

2. If a person board himself in garia, for him how much percent fare increase from rashbihari to hazra?

Sol.   **It is clearly understand that bus fare increases ₹ 5** so it is 50 % change in the fare.

$$\text{i.e., } \frac{5}{10} \times 100 = 50\,\%$$

(3) Bar Graph

A bar graph is a chart that uses either horizontal or vertical bars to show comparisons among categories. One axis of the chart shows the specific categories being compared, and the other axis represents a discrete value.

Example 1:

Directions: *Study the following graph carefully to answer the questions that follow:*

Number of runs scored by three different teams in six different cricket matches

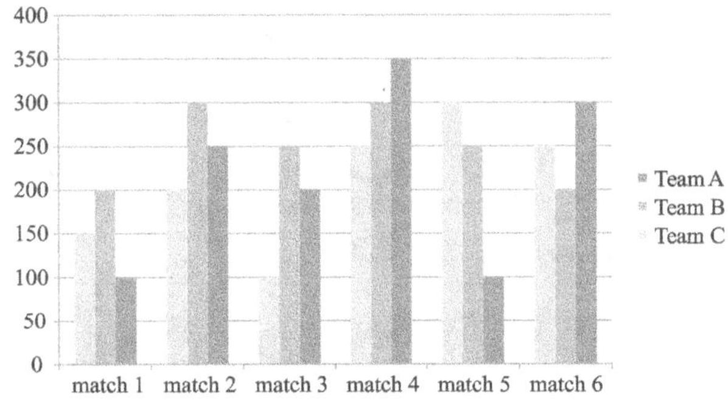

1. What is the percentage increase in the number of runs scored by Team B in match 4 as compared to that in the previous match (Match 3)?

(a)   40   (b) 30   (c)   20   (d) 25

Sol.(c) Score of team B in Match 4 = 300 runs
Score in match 3 = 250 runs, required % increase = (50/250) × 100 = 20%.

2. What is the ratio of the number of runs scored by team A in match 2 to the number of runs scored by Team C in Match 6?

(a) 5 : 4

(b) 2 : 5

(c) 2 : 3

(d) None of these

Sol.(d) Score of team A : score of team C = 200 : 10 = 20 : 1.

3. What is the average number of runs scored by Team B in all the matches together?

(a) 250　　(b) 275　　(c) 200　　(d) 300

Sol. Average runs scored by team B

$$= \frac{200 + 300 + 250 + 300 + 250 + 200}{6} = 250$$

Example 2: The following bar chart shows the consumption of fertilizers in nutrient terms. Examine the following graph to answer these questions:

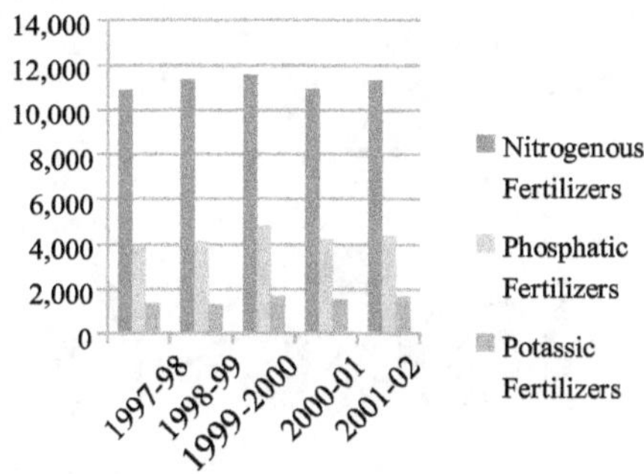

1. Total Consumption of Nitrogenous Fertilizers, Phosphatic fertilizers and Potassic Fertilizers during the period 1997-2002 has been in the ratio

(a) 10 : 28 : 74

(b) 37 : 14 : 5

(c) 5 : 2 : 1

(d) None of the above

Sol.(d) Required ratio = nitrogenous : phosphate : potassic = 54500 : 21500 : 3500 = 109;43:13.

2. Which of the following fertilizers has shown a consumption pattern of increase and decrease in alternate years?

(a) Nitrogenous Fertilizers

(b) Phosphatic Fertilizers

(c) Potassic Fertilizers

(d) No such trend is discernable

Sol. No such trend is encountered by any types of the fertilizers.

(4) PIE CHART

Pie charts are the circular representation of the data. Generally the data in the question represents the break ups of a whole into its parts. The share of each part in the pie diagram is proportionate to its share of the whole data. As we know that the total angle is 360 degree. Hence angle of sector = $\dfrac{\theta}{360} \times \pi r^2$ or $\dfrac{\theta}{360} \times$ total value

Example:

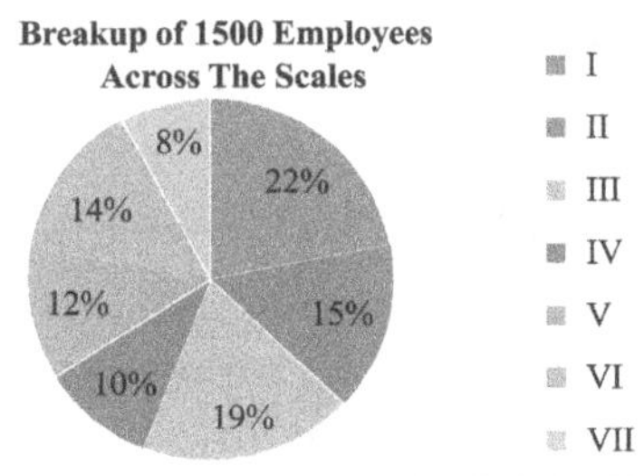

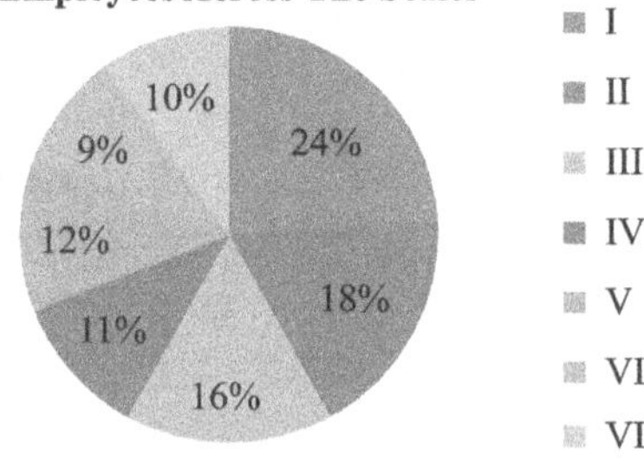

1. How many females are working in Scale II ?

   (a)   144   (b)   81

   (c)   96   (d)   138

Sol. (b) As total number of employees are 15% of 1500 = 225 total male employee in scale II are 18% of 800 = 144 therefore, total no of female employee in scale II = 225 – 144 = 81

2. What is the ratio of male to female employees working in Scale V?

   (a)   7 : 8   (b)   2 : 1

   (c)   8 : 7   (d)   1 : 2

Sol. (b) Total no. of employees in scale v are 12% of 1500 = 180 total no. of male employees in scale v are 12% of 800 =

96 total no. of female employees in scale v are (180 – 96)

= 84 required ratio = $\dfrac{96}{84}$ = 8 : 7

(5) Mixed Graph

Mixed graph is the another type of questions which is usually asked in different types of competitive exams to see whether the candidate is capable to interpret information given in different types of multi-graphs . Generally two or more graphs (either bar chart with pie or line graph with data table) are combined together. Let's start the exercise to understand the different levels of difficulties.

Example: Study the line and the bar graph and answer the question:

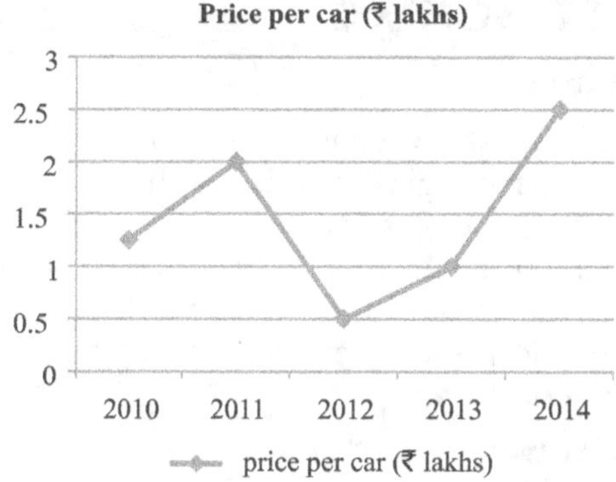

The two graphs above pertain to ABC LTD , a famous car maker of india. Follow the graph and questions based on graphs.

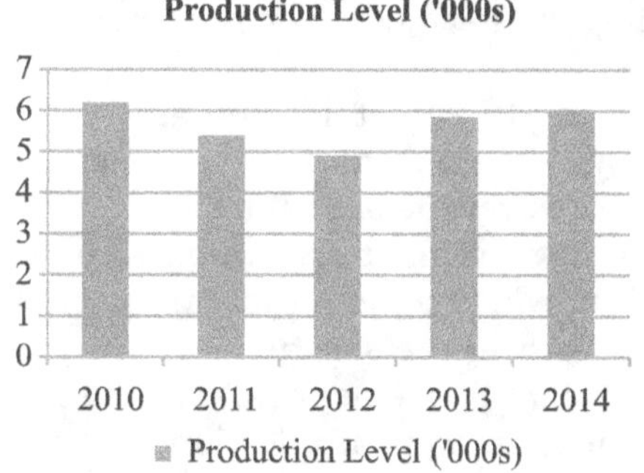

Q. No. of cars produced = (cost of production + profit margin)/ (price per car). If during 2014 , the cost of production was ₹ 1200 cr. Find profit margin?

(a) 10 crs   (b) 20 crs
(c) 30 crs   (d) 40 crs

Sol. (c) Using the information given in the questions, we know that –

Cost of production in year 2014 = 120 Crs

Production level = 6000

Price per car = 2.5 lakhs

Now using the formula, No. of cars produced = (cost of production + profit margin)/(price per car)

Or, profit margin = no. of cars produced x price per car – cost of production = 6000 × 2.5 lakhs – 120 crs = 15000 lakhs – 120, 00,00,000 = 15000,00,000 –120,00,00,000 = 30,00,00,000 = 30crs

LOGICAL REASONING

Data Sufficiency

Data Sufficiency questions consists of 2 or more statements and are generally in form logical puzzle.You have to select question in this form.First,if one statement is enough to answer the question.Second,Both the statements are true to answer the question.This type of questions need much practice and and it also needs time.So prefer them to solve after you have solved each and every question.

Direction to Solve:-

In each of the questions below consists of a question and two statements numbered I and II given below it. You have to decide whether the data provided in the statements are sufficient to answer the question. Read both the statements and

Give answer

(A) If the data in statement I alone are sufficient to answer the question, while the data in statement II alone are not sufficient to answer the question

(B) If the data in statement II alone are sufficient to answer the question, while the data in statement I alone are not sufficient to answer the question

(C) If the data either in statement I alone or in statement II alone are sufficient to answer the question

(D) If the data given in both statements I and II together are not sufficient to answer the question and

(E) If the data in both statements I and II together are necessary to answer the question.

Example 1: How is 'No' coded in the code language ?
Statements:
1. 'Ne Pa Sic Lo' means 'But No None And' and 'Pa Lo Le Ne' means 'If None And But'.
2. 'Le Se Ne Sic' means 'If No None Will' and 'Le Pi Se Be' means 'Not None If All'.

Example 2: Who among P, Q, T, V and M is exactly in the middle when they are arranged in ascending order of their heights ?
Statements:
1. V is taller than Q but shorter than M.
2. T is taller than Q and M but shorter than P.

MATRIX ARRANGEMENT

Matrix arrangement problems are the most common problem types in all aptitude test entrance exams. Unlike linear arrangement problems these are dealt with more than one variable / property of the objects. In linear arrangement, where the objects had only one property – their positioning, objects in matrix arrangement have multiple properties.

In general the information that is provided in these question is of two types:

1. Direct information: Information relating an object with its property

2. Indirect information: Information that relates two or more properties of an object.

To handle this type of questions 1st we have to note down all the given information, then find out the parameters about which more information is given and then make a table and co-relate the given parameters to find out exact match.

For example if it is given that four students A, B, C, and D belongs to 4 different cities namely Delhi, Kolkata, Mumbai and Chennai. If it is given that A doesn't belongs to Chennai and Delhi, B belongs to Kolkata then we can represent this information as-

	Delhi	Kolkata	Mumbai	Chennai
A	X	X	√	X
B	X	√	X	X
C		X	X	
D		X	X	

Lets proceed towards questions and see how to deal these types of questions.

EXAMPLE (Qs. 1-3) : *Study the following information carefully and answer the questions given below :*

Five friends Yash, Neeraj, Mehul, Ram and Prakash are students of five different disciplines – Medical, Engineering, Architecture, Arts, Management. Each plays a different musical instrument Sitar, Tabla, Sarod, Guitar and Violin.

Mehul, a medical student, does not play Sarod or Sitar nor Guitar. Prakash is neither a student of Engineering nor Management. Ram, who plays Tabla, is an Arts student.
Neither Prakash nor Yash plays Sarod.

1. Who among the following plays Sarod?
    (a) Yash   (b) Neeraj
    (c) Prakash   (d) Data inadequate
2. The guitarist is a student of which of the following disciplies?
    (a) Engineering
    (b) Either Engineering or Management
    (c) Data inadequate
    (d) None of these
3. Who among the following plays Sitar?
    (a) Yash   (b) Neeraj
    (c) Data inadequate   (d) None of these

EXAMPLE (Qs. 4-7): *Study the following information carefully and answer the questions given below it :*

(i) Seven subjects Sociology, Psychology, English, History, Geography, Economics and Hindi are taught between Monday and Friday by five persons A, B, C, D and E.

(ii) Each person teaches at least one subject. At least one subject is taught every day. No person teaches two subjects on the same day. B teaches Sociology on Wednesday. History is taught by E but not on Monday or Thursday. English is taught on Monday by A. Geography and Economics are taught on Monday and Tuesday respectively. D teaches only one subject Psychology on Tuesday. Geography is not taught by E or B.

4. Who teaches Geography?
   (a) C   (b) E
   (c) B   (d) Data inadequate
5. Which subject is taught on Friday?
   (a) Hindi   (b) Economics
   (c) History   (d) Data inadequate
6. Who teaches Economics?
   (a) E   (b) A
   (c) B   (d) Data inadequate
7. Which subject is taught on Thursday?
   (a) History   (b) Economics
   (c) Data inadequate   (d) None of these **11-13.**

SOLUTIONS

1-3

| | Discipline | | | | | Musical Instrument | | | | |
Name	Med	Eng	Ar	Art	Mg	Sit	Tab	Sar	Gui	Viol
Neeraj	×	—	×	×	—	×	×	✓	×	×
Yash	×	—	×	×	—	—	×	×	—	×
Mehul	✓	×	×	×	×	×	×	×	×	✓
Ram	×	×	×	✓	×	×	✓	×	×	×
Prakash	×	×	✓	×	×	—	×	×	—	×

1. (b)
2. (c) Guitarist is either Yash or Prakash. Therefore discipline may be Engineering or Architecture or Management.
3. (c)

Sol. (4 - 7).

As History is not taught on Monday or Thursday, it must be taught on Friday. Since it is given that at least one subject is taught every day, this helps to match Hindi — Thursday.

As D teaches only one subject (Psychology) and Geography is not taught by E or B and from the information: No person teaches two subjects on the same day, it is clear that C teaches Geography (since A teaches English on Monday).

Hence, the above information can be summerized in table as follows –

Subject	Person	Day
Sociology	B	Wednesday
History	E	Friday
English	A	Monday
Geography	C	
Economics	B/E/A/C	Tuesday
Psychology	D	
Hindi	_____	Thursday

From above table.

4. (a) C teaches Geography.

5. (c) History taught on Friday.

6. (d) From given dates it is not clear.

7. (d) Hindi is taught on Thursday.

LINEAR ARRANGEMENT

In Linear arrangement problems we are generally given a set of information about positioning of different elements with respect to other elements. From the given set of information we have to use the given information systematically to find the actual arrangement of the elements.

The arrangements can be in a straight line, on chair, in rooms or in a row. Another type of arrangement is arrangement in two rows parallel to each other.

Left and Right: We can use Left and Right as per Information that generally is given and its interpretation is as follows-

➢ Left and Right: We can use Left and Right as per our convenience. Generally (and in this book) we will use as follow-

Left End								Right End

➢ **A is 2 places right of B:** Generally students used to get confuse that how many gaps are there between A and B. Here in this case there is only 1 gap between A and B. As it is explained in the diagram below.

Left End	1st Place	2ndPlace	3rd Place	Right End
	B		A	

➢ **A is 3 places right of B:** Here in this case there is only 2 gaps between A and B. As it is explained in the diagram below. If B is at 1st place then A ia at 4th place.

Left End	1st Place	2nd Place	3rd Place	4th Place	Right End
	B			A	

➢ **A stays 2 places away of B:** Here in this case it is not given who is in right and who is in left so we have two different cases-

Left End	1st place	2nd place	3rd Place	Right End
	B/A		A/B	

➢ **A stays 2 places away of B who is 3 place left of C:** In this case, we can assume that B is at 3rd place then C is at 6th place,

Left End	1st place	2nd place	3rd Place	4th Place	5th Place	6th Place	Right End
	A		B		A	C	

Example 1

If four students are standing in a row such that A and B are always together, then draw a diagram and state all the possible cases.

Solution:

It is given that 4 students are in a row.

A is left of B but right of C: Here it is not mentioned that right or immediate right, as shown in the figure we have assumed that these are immediate right or left.

Left End	1st Place	2nd Place	3rd Place	Right End
	C	A	B	

A is left of B but Right of C, while D is right of E but left of C

We can represent this as, C > A > B, E > D > C by combining these we will get, E>D>C>A>B

Example 2

If four persons A, B, C and D are arranged in a row such that A and B are always together while C and D are never together. How many arrangements are possible.

Solution:

Here left and right of any arrangement is not mentioned hence we have following cases-

C	A	B	D
D	A	B	C
C	B	A	D
D	B	A	C

There are four such cases, we can represent these four cases in a line as-

C/d	A/B	B/A	D/C

EXAMPLE Qs. 3 to 5: *Six products - Ariel, Vivel, Rin, Nirma, Gillette Gel and Pepsodent - are to be placed in six display windows' of a shop numbered 1-6 from left to right of a shopper standing outside the shop. As per the company requirements, Rin and Ariel should be displayed next to each other, but Ariel should be at least three windows away from Nirma. Pepsodent is preferred to be kept between Gillette Gel and Rin but away from Vivel at least by two windows. Vivel cannot be displayed next to Rin for the reasons of mixed-product identity. Also Vivel cannot be displayed in window 1.*

3. Which of the following products is displayed left to Ariel?
    (a) Vivel   (b) Nirma
    (c) Rin   (d) Pepsodent

4. If the positions of Rin and Ariel are interchanged, which item will be displayed in window 5?
    (a) Ariel   (b) Nirma
    (c) Rin   (d) Vivel

5. Which of the following products except Rin will be displayed left of Ariel but right of Gillette Gel?
    (a) Vivel   (b) Rin
    (c) Pepsodent   (d) None of these

SOLUTIONS

(3 to 5)

Given that Six products - Ariel, Vivel, Rin, Nirma, Gillette Gel and Pepsodent

From 1st condition; Rin and Ariel are next to each other.

From 2nd condition at least two products are between Ariel&Nirma

From 3rd condition Pepsodent is kept between Gillette Gel and Rin, and at least 2 products between Pepsodent and Vivel.

From 4thcondition: Vivel and Rin cannot be next to each other.

From 5th condition Vivel is not kept at 1st window
Final arrangement would be Nirma Gillette Pepsodent Rin Ariel Vivel

3. **(c)** From case II of the above table Rin is left of Ariel. Hence, the answer is option (c).

4. **(c)** If we interchange the position of Rin and Ariel, the item displayed in window 5 will be Rin.

5. **(c)** Except Rin, the product displayed left of Ariel but right of Gillette Gel is Pepsodent.

CIRCULAR ARRANGEMENT

Circular arrangement is a type of arrangement of questions with more complexity. In this case, apart from normal arrangement, we have different variables/angles that have to be solved. Left or right information is given in both linear and circular arrangements but in circular arrangement for left or right, you can choose either clockwise or anti-clockwise. When people have to be seated in a row or in a circular table, the best way to determine the left hand and right hand position is to imagine yourself seated in that particular place.

In this book, we will take right as anti-clockwise and left as clockwise.

To solve these types of questions, we should follow the instructions given below-

(i) Draw the diagrammatic representation of the arrangement, e.g. draw a circle for a circular arrangement, draw a dashed line for position on a straight line, draw rectangle for rectangular table, etc.

(ii) Mark the right hand and left hand position of the people keeping in mind the direction in which the individuals are facing.

(iii) Mark the direction, i.e. North, South, West or facing towards the table or away from the table.

(iv) Identify the definite clues and locate them first on circular/ rectangular table whatever is given in the question.

(v) Identify the relative position and locate the same to get an indicative position.

(vi) Use definite clues in conjunction with relative position clues to arrive at the final arrangement.

(vii) If people are seated around a table with no direction mentioned, it has to be read as facing towards the table.

EXAMPLE Qn. 1 to 5: *Twelve people Abhishek, Binit, Chand, Dhiraj, Eshita, Fatima, Garima, Hena, Ishan, Jatin, Kamal and Lalit are sitting around a rectangular table. The following information is known*

The table has 12 chairs numbered from 1 to 12. 6 seats on one side of the table and 6 on the opposite side. The chairs are arranged in such a way that chair number 1 is just opposite to 12, 6 is opposite to 7 and so on-

Abhishek is sitting opposite to Kamal who is the only person sitting between Chand and Jatin. Eshita is sitting opposite to Ishan who is the only person sitting between Binit and Lalit. Fatima, sitting at chair number 1, is diagonally opposite to Chand who is sitting opposite to Dhiraj.

1. If Garima is sitting opposite to Fatima then who is sitting opposite to Hena?
    (a) Lalit
    (b) Binit
    (c) Ishan
    (d) Uniquely not determined.

2. If Lalit is sitting opposite to Hena, then who is sitting opposite to Garima?
    (a) Eshita or Fatima   (b) Jatin or Fatima
    (c) Jatin or Eshita   (d) None of these

3. How many persons are sitting between Binit and Dhiraj, if they are on the same side of the table?
    (a) 2 or 3   (b) 1 or 2
    (c) 1 or 3   (d) None of these

4. Which one of the following is correct?
    (a) Lalit is sitting at seat number 12
    (b) Lalit is sitting at seat number 10

    (c) Kamal is sitting at seat number 8

    (d) None of these

5.   Which one of the following is incorrect?

    (a) Lalit is opposite to Jatin.

    (b) Jatin is opposite to Hena.

    (c) Lalit is adjacent to Chand.

    (d) None of these

SOLUTIONS

]Let us denote these 12 students by their 1st letter of name, like Abhishek is A and so on.

From the given information we can conclude that (C) and (D) are at seat numbers 7 and 6, respectively. And (K) is the only person between (C) and (J) while (A) is opposite to (K). Hence, (A), (K) and (J) must be at seat numbers 5, 8 and 9. respectively.

Then we have following two cases:

Case I

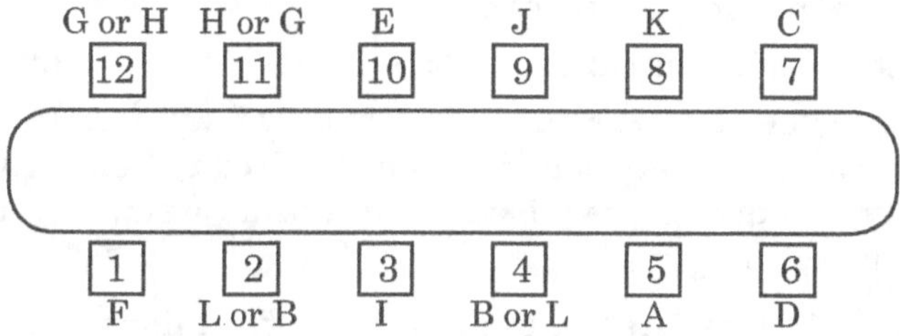

Case II

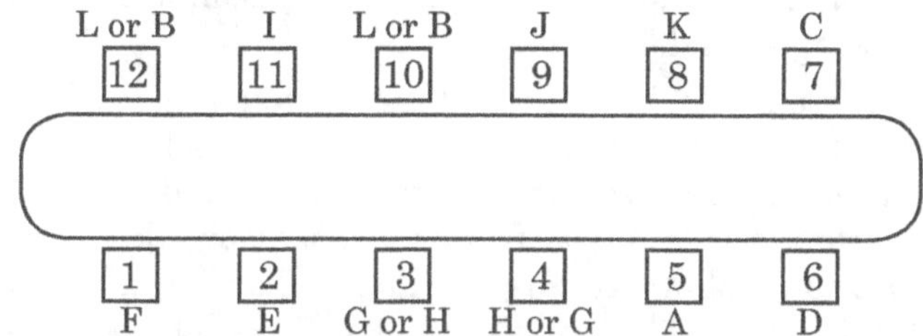

1.   (d) From the above 2 cases, it follows case (i) and opposite to Fatima is either Lalit or Binit.

2.   (b) From the above 2 cases,

    In case (i) if Lalit is sitting opposite to Hena then Fatima is sitting opposite to Garima.

In case (ii) if Lalit is sitting opposite to Hena then Jatin is sitting opposite to Garima.

3. (c) From the above 2 cases, it follows case (i) and number of persons sitting between Binit and Dhiraj is either 1 or 3.

4. (c) From the given options only option (c) is correct.

5. **(c)** From the given options option (c) is correct.

GROUP/TEAM FORMATION

Here, we will solve the questions related to group /Team formation. In these type of questions we have to form one or more group/teams from the given condition with the given members. Information provided are of two types-

(i) Positive information :- e.g A and B is together

(ii) Negative information:- e.g A and B are not together

(iii) Conditional information:- If A is with B then C is with D

(iv) Restrictive Information :- Number of members in a group can not be more/less than 3.

With the use of these information we have to form group/team.

In certain questions the main data has only few information and then in each and every question some more condition is given, in these type of questions we have to form team/group for each and every question.

Example 1: There are ten animals—two each of lions, panthers, bison, bears, and deer—in a zoo. The enclosures in the zoo are named X, Y, Z, P and Q and each enclosure is allotted to one of the following attendants:

Jack, Mohan, Shalini, Suman and Rita. Two animals of different species are housed in each enclosure. A lion and a deer cannot be together. A panther cannot be with either a deer or a bison. Suman attends to animals from among bison, deer, bear and panther only. Mohan attends to a lion and a panther. Jack does not attend to deer, lion or bison. X, Y, and Z are allotted to Mohan, Jack and Rita respectively. X and Q enclosures have one animal of the same species. Z and P have the same pair of animals. The animals attended by Shalini are:

    (a) bear and bison   (b) bison and deer

    (c) bear and lion   (d) bear and Panther

EXAMPLE QN. 2 to 6: *During one week, a human resource director conducts five interviews for a new job, one interview per day, Monday through Friday. There are six candidates for the job - Ram, Shyam, Trilochan, Usha, Veena, and Kishore. No more than two candidates are interviewed more than once. Neither Shyam nor Usha nor Veena is interviewed more than once, and no other candidate is interviewed more than twice. The schedule of interviews is subject to the following conditions:*

If Trilochan is interviewed, then Trilochan must be interviewed on both Monday and Friday.

If Shyam is interviewed, then Usha is also interviewed, with Shyam's interview taking place earlier than Usha's interview.

If Ram is interviewed twice, then Ram's second interview takes place exactly two days after Ram's first interview.

If Veena is interviewed, then Kishore is interviewed twice, with Veena's interview taking place after Kishore's first interview and before Kishore's second interview.

If Usha is interviewed, then Ram is also interviewed, with Usha's interview taking place on a day either immediately before or immediately after a day on which Ram is interviewed.

2. Which of the following could be a complete and accurate list of candidates the human resources director interviews and the days on which those interviews take place?
   (a) Monday: Shyam: Tuesday: Usha; Wednesday:Ram; Thursday: Kishore; Friday: Ram;
   (b) Monday: Shyam; Tuesday: Kishore; Wednesday: Ram; Thursday: Kishore; Friday: Usha;
   (c) Monday: Trilochan; Tuesday: Ram; Wednesday: Shyam; Thursday: Ram; Friday: Trilochan;
   (d) Monday: Trilochan; Tuesday: Ram; Wednesday: Kishore; Thursday: Veena; Friday: Trilochan;

3. If Veena is interviewed on Tuesday, then which one of the following MUST BE true?
   (a) Trilochan is interviewed on Friday
   (b) Usha is interviewed on Thursday
   (c) Ram is not interviewed
   (d) Shyam is not interviewed

4. If Kishore is not interviewed, then which one of the following MUST BE true?
   (a) Ram is interviewed on Thursday
   (b) Shyam is interviewed on Tuesday

    (c) Trilochan is interviewed on Monday

    (d) Usha is interviewed on Wednesday

5.   If Shyam is interviewed, then which one of the following could be true?

    (a) Kishore is interviewed on both Tuesday and Wednesday

    (b) Usha is interviewed on Monday.

    (c) Veena is interviewed on Tuesday

    (d) Shyam is interviewed on Thursday

6.   If neither Usha nor Trilochan is interviewed, then each of the following MUST BE true EXCEPT:

    (a) Ram is interviewed on Monday

    (b) Ram is interviwed on Thursday

    (c) Veena is interviewed on Tuesday

    (d) Kishore is interviewed on Wednesday

7.   If both Usha and Veena are interviewed, then which one of the following is a complete and accurate list of the days on which Kishore could be interviewed?

    (a) Monday, Friday

    (b) Tuesday, Thursday

    (c) Monday, Wednesday,Friday

    (d) Tuesday, Wednesday, Thursday

SOLUTIONS

1.   (c) Write down the information given

L→ -D (Lion and Dear cannot be together)

P→ -D & -Bs (A Panthor cannot be with a Dear or a Bison)

Suman → -L

Mohan →L + P

Jack → P or B

Hence we can short out following table

Keeper	Animal	Enclosure
Mohan	L + P (given)	X (given)
Jack	B + P	Y (given)
Shalini	B + L	Q
Suman	D + B	P
Rita	D + B	Z (given)

Since Z & P have the same pair of animals, the other 3 enclosures viz., X, Y and Q must contain the other

3 species within themselves. So apart from Lion and Panther, Bear must be third species in X, Y, Q.

Jack gets Bear and Panther as he doesn't handle lion (given) that leaves. Q with Lion and Bear; which goes to Shalini as Suman doesn't handle lion (given).

Solution (2 to 7)

Mon	Tues	Wed	Thrus	Fri
T_1		S		T_2
R_1		U	R_2	
	K_1		V	K_2

This is the case when Usha interviewed before a day when Ram interviewed.

Mon	Tues	Wed	Thrus	Fri
T_1		S		T_2
	R_1	U		R_2
K_1	V		K_2	

This is the case when Usha interviewed after a day when Ram interviewed

Mon	Tues	Wed	Thrus	Fri
T_1				T_2
S	U	R_1		R_2
	K_1	V	K_2	

This is the case when Shayam and Usha are not interviewed on same day.

2. (a)   3. (d)   4. (c)   5. (a)   6. (d)   7. (c)

CRITICAL REASONING

INTRODUCTION

Critical Reasoning (CR) is ability to reason clearly to evaluate and judge arguments. You are using this skill a lot during your everyday life while reading newspapers or watching movies. When you think that the movie is pushing the limit of the Reasonable or the news sounds less reasonable than the movie that was pushing the limit, you are using your Critical Reasoning skills to produce these conclusions. The argument you meet can be anything from a classical argument to an advertisement or a dialog. Critical Reasoning questions will ask you to manipulate the argument to weaken/strengthen it, find the conclusion, assumption, explanation, do an inference or supplement a statement, etc. Whatever it is that you have to do, you will need 2 things to succeed: know the basic structure of arguments and clearly understand the argument.

In general, most of them, arguments consist of evidence, usually 2 pieces, a conclusion - the main point of an argument, and an assumption - the bridge between the evidence and conclusion. The majority of the arguments you encounter on the test will be 3 step arguments:

Evidence 1 + Evidence 2 = Conclusion.

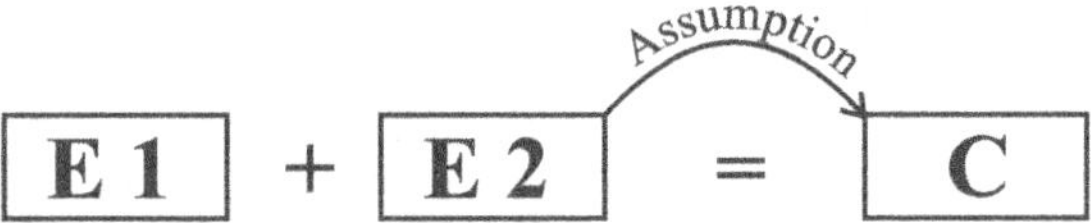

Example 1 :

Last week Mike was detained for shoplifting at a groceries store near his house, but he has been a Christian for 10 years, therefore, the police must have been wrong accusing him in stealing.

Note : There are two pieces of evidence: *'Mike was accused of stealing'* and that *'he is a Christian'.* The conclusion is that **'the police are wrong'**. Therefore, our huge assumption here is that *'a Christian could not have stolen anything.'*

Example 2.

There are a lot of mosquitoes outside today, please do not turn on the light in the room because a lot of them will fly in.

Note : Here the evidences are *'there are a lot of mosquitoes outside today'* and *'do not turn on the light'.* The conclusion is that 'Many will fly in' and the assumption is 'mosquitoes will approach the light.'

There is no set scheme for structure in CR, but since the majority of the arguments are only a few sentences long, the conclusion usually comes in the first or the last sentence. However, some of the arguments encountered will not have a conclusion at all or will have just an implied one.

Strategy to Crack Critical Reasoning Questions

This strategy is not the easiest way to do CR (the easiest would be read-and-answer), but it lets you get the most questions right spending less time per correct answer.

1. Read the questions first; this is needed so that you would know what to look for and what to do: find an assumption, strengthen/weaken, infer something or else; do not worry about the details in the question, read for keywords, such as strengthen, deny, or explain. [Use symbols for convenience, e.g. + for strengthen or – for weaken].

2. Read the passage very attentively because in contrast to Reading Comprehension, there is very little text here and mostly everything is important; try to read only once. Reread if required.

   As you read, look for the problem in the passage (evaluate how convincing it is)

3. Paraphrase (reword) the passage. It is a very important step because when you do a paraphrase, you check whether you understood the passage and at the same time you extract the skeleton of the argument, making it easier to identify the conclusion and the assumption. Very often, the paraphrase of the passage will be pretty close to the conclusion. It is not surprising, since the conclusion is the main point and evidence just supports it.) Your paraphrase should be as close to the text and as simple as possible so that you would understand it easily and at the same time could fully trust it. Do not make it too general nor too detail oriented. When you do a paraphrase, do it in three steps: Evidence1, Evidence2, and Conclusion; put "therefore" word before you start your conclusion, this will help you to set it off.

4. Read the question again (now with more understanding of what is being asked; reading the question 2 times, it will also help you to make sure your answer exactly what is stated and that you understand the question.)

5. Answer before reading the answer choices. There are two reasons for this :

   (i) if you can think of the correct answer or at least the general direction that the answer choice needs to be, you will identify it among the wrong choices much faster, thus spend less time reading the answers, which usually take 30 seconds to cover.

   (ii) Often students are seduced by the author's wording. One reads a few words that were used in the passage and the brain identifies this choice with the passage, thus making it seem more right that it needs to be. The more problems you practice with, the more chance is you will guess the right answer even before reading it.

6. Go through the answers, first time scan them for YOUR answer choice (usually you will guess correctly in 60-70% of cases), if you did not find it, reread them more attentively.

7. Draw a grid to eliminate the wrong answers easier. Use "✓" for a sure answer, "✖" for a definitely wrong answer choice, and "?" for an answer that may be right or questionable. This will help to concentrate only on a few answer choices and will prevent you from reading same answers several times if you get confused or keep having troubles locating the right answer.

Types of Critical Reasoning Questions

Critical reasoning questions will ask you to:

1. Identify the inference / Must be true question
2. Identify the assumption.
3. Strengthen an argument.
4. Weaken an argument.
5. Select the best conclusion / Main Point
6. Identify the paradox
7. Evaluation/ Reasoning
8. Identify a parallel argument/Structure.

1. Identify the inference/Must be true question

These type of questions are extremely common. An **Inference** means the same thing as "must be true". **Conclusions** differ from **inferences** in that conclusions are the result of premises and inferences are something that must be true. The following are the typical Inference (Must be true) based Questions:

- If the statements above are true, which of the following must also be true?

- Which of the following is [implied, must be true, implicit, most reasonably drawn] in the passage above?

- Which of the following inferences is best supported by the statement made above?

How to tackle "Identify the inference / Must be true questions":

- Read the stimulus and look for the argument.

- Note that Must Be True questions may not contain an argument. They may just be a series of facts. Nevertheless, try to find the argument.

- Avoid choices which contain absolute statements - never, always, none, only etc. Although these words might appear in some correct choice, you should be very sure about them.

- Some of the options can be eliminated as they go beyond the scope of the passage. Note that an inference can be based on only some of the information provided and not the complete passage.

Example 1 : Stimulus Argument

Increases in funding for police patrols often lower the rate of crimes of opportunity such as petty theft and vandalism by providing visual deterrence in high-crime neighborhoods. Levels of funding for police patrols in some communities are increased when federal matching grants are made available.

Question :

Which of the following can be correctly inferred from the statements above?

Options :

(a) Areas with little vandalism can never benefit from visual deterrence.

(b) Communities that do not increase their police patrols are at higher risk for crimes of opportunity late at night.

(c) Federal matching grants for police patrols lower the rate of crimes of opportunity in some communities.

(d) Only federal matching grants are necessary to reduce crime in most neighborhoods.

Sol. :(c) (c) is a summary of the information provided; it is the logical end of a chain of reasoning started in the stimulus argument. The sequence of events goes like this :

Increased funding Increased visual deterrence Lower crime

The last statement could be mapped as follows:
Federal grants Increased patrol funds
(c) makes the chain complete by correctly stating that federal grants can lead to lower crime in some communities. Now the logical chain becomes:
Federal grants Increased funding Increased visual deterrence Lower crime
The other answer choices may not be correctly inferred because they go beyond the scope of the argument. They may be objectively, factually correct, or they may be statements that you would tend to agree with. However, you are limited to the argument presented when choosing a correct answer.

2. Identify the assumption.

An assumption is an unstated premise that supports the author's conclusion. It's the connection between the stated premises and the conclusion. An assumption is something that the author's conclusion depends upon. Assumption questions are extremely common and have types that look like this:

- Which of the following most accurately states a hidden assumption that the author must make in order to advance the argument above?

- Which of the following is an assumption that, if true, would support the conclusion in the passage above?

How to approach "Identify the assumption Questions"

- Look for gaps between the premises and the conclusion. Ask yourself why the conclusion is true. Before you progress to the answer choices, try to get feel of what assumption is necessary to fill that gap between the premises.

- Beware of extreme language in the answer choices of assumption questions. Assumptions usually are not extreme. "Extreme" answer choices usually contain phrases such as always, never, or totally.

Example 2 : Stimulus Argument

Traditionally, decision making by doctors that is carefully, deductively reasoned has been considered preferable to intuitive decision making. However, a recent study found that senior surgeons used intuition significantly more than did most residents or mid-level doctors. This confirms the alternative view that intuition is actually more effective than careful, methodical reasoning.

Question :

The conclusion above is based on which of the following assumptions?

Options :

(a) Senior surgeons are more effective at decision making than are mid-level doctors.

(b) Senior surgeons have the ability to use either intuitive reasoning or deductive, methodical reasoning in making decisions.

(c) The decisions that are made by mid-level and entry-level doctors can be made as easily by using methodical reasoning as by using intuitive reasoning.

(d) Senior surgeons use intuitive reasoning in making the majority of their decisions.

Sol. : (a) The correct answer is (a), which provides a missing link in the author's reasoning by making a connection from the evidence: that intuition is used more by senior surgeons than other, less-experienced doctors, and the conclusion: that, therefore, intuition is more effective. None of the other choices helps bridge this gap in the chain of reasoning. Although some of the other statements may be true, they are not responsive to the question. In fact, they mostly focus on irrelevant factors such as appropriateness, ease of application, ability, etc.

3. Strengthen an Argument.

Assumptions connect premises to conclusions. An argument is strengthened by strengthening the assumptions. Here are some examples of Strengthen question types :

➢ The conclusion would be more properly drawn if it were made clear that...

➢ Which of the following, if true, would most strengthen the conclusion drawn in the passage above?

How to approach "Strengthen an argument"

➤ Once you have identified the argument of the passage, i.e. the evidence(s) + conclusion, try putting in each option with the argument. Check if the assumption(s) you have drawn is (are) strengthened if you accept the content of the option as true.

Example 3 : Stimulus Argument

Three years after the Bhakra Nangal Dam was built, none of the six fish species native to the area was still reproducing adequately in the river below the dam. Because the dam reduced the average temperature range of the water from approximately 40° to approximately 10°, biologists have hypothesized that sharp increases in water temperature must be involved in signaling the affected species to begin their reproduction activities.

Question :

Which of the following statements, if true, would most strengthen the scientists' hypothesis?

Options :

(a) The native fish species were still able to reproduce in nearby streams where the annual temperature range remains approximately 40°.

(b) Before the dam was built, the river annually overflowed its banks, creating temporary backwaters that were used as breeding areas for the local fish population.

(c) The lowest temperature ever recorded in the river prior to dam construction was 30°; whereas the lowest recorded river temperature after construction was completed has been 40°.

(d) Non-native fish species, introduced after the dam was completed, have begun competing with the native species for food.

Sol.: (a) (a) most strengthens the conclusion that the scientists reached. It does so by showing that there is a control group. In other words, a similar population, not subjected to the same change as the population near the dam, did not experience the same type of result. Here the basic assumption about the conclusion that scientists reached is that 'because of the reduction of average temperature range of the water, the reproduction of the native fish species has reduced drastically'. Option (a) clearly strengthens the assumption.

4. Weaken an argument

Assumptions connect premises to conclusions. An argument is weakened by weakening the assumptions. Here are some examples of Weaken question types :

➢ Which of the following, if true, would weaken the conclusion drawn in the passage above?

➢ The argument as it is presented in the passage above would be most strengthened if which of the following were true?

How to approach "Weaken an argument"

➢ Once you have identified the argument of the passage, i.e. the evidence(s) + conclusion, try putting in each option with the argument. Check if the assumption(s) you have drawn is (are) weakened if you accept the content of the option as true.

Example 4 : Stimulus Argument

A drug that is very effective in treating some forms of cancer can, at present, be obtained only from the bark of the Raynhu, a tree that is quite rare in the wild. It takes the bark of approximately 5,000 trees to make one pound of the drug. It follows, then, that continued production of the drug must inevitably lead to the raynhu's extinction.

Question :

Which of the following, if true, most seriously weakens the above conclusion?

Options :

(a) The drug made from Raynhu bark is dispensed to doctors from a central authority.

(b) The drug made from the Raynhu bark is expensive to produce.

(c) The Raynhu generally grows in largely inaccessible places.

(d) The Raynhu can be propagated from cuttings and cultivated by farmers.

Sol. :(d) (d) provides an alternate source of the Raynhu bark. Even though the tree is rare in the wild, the argument isn't silent on the availability of cultivated trees. The author of the argument must be assuming that there are no Raynhu trees other than those in the wild, in order to make the leap from the stated evidence to the conclusion that the Raynhu is headed for extinction.

The option (d) weakens the assupmtion - 'there are limited raynhu trees' - by saying that there are other ways as well for the propogation of Raynhu. The other answer choices all contain information that is irrelevant. Note that the correct choice does not make the conclusion of the argument impossible. In fact, it is possible that there may be domesticated Raynhu trees and the species could still become extinct. Answer choice (d) is correct because it makes the conclusion about extinction less likely to be true.

5. Conclusion/Main Point Question

In Main Point / Conlcusion questions, you have to identify the conclusion of an argument. You are trying to find the author's point and should approach this question in a similar way to the reading comprehension main point questions. They come in several different formats:

> The main point of the passage is that...

> Which of the following statements about... is best supported by the statements above?

> Which of the following best states the author's conclusion in the passage above?

> Which of the following conclusions can be most properly drawn from the data above?

The conclusion of arguments in Main Point questions is usually not directly stated. To find the conclusion, identify the premises and then identify the conclusion drawn from the premises. Main Point questions differ from the other Critical Reasoning questions in that the argument in the stimulus is usually valid. (In most other Critical Reasoning questions the reasoning is flawed.) Conclusion questions require you to choose the answer that is a summary of the argument.

How to approach "Main Point Questions":

> Main Point answers must be within the scope of the passage.

> Your opinions or information outside of the passage are always outside of the scope.

> Some of the options given can be out of the scope of the passage.

➢ Knock out answers with extreme wording. Main Point answers typically do not use *only, always, never, best* or any strong words that leave little room.

Example 5 : Stimulus Argument

People should be held accountable for their own behaviour, and if holding people accountable for their own behaviour entails capital punishment, then so be it. However, no person should be held accountable for behaviour over which he or she had no control.

Question :

Which of the following is the most logical conclusion of the argument above?

Options :

(a) People should not be held accountable for the behaviour of other people.

(b) People have control over their own behaviour.

(c) People cannot control the behaviour of other people.

(d) People have control over behaviour that is subject to capital punishment.

Sol.:(b) The correct response is (b). The argument includes the following two premises:

Premise 1: People are accountable for their own behaviour.

Premise 2: People are not accountable for behaviour they cannot control.

Here's the logical conclusion based on these two premises:

Conclusion: People can control their own behaviour.

(a) would require that people never have control over the behaviour of other people. Yet the argument does not provide this premise.

(b) would require that people should not be held accountable for the behaviour of other people. Yet the argument does not provide this premise.

(d) is not inferable. The argument allows for the possibility that a person might not have control over another person's behaviour which is subject to capital punishment.

6. Identify the Paradox

These questions present you with a paradox, a seeming contradiction or discrepancy in the argument, and ask you to resolve it or explain how that contradiction could exist. In other words, there are two facts that are both true, and yet they appear to be in direct conflict with one another. Here are some examples of the ways in which these questions are worded:

- Which of the following, if true, would help to resolve the apparent paradox presented above?
- Which of the following, if true, contributes most to an explanation of the apparent discrepancy described above?

How to approach "Identify the paradox questions"

- Read the argument and find the apparent paradox, discrepancy, or contradiction.
- State the apparent paradox, discrepancy, or contradiction in your own words.
- Use process of elimination. The best answer will explain how both sides of the paradox, discrepancy, or contradiction can be true. Eliminate answers that are out of scope.

Example 6 : Stimulus Argument

Town Y is populated almost exclusively by retired people and has almost no families with small children. Yet Town Y is home to a thriving business specializing in the rental of furniture for infants and small children.

Question :

Which of the following, if true, best reconciles the seeming discrepancy described above?

Options :

(a) The business specializing in the rental of children's furniture buys its furniture from distributors outside of Town Y.

(b) The few children who do reside in Town Y all know each other and often stay over night at each other's houses.

(c) Many residents of Town Y who move frequently prefer to rent their furniture rather than buy it outright.

(d) Many residents of Town Y must provide for the needs of visiting grandchildren several weeks a year.

Sol.: (d) The correct answer (d), explains why a town of mostly retired residents might need to rent children's furniture. The other answer choices all contain irrelevant information. This further illustrates the fact that, on all question types, if you eliminate the irrelevant choices, the remaining choice will most likely be correct.

7. Evaluation/Reasoning based Questions

Reasoning questions ask you to describe how the argument was made, not necessarily what it says. These questions are closely related to assumption, weakening, and strengthening questions. The correct answer identifies a question that must be answered or information that must be gathered to determine how strong the stimulus argument is. The information will be related to an assumption that the author is making. Another type of question that you will encounter asks you to *identify a flaw* in the stimulus argument. The question tells you that there is a problem with the logic of the argument. You just have to choose the answer that describes the flaw. Here are some examples of the ways in which these questions are worded:

- ➤ How does the author make his point?
- ➤ A major flaw in the argument above is that it...
- ➤ A's response has which of the following relationships to B's argument?

How to approach Reasoning Questions

- Read the argument and find the conclusion.

- State the reasoning in your own words.

- Check whether the reasoning given in the various options fall in line with the reasoning described above.

Example 7 : Stimulus Argument

Some observers have taken the position that the recently elected judge is biased against men in divorce cases that involve child custody. But the statistics reveal that in 40% of such cases, the recently elected judge awards custody to the fathers. Most other judges award custody to fathers in only 20%–30%of their cases. This record demonstrates that the recently elected judge has not discriminated against men in cases of child custody.

Question:

The argument above is flawed in that it ignores the possibility that

Options:

(a) A large number of the recently elected judge's cases involve child custody disputes.

(b) The recently elected judge is prejudiced against men in divorce cases that do not involve child custody issues.

(c) The majority of the child custody cases that have reached the recently elected judge's court have been appealed from a lower court.

(d) The evidence shows that men should have won custody in more than 40% of the recently elected judge's cases involving divorcing fathers.

Sol.: (d) The correct answer (d), points out a flaw in the argument. Specifically, it points out that the author of the argument was comparing the recently elected judge to other judges, not to the evidence presented in the recently elected judge's cases. In other words, the author of the argument made an unwarranted assumption that the recently elected judge did not rule against many men in custody battles where the evidence clearly favored the men. As with strengthening and weakening questions, the correct answer in flaw questions often involves unwarranted assumptions.

Example 8 : Stimulus Argument

Although dentures produced through a new computer-aided design process will cost more than twice as much as ordinary dentures, they should still be cost effective. Not only will fitting time and X-ray expense be reduced, but the new dentures should fit better, diminishing the need for frequent refitting visits to the dentist's office.

Question:

Which of the following must be studied in order to evaluate the argument presented above?

Options:

(a) The amount of time a patient spends in the fitting process versus the amount of money spent on X-rays

(b) The amount by which the cost of producing dentures has declined with the introduction of the new technique for producing them

(c) The degree to which the use of the new dentures is likely to reduce the need for refitting visits when compared to the use of ordinary dentures

(d) The amount by which the new dentures will drop in cost as the production procedures become standardized and applicable on a larger scale

Sol. : (c) The correct answer (c), highlights an assumption in the stimulus argument. It shows that the author must be assuming that the reduction in refitting with the new dentures compared to ordinary dentures is significant in order to conclude that that difference will help offset an initial outlay that is twice as much. In other words, if you answer the question posed by answer choice (c) with "not much," the argument is weakened. If you answer it with "a tremendous amount," the argument is strengthened. The other answer choices are all irrelevant because no matter what the answers are, there is no impact on the relationship between the evidence presented in the stimulus argument and its conclusion.

8. Identify a Parallel Argument/Structure.

The last type of Critical Reasoning question is the *parallel structure* question. In this type of question, you must choose the answer that has the same structure as the stimulus argument. In other words, you have to find the argument that is analogous to the given argument in that it includes the same relationship between the evidence presented and the conclusion. Here are some examples of the ways in which these questions are worded:

> Which of the following is most like the argument above in its logical structure?

> Which of the following is a parallel argument to the above given argument?

Example 9 : Stimulus Argument

It is true that it is against international law to provide aid to certain countries that are building nuclear programs. But, if

Russian companies do not provide aid, companies in other countries will.

Question :

Which of the following is most like the argument above in its logical structure?

Options :

(a) It is true that it is against United States policy to negotiate with kidnappers. But if the United States wants to prevent loss of life, it must negotiate in some cases.

(b) It is true that it is illegal to sell diamonds that originate in certain countries. But there is a long tradition in Russia of stockpiling diamonds.

(c) It is true that it is illegal for an attorney to participate in a transaction in which there is an apparent conflict of interest. But, if the facts are examined carefully, it will clearly be seen that there is no actual conflict of interest in the defendant's case.

(d) It is true that it is against the law to steal cars. But someone else certainly would have stolen that car if the defendant had not done so first.

Sol. : (d) The correct answer (d), has the same structure as the stimulus argument. If you just replace "aid to developing nuclear powers" with "car theft," and "Russian companies" with the "defendant," it is essentially the same argument. Sometimes the parallel structure is easier to see if you use symbols to represent the terms of the argument: It is true that X is illegal. But, if Y doesn't do it, others will. Granted, the stimulus argument is in the future tense and the credited answer is in the past tense. However, it certainly is most like the stimulus.

Chapter 6

TIPS & TECHNIQUES TO CRACK QUANTITATIVE ABILITY

IMPORTANCE OF QUANTITATIVE APTITUDE BY CAT GURU GAJENDRA KUMAR

Many of us think Mathematics is a subject which requires a magical brain but it's not true. It is a subject which requires logical brain. We have come across various examinations where quantitative section is common, then question arises why we need this section to test the ability of a candidate. The reason which I believe is that the candidate needs to be mentally alert to the changes happening around him/her. A high profile employee/manager or student struggles with challenges every minute. A major part of his/her work requires logical decision as well as to find solutions to deal with the problems.

Hence, solving QA section for CAT can be quite challenging for test takers especially for non-engineering students but they have to focus in this section so as to score good percentile in this section which in turn will impact their overall percentile. One should focus on the concepts building and must practice and practice from simple to moderate and different types of questions.

Topics that the aspirants must focus on in this section are-

- Number system.
- Arithmetic.
- Algebra.
- Geometry.
- Modern Math.

If we see the CAT 2017's sectional breakup of QA, we can understand the importance of the above mentioned chapters.

No. of Questions	Total no. of MC Questions	Total no. of non-MC Questions	Topic-wise Questions
34	27	7	Number System-4 Arithmetic-11 Algebra- 10-11 Geometry– 6-7 Modern Maths-2

Hence, aspirants should focus on the topics and must have concrete knowledge over these. Focus more on Algebra especially on quadratic equation and inequality. In Arithmetic, profit & loss and distance ,speed & time are the most important chapters to concentrate , along with Geometry and Permutation & Combination to fetch good score or percentile.

The following points will help you to prepare better in the days left to your CAT test day.

➢ **Know the areas well:** As the first step of any preparation is to know the basics. Go through the past years' analysis and question types to know which are the areas and topics with major weights. If you are not too strong with those topics, start with the basics. Don't hesitate to go back to your old school or college books to learn the basics. To know the question types, solving the previous years' question papers is the best solution.

➢ **Do not leave out important topics:** Although it is not possible to prepare for each and every topic that has appeared in the CAT paper over the years, ensure that you do not leave out the important areas or chapters from your scheme of things. Many Students usually find topics such as Modern Math tough but you must remember that Modern Math questions in the CAT are not always tough nor are Arithmetic questions always easy. The aim is to maximise your score in all sections, you can do that by solving all the easy questions. With 50 questions to a section, you cannot afford to leave questions out. If you leave out Modern Math entirely, you have narrowed your selection to only the easy questions in Arithmetic and Algebra. However, there would be some areas, which by now you have realized are not your cup of tea. In that case, focus on your strength areas and leave out the others.

➢ **Focus on important chapters** – As mentioned in the above point, there are certain important areas in the Quantitative Aptitude and Data Interpretation section which you must not leave out. But you must also take care that those areas or chapters get high focus during preparation. Don't be reluctant while preparing for important topics like Number System, Arithmetic, Modern Math or Geometry. Prepare in such a way that no matter how tricky the question is, you can crack the solving process within few minutes.

"For Quantitative Ability, the focus was on few chapters like arithmetic and geometry. I used to collate formulas from various sources and practiced problems every day."

-Says Sohini, CAT Topper

> **Practice** – Practice is the universal preparation strategy for the toppers and experts alike. There is no substitute for regular practice which will help you ace your weaker areas and make the areas of strength even stronger. Practice also includes taking regular mock tests, whether full length or sectional depending on your stage of preparation.

"For QA, practice makes a man perfect is the only mantra, like solving Quantitative aptitude problems from various books," suggests Gagandeep Singh Pannu who obtained 99.97 percentile in CAT.

SHORTCUTS TO CRACK QA SECTION

NUMBERS

I. SHORTCUTS FOR MULTIPLICATION

1. Line Segment Method of Multiplications of Two Whole Numbers of any Number of Digits

To clearly understand this method, we will discuss some examples.

(i) Consider the multiplication of two digit numbers,

$$\begin{array}{r} 7\quad 6 \\ \times\ 4\quad 9 \\ \hline \\ \hline \end{array}$$

The digit of the different places of the required product will be found out as follows.

(a) Finding the Units Place Digit

To Find the unit's digit of the product of any two numbers, we always find the product their unit's digits.

Here product of unit digits = $6 \times 9 = 54$

Unit's digit 4 of 54 is the unit's digit of the required product. Tenth digit 5 of 54 will be carry over to the tens place.

Thus

$$\begin{array}{r} 7\quad 6 \\ \times\ 4\quad 9 \\ \hline \quad 4 \\ \hline \end{array}$$

5 carry over to the tens place.

(b) Finding the Tens Place Digit

$$7 \times 4 \quad 6 \times 9$$
$$\overline{ 4}$$

$7 \times 9 + 6 \times 4 = 63 + 24 = 87$

$87 + 5$ (from carry over) $= 92$

Here unit's digit 2 of 92 is the tens place digit of the required product. Tens digit 9 of 92 will be carry over to the hundred's place digit.

Thus

$$\begin{array}{ccc} & 7 & 6 \\ \times & 4 & 9 \\ \hline & 2 & 4 \end{array}$$

9 carry over to the hundred's place.

(c) Finding the Hundred's Place Digit

$$\begin{array}{ccc} & 7 & 6 \\ \times & 4 & 9 \\ \hline & 2 & 4 \end{array}$$

$7 \times 4 = 28$

$28 + 9$ (from carry over) $= 37$

Since 7 and 4 are the last digits on the left in both the given numbers, so this is the last calculation in this multiplication and hence we can write 37 for the remaining 2 digits in the required product.

Thus

$$\begin{array}{cccc} & & 7 & 6 \\ \times & & 4 & 9 \\ \hline 3 & 7 & 2 & 4 \end{array}$$

(ii) Consider the following multiplication of more than 2 digits numbers,

$$\begin{array}{cccc} 5 & 4 & 0 & 2 \\ \times \ 3 & 1 & 5 \\ \hline \\ \hline \end{array}$$

Study the following table which explains the process of finding the digit at different places of the required product.

Finding the digit	Diagram showing the calculation process	Calculation	Required digit(s)	Carry on to the next place digit	Explanation of the diagram showing the calculation process
Unit digit	5 4 0 2 × 3 1 5 —————— 0	$5 \times 2 = 10$	0	1	Multiplication between unit's digit of both the number shows by line segment between 2 and 5.
Tens digit	5 4 0→2 × 3 1←5 —————— 3 0	$5 \times 0 + 1 \times 2 = 2$ $2 + 1$ (carry over) $= 3$	3	0	Multiplication of tens digit 0 of 5402 by unit's digit 5 of 315 shows by line segment between 0 and 5, then rotate this line segment in clockwise direction about their midpoint to find the next pair of digits to be multiplied
Hundred digit	5 4→0→2 × 3←1←5 —————— 6 3 0	$5 \times 4 + 1 \times 0 + 3 \times 2 = 26$	6	2	Multiplication of hundred's digit 4 of 5402 by unit's digit 5 of 315 shows by line segment between 4 and 5, then rotate this line segment in clockwise direction about their mid-point to find the next pair of digits to be multiplied.
Thousand digit	5→4→0→2 × 3←1←5 —————— 1 6 3 0	$5 \times 5 + 1 \times 4 + 3 \times 0 = 29$ $29 + 2$ (carry over) $= 31$	1	3	Similar explanation as given above for hundred digit but there is no digit in the left of 3 in 315, so the unit digit 2 of 5402 will not be multiplied by any digit.

Ten thousand digit	$5 \to 4 \quad 0 \quad 2$ $\times \quad 3 \leftarrow 1 \quad 5$ $\overline{0 \quad 1 \quad 6 \quad 3 \quad 0}$	$1 \times 5 + 3 \times 4 = 17$ $17 + 3$ (carry out) $= 20$	0	2	Since there is no ten thousand digit in 5402, So we can not find any digit in 5402 which will be multiply with unit digit 5 of 315. Hence we start multiplying thousand digit 5 of 5402 with the tens digit 1 of 315 by showing the line segment between thousand digit 5 of 5402 and tens digit 1 of 315 and rotate the line segment in clockwise direction between 1 and 5 about their mid-point to find the next pair of digits to be multiplied but there is no digit in the left of 3 in 315, so further rotation of line segment between 3 and 4 in clockwise direction will not find any two digits to be multiplied and hence the ten's and unit's digit of 5402 will not be multiplied by any digit.
Last digit(s)	$5 \quad 4 \quad 0 \quad 2$ $\times \quad 3 \quad 1 \quad 5$ $\overline{1 \; 7 \; 0 \; 1 \quad 6 \quad 3 \quad 0}$	$3 \times 5 = 15$ $15 + 2$ (carry over) $= 17$	17	0	Since ten's digit 1 of 315 is multiplied by left most digit 5 of 5402 in finding the ten thousand's digit, so hundred digit 3 of 315 multiplies the left most digit 5 of 5402. Since there is no digit in the left of 3 in 315, so rotation of line segment between 3 and 5 about their mid-point in anticlockwise direction will not find any two digits to be multiplied further and hence hundred, tens and unit digits of 5402 will not be multiplied by any digit.

Hence required product = 1701630

In CAT and CAT like competitions large multiplications might not be required but it might be required to find any specific digit of the product of large multiplication, then the above method of multiplication is quite useful.

2. Multiplication of Two Numbers Using

Formulae $(a - b)(a + b) = a^2 - b^2$

If the difference between two numbers x and y is a small even number, then the smaller is express as $(a - b)$ whereas larger is expressed as $(a + b)$, then the product of x and y is found out by the formulae

$x . y$ i.e., $(a - b)(a + b) = a^2 - b^2$

Here a should be such that a^2 is very easily calculated.

For example:

    (i) $38 \times 42 = (40 - 2) \times (40 + 2) = (40)^2 - (2)^2 = 1600 - 4$
$$= 1596$$

    (ii) $66 \times 74 = (70 - 4) \times (70 + 4) = (70)^2 - (4)^2 = 4900 - 16$
$$= 4884$$

    (iii) $2094 \times 2106 = (2100 - 6) \times (2100 + 6) = (2100)^2 - (6)^2$
$$= 4410000 - 36 = 4409964$$

If the difference between the two numbers is not even, still this method is used by modify as

$47 \times 54 = 47 \times 53 + 47$

$$= (50 - 3) \times (50 + 3) + 47$$
$$= (50)^2 - (3)^2 + 47$$
$$= 2500 - 9 + 47 = 2538$$

3. Multiplying Two Numbers Close to 100, 1000, 10000, 100000, etc

To multiply two numbers close to 100, 1000, 10000 or 100000; we can use a specific method which is discussed in the following illustrations.

(i) Let us multiply 92 and 97.

Step (a): Calculate the difference from 100 of both the numbers and write them as follows:

	Difference from 100
92	− 8
× 97	− 3

Step (b):

$$
\begin{array}{r}
92 \qquad\qquad -8 \\
\times\ 97 \qquad\qquad -3 \\
\hline
89 \quad\vert\quad 24 \\
\end{array}
$$

Initial digits of the required product is found out by cross addition as $92 + (-3)$ or $97 + (-8) = 89$	Last two digits of the required product $(-8) \times (-3) = 24$

Thus, $92 \times 97 = 8924$

(ii) Let us multiply 1008 and 994.

$$
\begin{array}{rcl}
& & \text{Difference} \\
& & \text{from } 1000 \\
1008 & & +8 \\
\times\ \ 994 & & -6 \\
\hline
1002 & \vert & 0\ 0\ 0 \\
- & \vert & 4\ 8 \\
\hline
1001 & \vert & 9\ 5\ 2 \\
\hline
\text{Initial} & \vert & \text{Last three} \\
\text{digits} & \vert & \text{digits} \\
\end{array}
$$

Here we first find the initial digits by cross addition as $1008 + (-6)$ or $994 + 8 = 1002$

Now write 1002 as initial digits and write last three digits as 000, (i.e., last three zeroes of 1000) which means numbers' value is 1002000. Now in 1002000 add the product $8 \times (-6) = -48$, which gives the required product i.e., 1001952.

Illustration 1: Find the product 108 $\times$ 104.

Solution:

$$
\begin{array}{rcl}
& & \text{Difference} \\
& & \text{from } 100 \\
108 & & +8 \\
\times\ 104 & & +4 \\
\hline
112 & \vert & 3\ 2 \\
\hline
\text{Last} & \vert & \text{First two} \\
\text{digits} & \vert & \text{digits} \\
\end{array}
$$

Hence $108 \times 104 = 11232$

II. SQUARES

When a number is multiplied by itself, then we get the square of the number.

For example, square of $5 = 5 \times 5$ (or 5^2) $= 25$

Square of 2 and 3 digits numbers and cube of 2 digits numbers are very useful in CAT and CAT like competitions.

For this it is advised to learn the square of 1 to 30 as given in the table:

Number	Square	Number	Square
1	1	16	256
2	4	17	289
3	9	18	324
4	16	19	361
5	25	20	400
6	36	21	441
7	49	22	484
8	64	23	529
9	81	24	576
10	100	25	625
11	121	26	676
12	144	27	729
13	169	28	784
14	196	29	841
15	225	30	900

1. Shortcuts to Find the Squares of Numbers From 31 to 49

  (i) The numbers from 31 to 49 is written in the form $(50 - x)$.

        Thus to find the square of 38, 38 can be written as $(50 - 12)$.

  (ii) The last two digits of the square of 38 is the last two digits of $(12)^2$ $= 144$

        Thus last two digits of $(38)^2$ is 44 and 1 is carry over.

 (iii) The first two digits of the square of $38 = 25 - 12 + 1 = 14$

        Here 25 is the standard number used for finding square of any number from 31 to 49.

        12 is the value of x, when the number from 31 to 49 written in the form $(50 - x)$ and 1 is the carry over.

        Thus square of $38 = 38^2 = 1444$

The whole process can be shown in a single line as

$38 \rightarrow 50 - 12 \rightarrow (12)^2 = 1\,\textcircled{44} \rightarrow 25 - 12 + 1 = \textcircled{14} \rightarrow 1444$

Illustration 2: Find the square of 31.

Solution: (i) $31 = 50 - 19$

       (ii) $(19)^2 = 361$

Thus last two digits of the square of 31 is 61 and carry over 3.

       (iii) $25 - 19 + 3 = 9$

Thus $(31)^2 = 961$

The whole process can be shown in a single line as

$$31 \rightarrow 50 - 19 \rightarrow 19^2 = 3\,\circled{61} \rightarrow 25 - 19 + 3 = \circled{9} \rightarrow 961$$

---

2. Shortcuts to Find the Squares of Numbers From 51 to 79

(i) The numbers from 51 to 79 is written in the form $(50 + x)$. Thus to find square of 78, 78 can be written as $(50 + 28)$.

(ii) The last two digits of the square of 78 is the last two digits of $(28)^2$ = 784.

    Thus last two digits of $(28)^2$ is 84 and carry over 2.

(iii) The first two digits of the square of $78 = 25 + 28 + 7 = 60$. Here 25 is the standard number used for finding square of any number from 51 to 79. 28 is the value of x, when 78 is written in the form $(50 + x)$ and 2 is the carry over.

    Thus square of $78 = 78^2 = 6084$.

    The whole process can be shown in a single line as

$$78 \rightarrow 50 + 28 \rightarrow (28)^2 = 7\,\circled{84} \rightarrow 25 + 28 + 7 = \circled{60} \rightarrow 6084$$

3. Shortcuts to Find the Squares of Numbers From 81 to 99

(i) The numbers from 81 to 99 is written in the form $(100 - x)$. Thus to find square of 83, 83 can be written as $(100 - 17)$.

(ii) The last two digits of the square of 83 is the last two digits of $(17)^2$ = 289.

    Thus last two digits of $(83)^2$ is 89 and carry over 2.

(iii) The first two digits of the square of 83

$$= 83 - 17 + 2 = 68$$

Here 83 is the number whose square is to be found out. 17 is the value of x when 83 is written as $(100 - x)$ and 2 is carry over. Thus square of $83 = (83)^2 = 6889$.

The whole process can be shown in a single line as

$$83 \rightarrow 100 - 17 \rightarrow (17)^2 = 2\,\circled{89} \rightarrow 83 - 17 + 2 \rightarrow \circled{68} \rightarrow 8968$$

4. Another Shortcut Method to Find the Square of any Two and Three Digits Numbers

This method of squaring is directly connected with a process known as 'Duplex Combination (D)'.

See the duplex (D) of some two and three digits numbers

(i) Duplex (D) of 7 = square of 7 = 7^2 = 49

(ii) Duplex (D) of 5 = $(5)^2$ = 25

(iii) Duplex (D) of 27 = Twice the product of the digits 2 and 7.

$$= 2 \times (2 \times 7) = 28$$

(iv) Duplex (D) of 54 = $2 \times (5 \times 4)$ = 40

(v) Duplex (D) of 69 = $2 \times (6 \times 9)$ = 108

(vi) Duplex (D) of 83 = $2 \times (8 \times 3)$ = 48

(vii) Duplex (D) of 97 = $2 \times (9 \times 7)$ = 126

(viii) Duplex (D) of 238 = Twice the product of extreem digits

+ Square of the central digit

$$= 2 \times (2 \times 8) + (3)^2 = 32 + 9 = 41$$

(ix) Duplex (D) of 789 = $2 \times (7 \times 9) + (8)^2$ = 126 + 64 = 190

In the same way, we can find the Duplex (D) of any two and three digits number.

Now see the squaring of some two and three digits numbers.

(i) $(57)^2$ = D of 5 / D of 57 / D of 7

$$= (5)^2 / 2 \times (5 \times 7) / (7)^2$$

$$= 25 / 70 / 49$$

$$= 25 + 7\ (= 32) / 70 + 4\ (= 74) / 49$$

$$= 3249 \qquad \text{carry over} \qquad \text{carry over}$$

(ii) $(78)^2$ = D of 7 / D of 78 / D of 8

$$= 49 / 112 / 64$$

$$= 49 + 11\ (= 60) / 112 + 6\ (= 118) / 64$$

$$= 6084 \qquad \text{carry over} \qquad \text{carry over}$$

(iii) $(83)^2$ = 64 / 48 / 9 = 6889

(iv) $(96)^2$ = 81 / 108 / 36 = 9216

(v) $(769)^2$ = D of 7 / D of 76 / D 769 / D of 69 / D of 9

$$= (7)^2 / 2 \times (7 \times 6) / 2 \times (7 \times 9) + (6)^2 / 2$$
$$\times (6 \times 9) / (9)^2$$

$$= 49 / 84 / 162 / 108 / 81$$

$$= 49+10\ (=\textcircled{59})/84+17(=10\textcircled{1})$$
$$/162+11(=17\textcircled{3})$$
$$/108+8(=11\textcircled{6})/8\textcircled{1}$$

carry over   carry over   carry over   carry over

$$= 591361$$

(vi) $(483)^2$ = D of 4 / D of 48 / D of 483 / D of 83 / D of 3
$$= 16 / 64 / 88 / 48 / 9 = 233289$$

(vii) $(238)^2 = 4 / 12 / 41 / 48 / 64 = 56644$

In the same way, we can find the square of two and three digits numbers.

III. CUBES

When a number multiplies itself three times, we get the cube of the number.

Cube of 4 = $4 \times 4 \times 4$ = 64

Cubes of large numbers are rarely used. It is advised to you to learn the cube of the integers from 1 to 10.

Number	1	2	3	4	5	6	7	8	9	10
Cube	1	8	27	64	125	216	343	512	729	1000

To find the cube of a two digit number, first write the square of tens digit of the number and then write three numbers separately right of the square of tens digit, which form a G.P. (geometrical progression) of four terms whose first term is the square of tens digit and common ratio is equal to the ratio of unit's digit to tens digit of the given numbers.

Note that the sequence 3, 6, 12, 24, ... is a G.P. whose first term is 3. In this sequence we get each number after multiplying just previous number by 2.

$$\therefore \quad \frac{6}{3} = \frac{12}{6} = \frac{24}{12} = ... = 2$$

Thus 2 is called common ratio.

Let us find the cube of a two digits number 26. For this we find the cube of tens digit i.e. $(2)^3 = 8$, then we find the ratio of its unit's digit to tens digit $= \dfrac{6}{2} = 3$.

Now we write square of tens digit i.e. 8 and the three numbers right of 8 separately in such a way that 8 and the three number are in G.P. whose common ratio is 3 as

8   24   72   216

(we get each of the numbers 24, 72 and 216 by multiplying just previous number of it by the common ratio 3.)

Now write twice the two middle number 24 and 72 just below to 24 and 72 respectively and add the numbers one below the other in two rows with carry over the digits except units digit of each sum from right to left as shown:

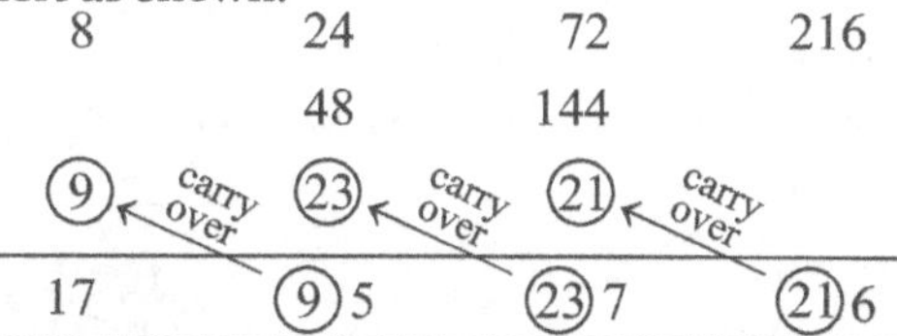

The final number 17576 obtained is the cube of 26 i.e.,

$(26)^3 = 17576$.

Illustration 3: Find the cube of 42.

Solution: Cube of tens digit 4 = 64.

Ratio of unit's digit to tens digit = $\dfrac{2}{4} = \dfrac{1}{2}$.

The next three numbers are

$$64 \times \frac{1}{2}, \left(64 \times \frac{1}{2}\right) \times \frac{1}{2}, \left(64 \times \frac{1}{2} \times \frac{1}{2}\right) \times \frac{1}{2} \text{ i.e. } 32, 16, 8.$$

$\therefore (42)^3 = 74088$

Illustration 4: Find the cube of 14.

Solution: $(1)^3 = 1$,

Ratio of unit digit to tens digit = $\dfrac{4}{1}$ = 4

$\therefore (14)^3 = 2744$

CLASSIFICATION OF NUMBERS

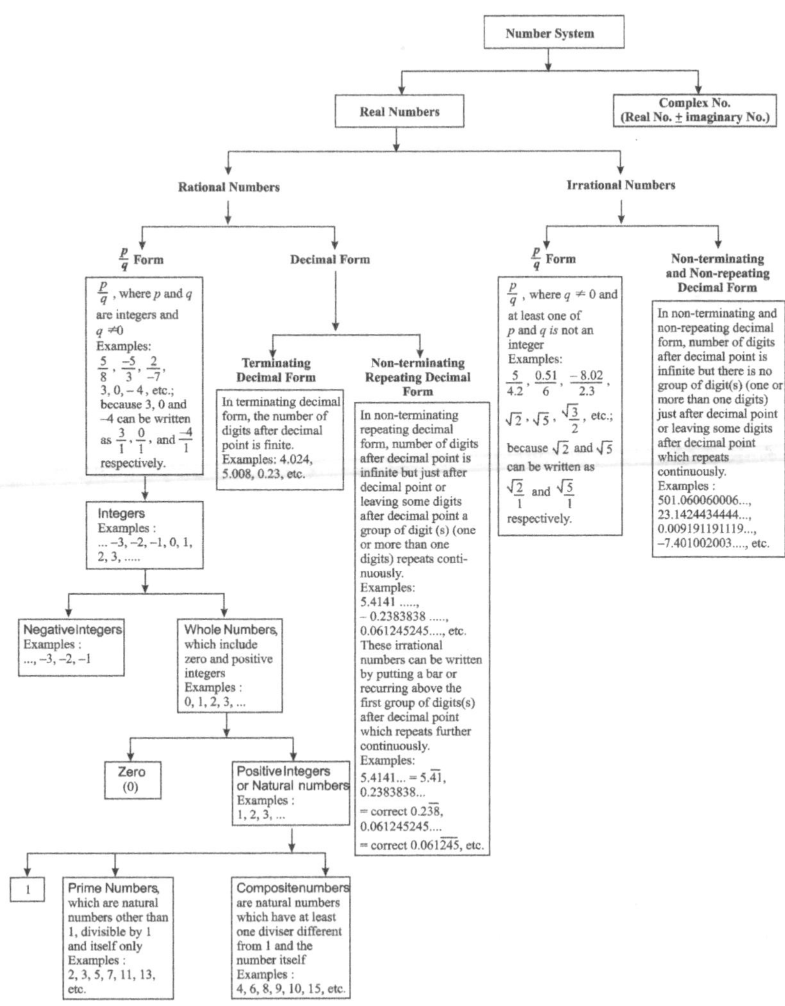

To Test Whether a Given Number is Prime Number or Not

In CAT and CAT like competitions you are required to check whether a given number maximum upto 400 is prime number or not.

If you want to test whether any number is a prime number or not, take an integer equal to the square root of the given number but if square root is not an integer then take an integer just larger than the approximate square root of that number. Let it be 'x'. Test the divisibility of the given number by every prime number less than 'x'. If the given number is not divisible by any prime number less than, then the given number is prime number; otherwise it is a composite number.

Square root of 361 is 19. Prime numbers less than 19 are clearly 2, 3, 5, 7, 11, 13 and 17. Since, 361 is not divisible by any of the numbers 2, 3, 5, 7, 11, 13 and 17. Hence, 361 is a prime number.

It is advisable to learn the squared numbers of all integers from 1 to 20, which are very useful to find whether a given number is a prime or not.

From the table it is clear that if any number, say 271 lies between 256 and 289, then its square root lies between 16 and 17, because $16^2 = 256$ and $17^2 = 289$. Thus square root of the given number is not an integer. So, we take 17 as an integer just greater than the square root of the given number. Now all the prime numbers less than 17 are 2, 3, 5, 7, 11 and 13. Since 271 is not divisible by any of the numbers 2, 3, 5, 7, 11 and 13. Hence 361 is a prime number.

Illustration 1: Is 171 is a prime number ?
Solution: Square root of 171 lies between 13 and 14, because $13^2 = 169$ and $14^2 = 196$. Therefore, the integer just greater than the square root of 171 is 14.
Now prime numbers less than 14 are 2, 3, 5, 7, 11 and 13.
Since 171 is divisible by 3, therefore 171 is not a prime number.

Illustration 2: Is 167 is a prime number ?
Solution: Square root of 167 lies between 12 and 13, because $12^2 = 144$ and $13^2 = 169$. Therefore the integer just greater than the square root of 167 is 13.
Now prime numbers less than 13 are 2, 3, 5, 7 and 11.
Since 167 is not divisible by any of the prime numbers 2, 3, 5, 7 and 11; therefore 167 is a prime number.

The Last Digit From Left (i.e., unit digit) of Any Power of a Number

The last digits (from left) of the powers of any number follow a cyclic pattern i.e., they repeat after certain number of steps. If we find out after how many steps the last digit of the powers of a number repeat, then we can find out the last digit of any power of any number.

Let us look at the powers of 2:

Last digit of 2^1 is 2 . Last digit of 2^6 is 4 .

Last digit of 2^2 is 4 . Last digit of 2^7 is 8 .

Last digit of 2^3 is 8 .   Last digit of 2^8 is 6 .

Last digit of 2^4 is 6 .   Last digit of 2^9 is 2 .

Last digit of 2^5 is 2 .

Since last digit of 2^5 is the same as the last digit of 2^1, then onwards the last digit will start repeating, i.e., digits of $2^5, 2^6, 2^7, 2^8$ will be the same as those of $2^1, 2^2, 2^3, 2^4$. Then the last digit of 2^9 is again the same as the last digit of 2^1 and so on. Thus, we see that when power of 2 increases, the last digits repeat after every 4 steps.

In above pattern, we can see that whenever the power of 2 is a multiple of 4, the last digit of that number will be the same as the last digit of 2^4.

Suppose we want to find out the last digit of 2^{66}, we should look at a multiple of 4 which is just less than or equal to the power 66 of 2. Since 64 is a multiple of 4, the last digit of 2^{64} will be the same as the last digit of 2^4.

Then the last digits of $2^{65}, 2^{66}$ will be the same as the last digits of 2^1, 2^2 respectively. Hence the last digit of 2^{66} is the same as the last digit of 2^2 i.e., 4.

Similarly, we can find out the last digit of 3^{75} by writing down the pattern of the powers of 3.

Last digit of 3^1 is 3.   Last digit of 3^4 is 1.

Last digit of 3^2 is 9.   Last digit of 3^5 is 3.

Last digit of 3^3 is 7.   Last digit of $3^6 = 9$

     Last digit of $3^7 = 7$

     Last digit of $3^8 = 1$

     Last digit of $3^9 = 3$

The last digit repeats after 4 steps (like in the case of powers of 2).

Whenever the powers of 3 is a multiple of 4, the last digit of that number will be the same as the last digit of 3^4.

To find the last digit of 3^{75}, we look for a multiple of 4 which is just less than or equal to the power 75 of 3. Since, 72 is multiple of 4, the last digit of 3^{72} will be the same as that of 3^4. Hence the last digit of 3^{75} will be the same as the last digit of 3^3 i.e., 7.

Last Digit (i.e., Unit Digit) of a Product

Last digit of the product $a \times b \times c \ldots$ is the last digit of the product of last digits of $a, b, c, \ldots$

Illustration 3: Find the last digit of $2^{416} \times 4^{430}$.

Solution: Writing down the powers of 2 and 4 to check the pattern of the last digits, we have

We have seen that whenever the power of 2 is a multiple of 4, the last digit of that number will be the same as the last digit of 2^4.

Now,   Last digit of $4^1 = 4$.

Last digit of $4^2 = 6$.

Last digit of $4^3 = 4$.

Last digit of $4^4 = 6$.

Thus last digit of any power of 4 is 4 for an odd power and 6 for an even power. The last digit of 2^{416} will be the same as 2^4 because 416 is a multiple of 4. So the last digit of 2^{416} is 6.

Last digit of 4^{430} is 6, since the power of 4 is even.

Hence the last digit of $2^{416} \times 4^{430}$ will be equal to the last digit of $6 \times 6 = 6$.

CONCEPT OF REMAINDERS

(I) Suppose the numbers N_1, N_2, N_3, ... give quotients Q_1, Q_2, Q_3, ... and remainder R_1, R_2, R_3, ... when divided by a common divisor D.

Let S be the sum of N_1, N_2, N_3,..

Therefore, $S = N_1 + N_2 + N_3 + ...$

$$= (D \times Q_1 + R_1) + (D \times Q_2 + R_2) +$$
$$(D \times Q_3 + R_3) + ...$$
$$= D \times K + (R_1 + R_2 + R_3...), \qquad ...(1)$$

where K is some number

Hence the remainder when S is divided by D is the remainder when $(R_1 + R_2 + R_3.....)$ is divided by D.

(II) Suppose the numbers, N_1, N_2, N_3,... give quotients Q_1, Q_2, Q_3,... and remainders R_1, R_2, R_3,... respectively, when divided by a common divisor D.

Therefore $N_1 = D \times Q_1 + R_1$, $N_2 = D \times Q_2 + R_2$,

$N_3 = D \times Q_3 \times R_3...$ and so on.

Let P be the product of N_1, N_2, N_3,...

Therefore,

$$P = N_1 N_2 N_3 ...$$
$$= (D \times Q_1 + R_1)(D \times Q_2 + R_2)(D \times Q_3 + R_3)...$$
$$= D \times K + (R_1 R_2 R_3...), \qquad ...(2)$$

where K is some number

In the above equation, since only the product $(R_1 R_2 R_3 ...)$ is free of D, therefore the remainder when P is divided by D is the remainder when the product $(R_1 R_2 R_3 ...)$ is divided by D.

Illustration 4: What is the remainder when the product 1991 × 1992 × 2000 is divided by 7 ?

Solution: The remainder when 1991, 1992 and 2000 are divided by 7 are 3, 4 and 5 respectively.

Hence the final remainder is the remainder when the product $3 \times 4 \times 5 = 60$ is divided by 7. Therefore, remainder = 4.

Illustration 5: What is the remainder when 2^{2010} is divided by 7 ?

Solution: 2^{2010} is a product $(2 \times 2 \times 2...(2010$ times$))$. Since, 2 is a number less than 7, we try to convert the product into product of numbers higher than 7. Notice that $8 = 2 \times 2 \times 2$. Therefore, we convert the product in the following manner

$2^{2010} = 8^{670} = 8 \times 8 \times 8...$ (670 times.)

The remainder when 8 is divided by 7 is 1. Hence the remainder when 8^{670} is divided by 7 is the remainder obtained when the product $1 \times 1 \times 1...$ (670 times) is divided by 7. Therefore, remainder = 1.

Illustration 6: What is the remainder when $39^{32^{32}}$ is divided by 7?

Solution: Steps for finding remainder when X^{Y^Z} is divided by D.

(i) Divide X by D. Let the remainder be R. Therefore, you have to find the remainder when R^{Y^Z} is divided by D. 39 gives a remainder 4 when divided by 7. Therefore, you have to find the remainder when $4^{32^{32}}$ is divided by 7.

(ii) Find a power of R that gives a remainder +1 when divided by D. If you find a power that gives a remainder –1, twice of that power will give a remainder of +1. Now we know that $4^3 = 64$ gives a remainder 1 when divided by 7.

(iii) Find the remainder when Y^Z is divided by the power R. Here, find the remainder when 32^{32} is divided by 3. The remainder is 1. Therefore, when 32^{32} is divided by 3. The remainder is 1. Therefore, 32^{32} can be written as $3k + 1$ and $4^{32^{32}}$ can be written as $4^{3k+1} = (4^3)^k \times 4$.

(iv) Now 4^3 gives a remainder 1 when divided by 7. Therefore, the required remainder is the remainder when 4 is divided by 7. Hence, the required remainder is 4.

Some Special Cases

(A) When Both the Dividend and the Divisor have a Factor in Common

To find the remainder,

- Divide both dividend and divisor by the common factor (K) i.e. HCF of dividend and divisor.

- Divide the resulting dividend (A) by resulting divisor (B) and find the remainder (R_1).

- The real remainder R is the remainder R_1 multiplied by the common factor (K).

Illustration 7: What is the remainder when 2^{96} is divided by 96?

Solution: The common factor between 2^{96} and 96 is $32 = 2^5$.

Divide both dividend and divisor by 32 i.e., 2^5

You will get the resulting dividend and the divisor as the numbers 2^{91} and 3 respectively.

Now, $2^{91} = (2^4)^{22} \, 2^3 = (16)^{22} \cdot 8$

When 16 and 8 are divided by 3, remainder are 1 and 2 respectively.

Hence when $(16)^{22}$ when divided by 3, we get the remainder $(1)^{22}$ i.e. 1.

Hence the remainder when $(2)^{91}$ is divided by 3 is the remainder when 1×2 is divided by 3. Hence the remainder when $(2)^{91}$ is divided by 3 is 2.

Hence the real remainder will be 2 multiplied by common factor 32.

i.e. real remainder = 64

(B) The Concept of Negative Remainder

$$15 = 16 \times 0 + 15 \quad \text{or} \quad 15 = 16 \times 1 - 1.$$

The remainder when 15 is divided by 16 is 15 in the first case and -1 in the second case. Hence, the remainder when 15 is divided by 16 is 15 or -1.

Also $23 = 7 \times 3 + 2 \quad \text{or} \quad 23 = 7 \times 4 - 5$.

Thus, when 23 is divided by 7, then remainder is 2 or -5.

Thus, when a number is divided by A gives a negative remainder B, then positive remainder $= A + B$.

For example, when a number gives a negative remainder of -2 when divided by 23, it means that the number gives a positive remainder of $23 - 2 = 21$ when divided by 23.

Using the concept of positive and negative remainders, you can find the remainder more easily by reducing calculations. You must remember that we always take the positive remainder in final answer.

(i) To find the remainder when $76 \times 55 \times 67 \times 51$ is divided by 8, we can follow as

$$\frac{76 \times 55 \times 67 \times 51}{8} \xrightarrow{\text{Remainder}} \frac{4 \times (-1) \times 3 \times 3}{8} \xrightarrow{\text{Remainder}}$$

$$\frac{-36}{8} \xrightarrow{\text{Remainder}} -4 \xrightarrow{\text{Remainder}} -4 + 8 = 4$$

Thus required remainder = 4

To convert the negative remainder into positive remainder, we add the divisor to the negative remainder.

Note that if you transform $\dfrac{-36}{8}$ into $\dfrac{-9}{2}$ by dividing both numerator and denominator by common factor 4 of -36 and 8, then original remainder -4 is also divided by 4 giving -1 as remainder. So to find the correct answer, we multiply the incorrect remainder by 4.

(ii) When $69 \times 68 \times 71 \times 66$ is divided by 72 to find the remainder, we can follow as

$$\frac{69 \times 68 \times 71 \times 66}{72} \xrightarrow{\text{Remainder}} \frac{(-3) \times (-4) \times (-1) \times (-6)}{72}$$

$$\xrightarrow{\text{Remainder}} \frac{72}{72} \xrightarrow{\text{Remainder}} 1.$$

Thus required remainder = 1.

(iii) When $53 \times 55 \times 57 \times 61$ is divided by 60, then to find the remainder we can follow as

$$\frac{53 \times 55 \times 57 \times 61}{60} \xrightarrow{\text{Remainder}} \frac{(-7) \times (-5) \times (-3) \times 1}{60}$$

$$\xrightarrow{\text{Remainder}} \frac{-105}{60} \xrightarrow{\text{Remainder}} -45$$

Thus Remainder $= -45 + 60 = 15$

(C) Remainder in Case of a Number with Large Power

(i) When remainder becomes 1 directly. In such a case, no matter how large the value of the power n is, the remainder is 1.

For example,

$$\frac{(33)^{24139}}{8} \xrightarrow{\text{Remainder}} \frac{(8 \times 4 + 1)^{24139}}{8}$$

$$\frac{(1)^{24139}}{8} \xrightarrow{\text{Remainder}} 1$$

If a is the divisor and dividend can be expressed as $(ax - 1)^n$, where x and n are two natural numbers, then

(ii) Remainder will be + 1, if n is even and –1, if n is odd and hence positive remainder is $(a - 1)$, when n is odd.

For example,

$$\frac{41^{127}}{7} \xrightarrow{\text{Remainder}} \frac{(7 \times 6 - 1)^{127}}{7} \xrightarrow{\text{Remainder}} \frac{(-1)^{127}}{7}$$

$$\xrightarrow{\text{Remainder}} (-1) \xrightarrow{\text{Remainder}} 7 - 1 = 6.$$

Illustration 8: Find the remainder when 7^{52} is divided by 2402.

Solution:

$$\frac{7^{52}}{2402} \xrightarrow{\text{Remainder}} \frac{(7^4)^{13}}{2402} \xrightarrow{\text{Remainder}} \frac{(2401)^{13}}{2402}$$

$$\xrightarrow{\text{Remainder}} \frac{(2402 - 1)^{13}}{2402} \xrightarrow{\text{Remainder}} (-1)^{13} = -1.$$

Hence, the remainder when 7^{52} is divided by 2402 is equal to $- 1$ or $2402 - 1 = 2401$.

To find the last digits of the

EXPRESSION LIKE $a_1 \times a_2 \times a_3 \times \ldots \times a_n$

Last r digits (from right) of the product $a_1 \times a_2 \times a_3 \times \ldots \times a_n$ is the remainder when $a_1 \times a_2 \times a_3 \times \ldots \times a_n$ is divided by $(10)^r$.

Let us find the last two digits of $29 \times 47 \times 53 \times 76 \times 89$.

$$\text{Now } \frac{29 \times 47 \times 53 \times 76 \times 89}{100} \xrightarrow{\text{Remainder}}$$

$$\frac{29 \times 47 \times 53 \times 19 \times 89}{25} \xrightarrow{\text{Remainder}} \frac{4 \times (-3) \times 3 \times (-6) \times (-11)}{25}$$

$$\xrightarrow{\text{Remainder}} \frac{-2376}{25} \xrightarrow{\text{Remainder}} - 1$$

(on dividing by 4 in both numerator and denominator)

Thus remainder is –1 (after dividing by 4)

Hence actual remainder = $-1 \times 4 = - 4$, which is negative

Now actual positive remainder = $- 4 + 100 = 96$

Hence required last two digits = 96

Similarly you can find any number of last digits of a product.

Theorem 1: $(a^n + b^n)$ is divisible by $(a + b)$ when n is odd.

Theorem 2: $(a^n - b^n)$ is divisible by $(a + b)$ when n is even.

Theorem 3: $(a^n - b^n)$ is always divisible by $(a - b)$ when n is an integer.

Hence $(a^n - b^n)$ is divisible by both $(a + b)$ and $(a - b)$ when n is even and $(a^n - b^n)$ is divisible by only $(a - b)$ when n is odd.

Illustration 9: What is the remainder when $3^{444} + 4^{333}$ is divided by 5 ?

Solution: The dividend is in the form $a^x + b^y$. We need to change it into the form $a^n + b^n$.

$3^{444} + 4^{333} = (3^4)^{111} + (4^3)^{111}$. Now $(3^4)^{111} + (4^3)^{111}$ will be divisible by $3^4 + 4^3 = 81 + 64 = 145$.

Since the number is divisible by 145, it will certainly be divisible by 5. Hence, the remainder is 0.

Illustration 10: $20^{2008} + 16^{2008} - 3^{2008} - 1$ is divisible by:

(a) 314   **(b) 323**

(c) 253   **(d) 91**

Solution: (b) $20^{2008} + 16^{2008} - 3^{2008} - 1 = (20^{2008} - 3^{2008}) + (16^{2008} - 1^{2008})$. Now $20^{2008} - 3^{2008}$ is divisible by 17 (Theorem 3) and $16^{2008} - 1^{2008}$ is divisible by 17 (Theorem 2). Hence the complete expression is divisible by 17.

$20^{2008} + 16^{2008} - 3^{2008} - 1 = (20^{2008} - 1^{2008}) + (16^{2008} - 3^{2008})$. Now $20^{2008} - 1^{2008}$ is divisible by 19 (Theorem 3) and $16^{2008} - 3^{2008}$ is divisible by 19 (Theorem 2). Hence the complete expression is also divisible by 19.

Hence the complete expression is divisible by $17 \times 19 = 323$.

Illustration 11: If $p = 1! + (2 \times 2!) + (3 \times 3!) + \ldots + (10 \times 10!)$, where $n! = 1 \times 2 \times 3 \times \ldots n$ for integer $n \geq 1$, then $p + 2$ when divided by 11!, leaves a remainder

(a) 10   **(b) 0**   **(c) 7**   **(d) 1**

Solution: (b) nth term of series

$$= \quad n \times n! = (n + 1 - 1) \times n! = (n + 1)! - n!$$

Therefore, $p = 2! - 1! + 3! - 2! + 4! - 3! + \ldots + 11! - 10!$

$$= 11! - 1! \Rightarrow p + 2 = 11! + 1$$

Hence when $(p + 2)$ is divided by 11!, then remainder = 1.

Illustration 12: Find the remainder when
$1 \times 2 + 2 \times 3 + 3 \times 4 + \ldots + 99 \times 100$ is divided by 101.

Solution: nth term of the series $= n \times (n + 1) = n^2 + n$.
Therefore, sum of the series,

$$\sum (n^2 + n) = \frac{n\,(n+1)\,(2n+1)}{6} + \frac{n\,(n+1)}{2}$$

$$= \frac{n\,(n+1)\,(n+2)}{3} = \frac{99 \times 100 \times 101}{3}$$

$$= 33 \times 100 \times 101$$

$\Rightarrow$ Remainder on dividing by $101 = 0$.

Note:

(i) $1 + 2 + 3 + \dots + n = \dfrac{n(n+1)}{2} \Rightarrow \sum n = \dfrac{n(n+1)}{2}$

(ii) $1^2 + 2^2 + 3^2 + \dots + n^2$

$$= \frac{n(n+1)\,(2n+1)}{6} \Rightarrow \sum n^2 = \frac{n(n+1)\,(2n+1)}{6}$$

(iii) $1^3 + 2^3 + 3^3 + \dots + n^3$

$$= \left(\frac{n(n+1)}{2} \right)^2 \Rightarrow \sum n^3 = \left(\frac{n(n+1)}{2} \right)^2$$

Last Two Digits of a Number with Large Power

Last Two Digits of Numbers Ending in 1

Let's start with an example $(31)^{786}$.

Multiply the tens digit of the number (3 here) with the last digit of the exponent (6 here) to get the tens digit $3 \times 6 = 18$.

The unit digit 8 of the product 18 is tens digit of the required number.

Unit digits of the required number is equal to 1.

Last two digits of 41^{2789} is 61

(Since $4 \times 9 = 36$. Therefore, 6 is the tens digit and 1 is the units digit).

Last Two Digits of Numbers Ending in 3, 7 or 9

Convert the number till the base of the number ends in 1 and then find the last two digits according to the previous method.

To find the last two digits of 19^{266}:

$19^{266} = (19^2)^{133}$. Now, 19^2 ends in 61 ($19^2 = 361$) therefore, we need to find the last two digits of $(61)^{133}$.

Last two digits of $(61)^{133}$ and hence $(19)^{266}$ is 81 by the previous method (tens digit = unit digit of $(6 \times 3 = 18)$ and unit digit = 1).

To find the last two digits of 33^{288}:

$33^{288} = (33^4)^{72}$. Now 33^4 ends in 21 ($33^4 = 33^2 \times 33^2 = 1089 \times 1089 =$ xxxxx21), therefore we need to find the last two digits of 21^{72}. By the previous method, the last two digits of $21^{72} = 41$ (tens digit = $2 \times 2 = 4$, unit digit = 1).

Now try the method with a number ending in 7 :

$87^{474} = 87^{472} \times 87^2 = (87^4)^{118} \times 87^2 \rightarrow (69 \times 69)^{118} \times 69$

(The last two digits of 87^2 are 69) $\rightarrow 61^{118} \times 69 \rightarrow 81 \times 69 \rightarrow 89$.

Last Two Digits of Numbers Ending in 2, 4, 6 or 8

   (i)   There is only one even two-digit number 76, raised to any power gives the last two digits as 76.

  (ii) 2^{10} ends in 24.

 (iii)   24 raised to an even power always ends with 76 and 24 raised to an odd power always ends with 24. Therefore, 24^{34} will end in 76 and 24^{53} will end in 24.

          Now apply this concept in the following examples.

 (iv)   When 76 is multiplied with 2^n for $n \geq 2$, the last two digits of the product is the same as the last two digits of 2^n. Therefore, the last two digits of 76×2^7 will be the last two digits of $2^7 = 28$.

Illustration 13: Find the last two digits of 2^{543}.

Solution: $2^{543} = (2^{10})^{54} \times 2^3$

$= (24)^{54}$ (i.e. 24 raised to an even power) $\times 2^3 \rightarrow 76 \times 8 \rightarrow 08$.

Number of Zeroes in an Expression like $a \times b \times c \times \ldots$, where a, b, c,... are Natural Numbers

Consider an expression $8 \times 15 \times 20 \times 30 \times 40$.

The expression can be written in the standard form as :

$8 \times 15 \times 20 \times 30 \times 40$

     $= (2^3) \times (3 \times 5) \times (2^2 \times 5) \times (2 \times 3 \times 5) \times (2^3 \times 5)$

     $= 2^9 \times 3^2 \times 5^4$, in which base of each factor is a prime number.

A zero is formed by the product of 2 and 5 i.e. 2×5. Hence number of zeroes is equal to the number of pair(s) of 2's and 5's formed.

In the above standard form of the product there are 9 twos and 4 fives. Hence number of pairs of 2 and 5 i.e. (2×5) is 4. Hence, there will be 4 zeroes at the end of the final product.

In the same above way, we can find the number of zeroes at the end of any product given in the form of an expression like $a \times b \times c \times \ldots$, where a, b, c,... are natural numbers.

If there is no pair of 2 and 5 i.e. 2×5, then there is no zero at the end of the product. For example, consider the expression $9 \times 21 \times 39 \times 49$.

The given expression in standard form,

$$9 \times 21 \times 39 \times 49 = (3^2) \times (3 \times 7) \times (3 \times 13) \times (7^2)$$
$$= 3^4 \times 7^3 \times 13$$

There is no pair of 2 and 5 in the standard form of expression given as product, therefore there will be no zero at the end of the final product.

Illustration 14: Find the number of zeroes in the product
$$1^1 \times 2^2 \times 3^3 \times 4^4 \times 5^5 \times 6^6 \times \ldots\ldots\ldots \times 49^{49}$$

Solution: Clearly the fives will be less than the twos. Hence, we need to count only the fives.

Now, $5^5 \times 10^{10} \times 15^{15} \times 20^{20} \times 25^{25} \times 30^{30} \times 35^{35} \times 40^{40} \times 45^{45}$

$$= (5)^5 \times (5 \times 2)^{10} \times (5 \times 3)^{15} \times (5 \times 4)^{20} \times (5 \times 5)^{25} \times$$
$$(5 \times 6)^{30} \times (5 \times 7)^{35} \times (5 \times 8)^{40} \times (5 \times 9)^{45}$$

It gives us $5 + 10 + 15 + 20 + 25 \times 25 + 30 + 35 + 40 + 45$ fives *i.e.*, 825 fives

Thus the product has 825 zeroes.

Illustration 15: Find the number of zeroes in:
$$100^1 \times 99^2 \times 98^3 \times 97^4 \times \ldots\ldots\ldots \times 1^{100}$$

Solution: Clearly the fives will be less than the twos. Hence we need to count the number of fives only. This can get done by :

$100^1 \times 95^6 \times 90^{11} \times 85^{16} \times 80^{21} \times 75^{26} \times \ldots\ldots\ldots 5^{96}$

$= (5^2 \times 4)^1 \times (5 \times 19)^6 \times (5 \times 18)^{11} \times (5 \times 17)^{16} \times (5 \times 16)^{21} \times (5^2 \times 3)^{26} \times$

$(5 \times 14)^{31} \times \ldots\ldots\times (5 \times 11)^{56} \times (5^2 \times 2)^{51} \times (5 \times 9)^{56} \times \ldots\ldots \times (5 \times 6)^{71} \times$

$(5^2)^{76} \times (5 \times 4)^{81} \times \ldots \times (5 \times 2)^{91} \times (5)^{96}$

$\rightarrow (1 + 6 + 11 + 16 + 21 + 26 + 31 + 36 + 41 + 46 + \ldots\ldots\ldots + 96) + (1 + 26 + 51 + 76)$

In $1 + 6 + 11 + 16 + \ldots + 96$, if any term is subtract from just next term, we get the same number

$5 (= 6 - 1 = 11 - 6 = \ldots = 96 - 91)$. This difference 5 is called common difference and any series having a common difference is called an A.P. (Arithmetic Progression).

Hence $1 + 6 + 11 + 16 + \ldots + 96$ is an A.P.

The formula to find the number of terms in an A.P. is

$$l \quad = \quad a + (n - 1)\,d$$

where, l is the last term (here $l = 96$)

a is the first term (here $a = 1$)

d is the common difference (here $d = 5$)

and $\quad$ n is the number of terms.

$\therefore \quad 96 = 1 + (n - 1) \times 5 \implies n = 20$

The formula to find the sum of all terms of an A.P. is

$$S = \frac{n}{2}(a + l), \text{ where } S \text{ is the sum of all terms}$$

$$\therefore \quad S = \frac{20}{2}(1 + 96) = 970$$

i.e. $\quad 1 + 6 + 11 + 16 + ... + 96 = 970$

We will study A.P. in detail in the chapter: Progressions.

Now $\quad 1 + 26 + 51 + 76 = 154$

$\therefore \quad (1 + 6 + 11 + 16 + ... + 96) + (1 + 26 + 51 + 76)$

$$= 970 + 1124.$$

POWERS OF A NUMBER CONTAINED IN A FACTORIAL

(I) First Method

Highest power of prime number p in $n!$

$$= \left[\frac{n}{p}\right] + \left[\frac{n}{p^2}\right] + \left[\frac{n}{p^3}\right] + \left[\frac{n}{p^4}\right] + ... + \left[\frac{n}{p^r}\right],$$

where $[x]$ denotes the greatest integer less than or equal to x and r is a

natural number such that $p^r < n$.

Illustration 16: Find the highest power of 2 in 50!

Solution: The highest power of 2 in 50!

$$= \left[\frac{50}{2}\right] + \left[\frac{50}{4}\right] + \left[\frac{50}{8}\right] + \left[\frac{50}{16}\right] + \left[\frac{50}{32}\right]$$

$$= 25 + 12 + 6 + 3 + 1 = 47$$

Illustration 17: Find the highest power of 6 in 60!.

Solution: Here given number 6 is not a prime number so first convert 6 as a product of primes. $6 = 2 \times 3$, therefore we will find the highest power of 2 and 3 in 60!.

Highest power of 2 in 60!

$$= \left[\frac{60}{2}\right] + \left[\frac{60}{4}\right] + \left[\frac{60}{8}\right] + \left[\frac{60}{16}\right] + \left[\frac{60}{32}\right]$$

$$= 30 + 15 + 7 + 3 + 1 = 56$$

Highest power of 3 in 60!

$$= \left[\frac{60}{3}\right] + \left[\frac{60}{9}\right] + \left[\frac{60}{27}\right] = 20 + 6 + 2 = 28$$

So 60! contains $(2)^{56} \times (3)^{28}$. Hence it contains 28 pairs of 2 and 3. Therefore, required power of 6 is 28, which is actually the power of the largest prime factor 3 of 6, because power of largest prime factor is always equal or less than the other prime factors of any number.

(II) Second Method

We will discuss this method through an example,

Let us find the highest power of prime number 7 in 400! to find the highest power of prime number 7 in 400! we divide 400! by 7 and find the quotient. Divide this quotient by 7 again and find the next quotient and proceed as given below. In this way, we will find the last quotient, which is less than the divisor 7 as follows :

```
7| 400
7| 57 ←—— First quotient
7| 8  ←—— Second quotient
   1  ←—— Third quotient
```

Here the last quotient is 1, which is less than 7.

In this method, highest power of 7 in 400!

$$= \text{Sum of all the quotients}$$

$$= \text{First Quotient} + \text{Second Quotient} + \text{Third Quotient}$$

$$= 57 + 8 + 1 = 66$$

Above rule is valid only for prime numbers not for composite numbers. If we need to find the highest power of composite number in a given factorial, then first convert the composite number as product of primes and then find the highest power of largest prime factor of the given composite number, which is the required highest power of the given composite number.

Illustration 18: Find the number of zeroes present at the end of 100!

Solution: We get a zero at the end of a number when we multiply that number by 10. So, to calculate the number of zeroes at the end of 100!, we have to find highest power of 10 present in the number. Since, 10 (a composite number) = 2 × 5 and hence 5 is the largest prime factor of 10, therefore we have to find the highest power of 5 in 100!

```
5 | 100
5 |  20
  |   4
```

The highest power of 5 in 100!

$$= \text{First Quotient} + \text{Second Quotient} = 20 + 4 = 24$$

Therefore, the number of zeroes at the end of 100! = 24.

SHORTCUT FOR FINDING HCF OR GCD

To find the HCF of any number of given numbers, first find the difference between two nearest given numbers. Then find all factors (or divisors) of this difference. Highest factor which divides all the given numbers is the HCF.

Illustration 19: Find the HCF of 12, 20 and 32.

Solution: Difference of nearest two numbers 12 and 20 = 20 − 12 = 8

All factors (or divisor) of 8 are 1, 2, 4 and 8.

1, 2 and 4 divides each of the three given numbers 12, 20 and 32. Out of 1, 2 and 4; 4 is the highest number. Hence, HCF = 4.

Shortcut For Finding LCM

Using idea of co-prime, you can find the LCM by the following shortcut method:

LCM of 9, 10, 15 and 36 can be written directly as 9 × 10 × 2.

The logical thinking that behind it is as follows:

Step 1: If you can see a set of 2 or more co-prime numbers in the set of numbers of which you are finding the LCM, write them down by multiply them.

In the above situation, since we see that 9 and 10 are co-prime to each other, we start off writing the LCM by writing 9 × 10 as the first step.

Step 2: For each of the other numbers, consider what prime factor(s) of it is/are not present in the LCM (if factorised into primes) taken in step 1. In case you see some prime factors of each of the other given numbers separately are not present in the LCM (if factorised into primes) taken in step 1, such prime factors will be multiplied in the LCM taken in step 1.

Prime factorisation of $9 \times 10 = 3 \times 3 \times 2 \times 5$

Prime factorisation of $15 = 3 \times 5$

Prime factorisation of $36 = 2 \times 2 \times 3 \times 3$

Here we see that both prime factors of 15 are present in the prime factorisation of 9×10 but one prime factor 2 of 36 is not present in the LCM taken in step 1. So to find the LCM of 9, 10, 15 and 36; we multiply the LCM taken in step 1 by 2.

Thus required LCM = $9 \times 10 \times 2 = 180$

TIME AND WORK

I. WORK DONE EQUATION (UNITY METHOD)

If man A do any work in D days then– work by A in one day = $\dfrac{1}{D}$

Note: If n men do any work in D days then - work by one man in one day = $\dfrac{1}{nD} \Rightarrow w$

So that, if n, men do, any work in D_1 days and n_2 men do this work D_2 days then relationship b/w them

$$W_1 = \dfrac{1}{n_1 D_1}$$

$$W_2 = \dfrac{1}{n_2 D_2}$$

$$W_1 = W_2 \qquad\qquad\qquad \text{[only day work]}$$

$$\dfrac{1}{n_1 D_1} = \dfrac{1}{n_2 D_2}$$

$$\boxed{n_1 D_1 = n_2 D_2}$$

Note 1: If both group take H_1 hours and H_2 hours then relation will be -

$$\boxed{n_1 D_1 H_1 = n_2 D_2 H_2}$$

Note 3: If both group work efficiency E_1 and E_2 then

$$\boxed{n_1 D_1 H_1 E_1 = n_2 D_2 H_2 E_2}$$

Illustration 1: 12 men can make 80 tables in 20 days working 8 hours a day. In how many days 30 men can make 120 tables working 6 hours a day?

Solution: $\qquad M_1D_1T_1W_2 = M_2D_2T_2W_1$

Here $M_1 \qquad = 12, \ D_1 = 20, \ T_1 = 8, \ W_1 = 80$

$$M_2 = 30, \ D_2 = ? \ T_2 = 6, \ W_2 = 120$$

$\therefore \qquad 12 \times 20 \times 8 \times 120 = 30 \times D_2 \times 6 \times 80$

$$\Rightarrow \qquad\qquad D_2 = \frac{12 \times 20 \times 8 \times 120}{30 \times 6 \times 80} = 16$$

Hence required number of days = 16 days.

Illustration 2: 5 men can prepare 150 toys in 5 days working 6 hours a day. In how many hours 10 boys can prepare 200 toys in 10 days, if a man works thrice as fast as a boy?

Solution: Since a man works thrice as fast as a boy.

$\therefore \qquad$ (Efficience of a man) : (Efficiency of a boy) = 3 : 1

$$\therefore \qquad\qquad E_1 : E_2 = 3 : 1 \quad \text{or} \quad \frac{E_1}{E_2} = \frac{3}{1}$$

Since $M_1D_1T_1W_2 \qquad = M_2D_2T_2W_1$

Here $M_1 \qquad\qquad = 5, D_1 = 5, T_1 = 6, W_1 = 150$

$$M_2 = 10, D_2 = 10, T_2 = ? \ W_2 = 200$$

$\therefore \qquad\qquad 5 \times 5 \times 6 \times 200 = 10 \times 10 \times T_2 \times 150$

$$\Rightarrow \qquad\qquad T_2 = \frac{5 \times 5 \times 6 \times 200}{10 \times 10 \times 150} = 2$$

Hence required number of hours = 2 hours.

Illustration 3: *A* works twice as much as *B* in the same time period. Together, they finish the work in 14 days. In how many days can it be done by each separately?

Solution: Let E_1 and E_2 be the efficiency of A and B respectively.

$$\therefore \qquad\qquad E_1 : E_2 = 2 : 1, \ \Rightarrow \ \frac{E_1}{E_2} = \frac{2}{1} \ \text{or} \ \frac{E_2}{E_1} = \frac{1}{2}$$

$$(1 \times E_1 + 1 \times E_2) \times 14 = 1 \times E_1 \times D_2,$$

where D_2 is the number of days in which A can complete the work separately.

$$\Rightarrow \qquad \left(1 + \frac{E_2}{E_1}\right) \times 14 = D_2 \Rightarrow D_2 = 21$$

Hence A can do the work separately in 21 days. Since A works twice as much as B in the same time period, hence B will take twice as much time as A. Therefore B can complete the work separately in 42 days.

Illustration 4: A and B can do a work in 45 and 40 days respectively. They began the work together, but A left after some time and B finished the remaining work in 23 days. After how many days did A leave ?

Solution: A and B can do a work in 45 and 40 days respectively

$$\therefore \qquad 1 \times E_1 \times 45 = 1 \times E_2 \times 40 \quad [\because M_1 D_1 E_1 = M_2 D_2 E_2]$$

$$\Rightarrow \qquad \frac{E_1}{E_2} = \frac{8}{9} \quad \text{or} \quad \frac{E_2}{E_1} = \frac{9}{8},$$

where E_1 and E_2 are efficiency of A and B respectively.

Since A and B began the work together to do the same work which A can do in 45 days (or B can do in 40 days), but A left after some time and B finished the remaining work in 23 days.

$$\therefore \qquad E_1 \times D_3 + E_2 \times (D_3 + 23) = E_1 \times 45, \text{ where } D_3 \text{ is the number of}$$
days after which A left.

$$\Rightarrow \qquad D_3 + \frac{E_2}{E_1} \times (D_3 + 23) = 45$$

$$\Rightarrow \qquad D_3 + \frac{9}{8} \times (D_3 + 23) = 45$$

$$\Rightarrow \qquad D_3 + \frac{9}{8} D_3 + \frac{9}{8} \times 23 = 45$$

$$\Rightarrow \qquad 17 D_3 = 45 \times 8 - 9 \times 23 = 360 - 207 = 153$$

$$\therefore \qquad D_3 = 9$$

Hence required number of days = 9.

II. WORK IN TERMS OF VOLUME (SPECIAL CASE AS BUILDING A WALL)

In some problems work is considered in terms of volume of work. For example volume of a wall of a certain length (L), breadth (B) and height (H) is LBH. In such type of problems the following equation is used:

If $\qquad\qquad$ work = volume

Then $\qquad M_1 T_1 D_1 W_2 = M_2 T_2 D_2 W_1$

$$\Rightarrow \qquad \frac{W_1}{W_2} = \frac{M_1 T_1 D_1}{M_2 T_2 D_2}$$

$$\Rightarrow \qquad \frac{L_1 B_1 H_1}{L_2 B_2 H_2} = \frac{M_1 T_1 D_1}{M_2 T_2 D_2}$$

Where L_1, B_1, H_1 are the length, breadth and height of the wall to be built in first work situation and L_2, B_2, H_2 are the length, breadth and height of the wall to be built in second work situation.

M_1, T_1, D_1 are the number of men, number of hours and number of days in first work situation and M_2, T_2, D_2 are number of men, number of hours and number of days in second work condition.

Illustration 5: 5 men working 8 hours a day can completely build a wall of length 20 metres, breadth $\frac{1}{4}$ metre and height 6 metres in 3 days. How many days will 8 men working 6 hours a day require to build a wall of length 120 meters, breadth $\frac{1}{2}$ metre and height 4 metres.

Solution: $\qquad \dfrac{L_1 B_1 H_1}{L_2 B_2 H_2} = \dfrac{M_1 T_1 D_1}{M_2 T_2 D_2}$

Here $\qquad L_1 = 20,\ B_1 = \frac{1}{4},\ H_1 = 6,\ M_1 = 5,\ T_1 = 8,\ D_1 = 3,$

$\qquad\qquad L_2 = 120,\ B_2 = \frac{1}{2},\ H_2 = 4,\ M_2 = 8,\ T_2, = 6,\ D_2 = ?$

$$\therefore \qquad \frac{20 \times \frac{1}{4} \times 6}{120 \times \frac{1}{2} \times 4} = \frac{5 \times 8 \times 3}{8 \times 6 \times D_2} \quad \Rightarrow D_2 = 20$$

Hence required number of days = 20 days.

TIME SPEED AND DISTANCE

I. TO AND FRO MOTION IN A STRAIGHT LINE BETWEEN TWO POINTS A AND B

To and fro motion in a straight line between two points A and B means motion of one or more bodies between two fixed points A and B such that when any body reached at any end point A or B, they start moving towards the opposite end point.

1. When two bodies start moving towards each other from two points A and B

(a) If distance between A and B is D, then the two bodies together have to cover D unit of distance for the first meeting.

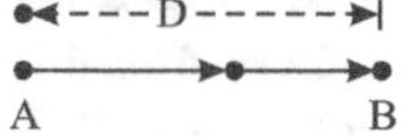

(b) For the next number of meeting (*i.e.* second, third, fourth meeting and so on) both A and B together have to cover $2D$ distance more from the previous meeting.

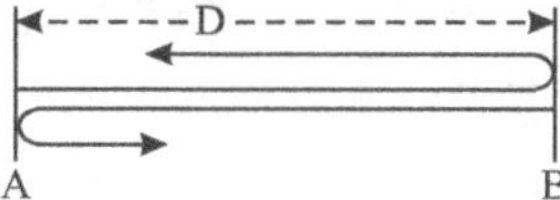

Hence to meet the fifth time they have to cover together $D + (4 \times 2D) = 9D$ unit of distances. Similarly for the ninth meeting they have to cover together $D + (8 \times 2D) = 17D$ units of distance. Thus, for the nth meeting they have to cover together $D + (n - 1) \times 2D$ *i.e.* $(2n - 1)$ D units of distance.

(c) At any point of time ratio of the distances covered by the two bodies will be equal to the ratio of their speeds.

2. When two bodies start moving towards the same direction from the point A

(a) Since the faster body reaches the next end (or opposite end) first than the slower body and the faster body starts returning before the slower body reaches the same opposite end and hence the two bodies meet somewhere between the two ends. For the first meeting after they start to move they have to cover $2D$ distance, where D is the distance between two particular end points (*i.e.* A and B)

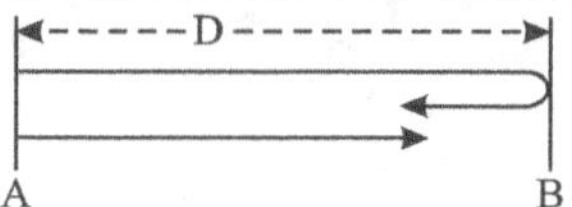

(b) For every subsequent meeting they have to cover together $2D$ unit distance more from the previous meeting.

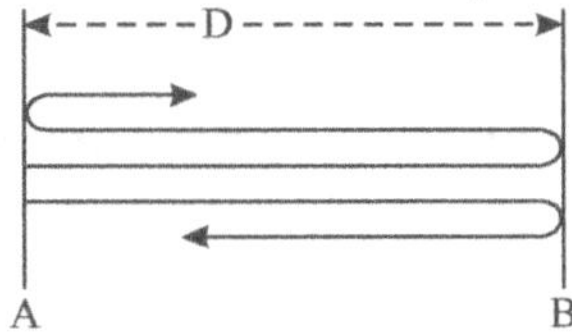

Thus, for the nth meeting they have to cover together $(n \times 2D)$ units of distance.

(c) At any point of time ratio of the distances covered by the two bodies will be equal to the ratio of their speeds.

Illustration 6: Two runners Shiva and Abhishek start running to and fro between opposite ends A and B of a straight road towards each other from A and B respectively. They meet first time at a point 0.75D from A, where D is the distance between A and B. Find the point of their 6th meeting.

Solution: At the time when Shiva and Abhishek meet first time,

Ratio of their speeds = Ratio of distance covered by them

$$= 0.75 : 0.25$$

$$= 3 : 1$$

Total distance covered by Shiva and Abhishek together till they meet at 6th time = $D + 5 \times 2D = 11D$

Total distance covered by Shiva till he meets Abhishek 6th time = $\dfrac{3}{3+1} \times 11D = 8.25D$

After covering a distance of 8.25D, Shiva will be at a point at a distance of 0.25D from A or 0.75D from B.

II. CONCEPT RELATED TO MOTION OF TRAINS

The following things need to be kept in mind before solving questions on trains.

(i) When the train is crossing a moving object, the speed of the train has to be taken as the relative speed with respect to the object.

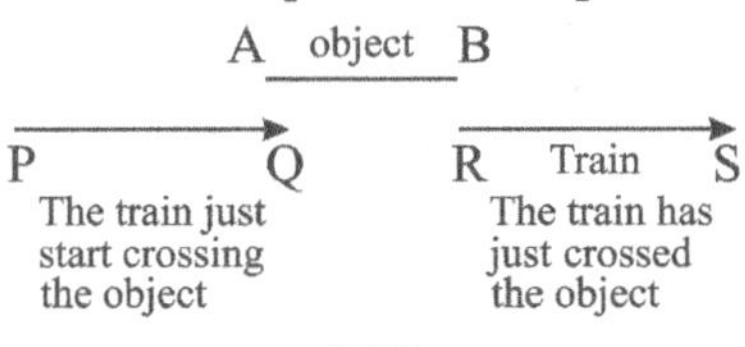

$$\left(\begin{array}{l}\text{Relative speed of the train}\\ \text{with respect to the object}\end{array}\right) \times \left(\begin{array}{l}\text{Time taken}\\ \text{by the train}\\ \text{to cross the}\\ \text{object}\end{array}\right) = \left(\begin{array}{l}\text{Distance}\\ \text{travelled}\\ \text{by the}\\ \text{train}\end{array}\right)$$

For object moving in opposite direction of the train,

$$\left(\begin{array}{l}\text{Relative speed of the train}\\ \text{with respect to the object}\end{array}\right) = \left(\begin{array}{l}\text{Speed of}\\ \text{the train}\end{array}\right) + \left(\begin{array}{l}\text{Speed of}\\ \text{the object}\end{array}\right)$$

And for object moving in the same direction of the train,

$$\left(\begin{array}{l}\text{Relative speed of the train}\\ \text{with respect to the object}\end{array}\right) = \left(\begin{array}{l}\text{Speed of}\\ \text{the train}\end{array}\right) - \left(\begin{array}{l}\text{Speed of}\\ \text{the object}\end{array}\right)$$

(Distance travelled by the train when crossing the object)

$$\begin{aligned} &= \quad \text{Distance travelled by the engine from } Q \text{ to } S\\ &= \quad QR + RS\\ &= \quad AB + RS\\ &= \quad \text{Length of the object + Length of the train} \end{aligned}$$

In the case of a train crossing a man, tree or a pole, the length of the man, tree or pole is actually its diameter (or width) which is generally considered as negligible *i.e.* a man, a tree, a pole or a point etc. has no length.

The various situations of motion of the train in which the questions are asked in CAT and all other aptitude examinations and formulae used in various situations are given in the following table:

CONCEPT RELATED TO MOTION OF TRAINS

The following things need to be kept in mind before solving questions on trains.

(i) When the train is crossing a moving object, the speed of the train has to be taken as the relative speed with respect to the object.

A ____object____ B

P   Q   R   Train   S

The train just start crossing the object   The train has just crossed the object

$$\left(\begin{array}{l}\text{Relative speed of the train}\\ \text{with respect to the object}\end{array}\right) \times \left(\begin{array}{l}\text{Time taken}\\ \text{by the train}\\ \text{to cross the}\\ \text{object}\end{array}\right) = \left(\begin{array}{l}\text{Distance}\\ \text{travelled}\\ \text{by the}\\ \text{train}\end{array}\right)$$

S. No.	Situations	Basic Formulae	Expenced Form of Basic Formulae	Expended Formulae in Symbolic Form
1.	When a train crossing a moving object with length in opposite direction	Relative Speed × Time = Distance	$\left[\begin{pmatrix}\text{Speed}\\\text{of the}\\\text{train}\end{pmatrix}+\begin{pmatrix}\text{Speed}\\\text{of the}\\\text{object}\end{pmatrix}\right]\times\begin{pmatrix}\text{Time taken by}\\\text{the train to cross}\\\text{the moving object}\end{pmatrix}=\begin{pmatrix}\text{Length}\\\text{of the}\\\text{train}\end{pmatrix}+\begin{pmatrix}\text{Length}\\\text{of the}\\\text{object}\end{pmatrix}$	$(S_T + S_0) \times t =$ $(L_T + L_0)$
2.	When a train crossing a moving object with length in the same direction	Relative Speed × Time = Distance	$\left[\begin{pmatrix}\text{Speed}\\\text{of the}\\\text{train}\end{pmatrix}-\begin{pmatrix}\text{Speed}\\\text{of the}\\\text{object}\end{pmatrix}\right]\times\begin{pmatrix}\text{Time taken by}\\\text{the train to cross}\\\text{the moving object}\end{pmatrix}=\begin{pmatrix}\text{Length}\\\text{of the}\\\text{train}\end{pmatrix}+\begin{pmatrix}\text{Length}\\\text{of the}\\\text{object}\end{pmatrix}$	$(S_T - S_0) \times t$ $= (L_T + L_0)$
3.	When a train crossing a moving object without length like a man, a tree, a pole, a point etc. in opposite direction	Relative Speed × Time = Distance	$\left[\begin{pmatrix}\text{Speed}\\\text{of the}\\\text{train}\end{pmatrix}+\begin{pmatrix}\text{Speed}\\\text{of the}\\\text{object}\end{pmatrix}\right]\times\begin{pmatrix}\text{Time taken by}\\\text{the train to cross}\\\text{the moving object}\end{pmatrix}=\begin{pmatrix}\text{Length}\\\text{of the}\\\text{train}\end{pmatrix}$	$(S_T + S_0) \times t$ $= L_T$

S. No.	Situations	Basic Formulae	Expended Form of Basic Formulae	Expended Formulae in Symbolic Form
4.	When a train crossing a moving object without length in the same direction	Relative Speed × Time = Distance	$\left[\left(\begin{array}{c}\text{Speed}\\\text{of the}\\\text{train}\end{array}\right) - \left(\begin{array}{c}\text{Speed}\\\text{of the}\\\text{object}\end{array}\right)\right] \times \left(\begin{array}{c}\text{Time taken by}\\\text{the train to cross}\\\text{the moving object}\end{array}\right) = \left(\begin{array}{c}\text{Length}\\\text{of the}\\\text{train}\end{array}\right)$	$(S_t - S_0) \times t = L_T$
5.	When a train crossing a stationary object with length	Speed × Time = Distance	$\left(\begin{array}{c}\text{Speed}\\\text{of the}\\\text{train}\end{array}\right) \times \left(\begin{array}{c}\text{Time taken to cross}\\\text{the stationary object}\end{array}\right) = \left[\left(\begin{array}{c}\text{Length}\\\text{of the}\\\text{train}\end{array}\right) + \left(\begin{array}{c}\text{Length}\\\text{of the}\\\text{object}\end{array}\right)\right]$	$S_T \times t = L_T + L_0$
6.	When a train crossing a stationary object without length	Speed × Time = Distance	$\left(\begin{array}{c}\text{Speed}\\\text{of the}\\\text{train}\end{array}\right) \times \left(\begin{array}{c}\text{Time taken to cross}\\\text{the stationary object}\end{array}\right) = \left(\begin{array}{c}\text{Length}\\\text{of the}\\\text{train}\end{array}\right)$	$S_T \times t = L_T$

For object moving in opposite direction of the train,

$$\left(\begin{array}{c}\text{Relative speed of the train}\\ \text{with respect to the object}\end{array}\right)=\left(\begin{array}{c}\text{Speed of}\\ \text{the train}\end{array}\right)+\left(\begin{array}{c}\text{Speed of}\\ \text{the object}\end{array}\right)$$

And for object moving in the same direction of the train,

$$\left(\begin{array}{c}\text{Relative speed of the train}\\ \text{with respect to the object}\end{array}\right)=\left(\begin{array}{c}\text{Speed of}\\ \text{the train}\end{array}\right)-\left(\begin{array}{c}\text{Speed of}\\ \text{the object}\end{array}\right)$$

(Distance travelled by the train when crossing the object)

$$= \text{Distance travelled by the engine from } Q \text{ to } S$$

$$= QR + RS$$

$$= AB + RS$$

$$= \text{Length of the object + Length of the train}$$

In the case of a train crossing a man, tree or a pole, the length of the man, tree or pole is actually its diameter (or width) which is generally considered as negligible *i.e.* a man, a tree, a pole or a point etc. has no length.

The various situations of motion of the train in which the questions are asked in CAT and all other aptitude examinations and formulae used in various situations are given in the following table:

Illustration 2: A train of length 100 m takes 1/6 hour to pass over another train 150 m long coming from the opposite direction. If the speed of first train is 60 km/h, then find speed of the second train.

Solution: Let speed of the second train be x km/h.

$$\text{Relative Speed} = \text{Sum of speed of two trains}$$

$$= (60 + x) \text{ km/h} = (60 + x)\frac{5}{18} \text{ m/s}$$

$$\text{Time} = \frac{\text{Sum of length of two trains}}{\text{Relative Speed}}$$

$$\Rightarrow \quad 10 = \frac{250 \times 18}{(60 + x) \times 5} \Rightarrow x = 30 \text{ km/h}.$$

Illustration 3: **Two trains 137 metres and 163 metres in length are running towards each other on parallel lines, one at the rate of 42 kmph and another at 48 kmph. In what time will they be clear of each other from the moment they meet?**

    (a) 10 sec   (b) 12 sec

    (c) 14 sec   (d) cannot be determined

Solution: (b) Relative speed of the trains

$$= (42 + 48) \text{ kmph} = 90 \text{ kmph}$$

$$= \left(90 \times \frac{5}{18}\right) \text{ m/sec} = 25 \text{ m/sec.}$$

Time taken by the trains to pass each other

$$= \text{Time taken to cover } (137 + 163) \text{ m at } 25 \text{ m/sec}$$

$$= \left(\frac{300}{25}\right) \text{ sec} = 12 \text{ seconds.}$$

III. BASIC TERMINOLOGY RELATED TO RACES

1. Startup or Head Start

When a runner allows to another runner to stay ahead in the same race, then it is said that there is a startup in the race.

For example if A allows B to go ahead before starting the race, then it is said that A gives startup to B and B has the startup. If before starting the race B goes ahead of x metre, then we can say A gives x metre startup to B or B has startup (or headstart) of x metre.

2. Dead Heat

When the runners reach the finishing line (or the final post) then it is said that these runners finish (or end) the race in dead heat.

Some Useful Concepts

    (i) When it is said that A can give B a startup x metre in y metre race, then it means in y metre race B runs x metre less than A in the same time.

   (ii) When A beats B by t second in a race of y metre then it means B is the loser and A is the winner and when A reaches the finishing line, B is still some distance back to A, from which B takes t

seconds to cover the remaining distance. Hence we can calculate the speed of loser B.

(iii) The ratio of speed of the runners is always maintained throughout the race.

Illustration 4: In 2 km race A gives a startup of 300 m to B. Despite this, A wins the race by 400 m. Find the ratio of speed of A and B.

Solution: A and B covers 2000 m and 1300 m respectively in same time intervals.

Since time period for both runners A and B are the same, hence ratio of speeds of A and B = 2000 : 1300 = 20 : 13

Illustration 5: In a 2 km race A wins over B by 200 m or 20 seconds. B can give a startup 500 m to C in 2 km race. Find out by how much time A will win over C?

Solution:

Ratio of speeds of A and B = 2000 : 1800 = 10 : 9

Ratio of speeds of B and C = 2000 : 1500 = 4 : 3

Ratio of speeds of A, B and C = 2000 : 1800 : 1350

$$\text{Speed of } B = \frac{200}{20} = 10 \text{ m/s}$$

$\therefore$ Speed of C = 7.5 m/s [$\because$ Ratio of speed of B to C = 4 : 3]

Now C has to cover 650 m in extra time. Therefore, the time taken by C to cover the remaining distance = $\dfrac{650}{7.5}$ = 86.7 seconds.

Hence, required time = 1 minute 27 second (approx)

IV. CIRCULAR MOTION

When two bodies start moving from a place on a circular track simultaneously in the same direction, the faster body keeps increasing the distance by which the slower body is behind the faster body. When the distance by which the faster body is in front of the slower body becomes equal to the circumference of the track, the faster body meets the slower body first time *i.e.* faster body comes in line with the slower body.

(i) When two bodies are moving in the opposite directions, their relative speed is equal to the sum of their individual speeds.

(ii) When two bodies are moving in the same direction, their relative speed is equal to the difference of the speeds of the two bodies.

First Meeting

(i) Let A and B are two runners.

Time taken by A and B to meet for the first time

$$= \frac{\text{Circumference of the circular Track}}{\text{Relative speed}}$$

(ii) When there are more than two runners, suppose A is the fastest runner and A meets B first time in time t_{AB}, A meets C first time in time t_{AC}, A meets D first time in time t_{AD} and so on. Then time taken by all of them to meet for the first time is the LCM of t_{AB}, t_{AC}, t_{AD}, etc.

First Meeting at the Starting Point

Let A take, t_A time, B takes t_B time, C takes t_C times and so on, to complete one round, then the time taken to meet all the runners for the first time at the starting point

$$= \text{LCM of } t_A, t_B, t_C \text{ etc.}$$

Illustration 6: The jogging track in a sports complex is 726 metres in circumference. Pradeep and his wife start from the same point and walk in opposite directions at 4.5 km/h and 3.75 km/h, respectively. They will meet for the first time in

(a) 5.5 min   **(b) 6.0 min**

(c) 5.28 min   **(d) 4.9 min**

Solution: (c) Let the husband and the wife meet after x minutes 4500 metres are covered by Pradeep in 60 minutes.

In x minutes, he will cover $\dfrac{4500}{60} x$ metres.

Similarly,

In x minutes, his wife will cover $\dfrac{3750}{60} x$ m.

Now, $\dfrac{4500}{60} x + \dfrac{3750}{60} x = 726$

$\Rightarrow \quad x = \dfrac{726 \times 60}{8250} = 5.28 \, \text{min}$

Illustration 7: *A and B run on a circular track of circum-ference 800 m in the opposite direction. Speeds of A and B are 50 m/s and 30 m/s respectively. Initially A and B are diametrically opposite to each other.*

  (i) **When will they meet for the first time ?**
  (ii) **What is the ratio of distances covered by each one to meet for the first time ?**

Solution:

(i) Relative speed of A with respect to B = 50 + 30 = 80 m/s

Initially A and B are diametrically opposite to each other means B is 400 m ahead of A in the race.

Time taken by A to meet B first time = $\dfrac{400}{80}$ = 5 s

(ii) To meet second time A and B have to cover 800 m

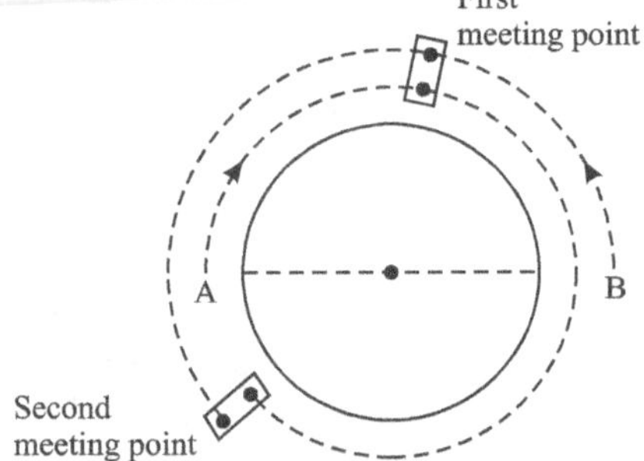

Hence time taken to meet second time = $\dfrac{800}{80}$ = 10 seconds

---

V. CLOCKS

Problems on clocks are based on the movement of the minute hand and hour hand. We consider the dial of a clock as a circular track having a circumference of 60 km. minute hand and hour hand are two runners running with the speed of 60 km/h and 5 km/hr respectively in the same direction. Hence relative speed of minute hand with respect to hour hand is 55 km/h. This means that for every hour elapsed, the minute hand goes 55 km more than the hour hand.

Degree Concept of a Clock

Total angle subtended at the centre of a clock = 360°

Angle made by hour hand at the centre = 30° per hour

$$= 0.5° \text{ per minute}$$

Angle made by minute hand at the centre = 360° per hour

$$= 6° \text{ per minute}$$

Number of Right Angles and Straight Angles Formed by Minute Hand and Hour Hand

A right angle is formed by hour hand and minute hand when distance between tip of hour hand and tip of minute hand is 15 km. A straight line is formed by hour hand and minute hand when distance between their tips is 30 km.

A clock makes two right angles in every hour. Thus there are 2 right angles between marked 1 to 2, 2 to 3, 3 to 4 and so on the dial.

Two straight lines are formed by hour hand and minute hand in every hour.

Thus two straight lines are formed by hour hand and minute hand between marked 1 to 2, 2 to 3, 3 to 4 and so on.

(iii) Hour hand and minute hand of a clock are together after every $65\dfrac{5}{11}$ minutes. So, if hour hand and minute hand of a clock are meeting in less than $65\dfrac{5}{11}$ minutes, then the clock is running fast and if hour hand and minute hand are meeting in more than $65\dfrac{5}{11}$ minutes, then clock is running slow.

Illustration 8: Between 5 O' clock and 6 O' clock, when hour hand and minute hand of a clock overlap each other ?

Solution: At 5 O' clock, distance between tips of two hands

$$= 25 \text{ km}$$

Relative speed = 55 km/h

Required time to overlap the two hands

$$= \frac{25 \text{ km}}{55 \text{ km / h}} = \frac{5}{11}\text{h}$$

$$= \frac{5 \times 60}{11} \text{ min}$$

$$= 27 \text{ min} + \frac{3 \times 60}{11} \text{ sec}$$

$$= 27 \text{ min} + 16 \text{ sec.}$$

$$= 27 \text{ minutes } 16 \text{ seconds.}$$

Illustration 9: Mrs. Veena Gupta goes for marketing between 5 P.M. and 6 P.M. When she comes back, she finds that the hour hand and the minute hand have interchanged their positions. For how much time was she out of her house ?

Solution: Since two hands are interchange their positions, so sum of the angles subtended at the centre by hour hand and minute hand = 360°

Let us suppose that she was out of house for 't' minutes.

So, the sum of the angles subtended at the centre by the hour hand and minute hand = $(0.5 \times t)° + (6t)°$

$$\therefore \qquad 0.5t + 6t = 360$$

$$\Rightarrow \qquad 6.5t = 360 \Rightarrow t = 55.4 \text{ (app.)}$$

Hence required time = 55.4 minutes.

PROGRESSIONS

CONVERGENT SERIES

Consider a series,

$$\frac{1}{5}, \frac{3}{5^2}, \frac{5}{5^3}, \frac{7}{5^4} \cdots$$

you can observe that subsequent terms of this series keep getting smaller. If taken to infinite terms, the sum of this series will reach a value which it will never cross i.e. the sum of this series reaches to a limit. Such type of series are called convergent series.

Some other examples of convergent series are

(a) $\dfrac{1}{10}, \dfrac{2}{10^2}, \dfrac{3}{10^3}, \dfrac{4}{10^4} \cdots$
(b) $\dfrac{1}{1^2}, \dfrac{2}{2^2}, \dfrac{3}{3^2}, \dfrac{4}{4^2} \cdots$

(c) $\dfrac{1}{3^2}, \dfrac{2}{3^3}, \dfrac{3}{3^4}, \dfrac{4}{5^5} \cdots$

This type of series cannot be strictly said to be under the domain of progressions. But since questions on finding sum of infinite terms of convergent series are very commonly asked in CAT and CAT like competitive exams.

Let's see an example based on multiple choice.

Illustration 1: Sum of infinite terms of the series

$$1 + \frac{4}{7} + \frac{9}{7^2} + \frac{16}{7^2} + \frac{25}{7^4} + ..., \text{ is}$$

(a) 27/14 (b) 21/13
(c) 49/27 (d) 256/147

Solution: There are two methods to solve the problem. One method requires lengthy mathematical process which we do not advise you.

The other process is one where we try to predict the approximate value of the sum by taking into account the first few significant terms. (This approach is possible to use because of the fact that in such series we invariably reach the point where the value of the next term becomes insignificant and does not add substantially to the sum). After adding the significant terms we are in a position to guess the approximate value of the sum of the series.

Let us look at the above question in order to understand the process.

In the given series the values of the terms are:

$$\text{First term} = 1$$
$$\text{Second term} = 4/7 = 0.57$$
$$\text{Third term} = 9/63 = 0.14$$
$$\text{Fourth term} = 16/343 = 0.04$$
$$\text{Fifth term} = 25/2401 = 0.01$$

Addition upto the fifth term is approximately 1.76

LINEAR EQUATIONS

STEPS TO BE FOLLOWED TO SOLVE A WORD PROBLEM USING LINEAR EQUATION(S)

Step (i): Read the problem carefully and note what is/are given and what is/are required.

Step (ii): Denote the unknown quantity by some letters, say p, q, r, x, y etc.

Step (iii): Translate the statements of the problem into mathematical statements i.e., equations using the condition(s) given in the problem and extra information(s) related to the variable(s) derived from the statement(s) in the problem.

Step (IV): Solve the equation(s) for the unknown(s).

Step (V): Check whether the solution satisfies the equation(s).

Most of the time in solving the word problem you get struck. It could be due to one or more of the following four reasons:

Reason (i): You are not able to interpret one or more statements in the problem. In this case you concentrate on developing your ability to decode the mathematical meaning of the statement(s) in the problems.

Reason (ii): You have either not used all the information given in the problem or have used them in the incorrect order.

In such a case, go back to the problem and try to identify each statement and see whether you have utilized it or not. If you have already used all the information, then check whether you have used the information given in the problem in the correct order.

Reason (iii): Even though you might have used all the information given in the problem, you have not utilized some of the information completely.

In such a case, you need to review each part of each information given in the problem and look at whether any additional details can be derived out from the same informations. If derived any additional details, use them in forming or solving the equation(s). Sometimes a statement can be used for more than one perspective. In this case, if you have used that statement for one perspective, then using it in the other perspective will solve the problem.

Reason (iv): You are struck because the problem does not have a solution. In such a case, check the solution once and if it is correct go back to reason (i), (ii) and (iii).

Illustration 1: Find the two odd numbers whose sum is 12.

Solution: Let the two odd numbers are x and y.

Then $x + y = 12$

There is no other information about the two variable x and y.

Hence, there will be no other equation between the variable x and y. So, we can not find the exact solution of the problem. The equation formed above yields a set of possibilities for the value of x and y as (1, 11), (3, 9), (5, 7), (7, 5), (9, 3), (11, 1). One of these possibilities has to be the correct answer.

Illustration 2: A piece of wire is 80 metres long. It is cut into three pieces. The longest piece is 3 times as long as the middle-sized and the shortest piece is 46 metres shorter than the longest piece. Find the length of the shortest piece (in metres).

Solution: Let the length of the longest piece = a metres

Length of middle-sized piece = b metres

Since sum of the length of three pieces of wire = 80 metres

$\therefore$ length of shortest piece = $80 - (a + b)$ metres

Now $\quad a = 3b$ $\hfill ...(1)$

and $\quad\quad 80 - (a + b) = a - 46$ $\hfill ...(2)$

From (1) and (2),

$$80 - \left(a + \frac{a}{3}\right) = a - 46$$

$\Rightarrow \quad\quad 80 - \dfrac{3a + a}{3} = a - 46$

$\Rightarrow \quad\quad 80 + 46 = a + \dfrac{4a}{3}$

$\Rightarrow \quad\quad \dfrac{7a}{3} = 126 \Rightarrow a = 126 \times \dfrac{3}{7} = 54$

$\therefore \quad\quad b = \dfrac{a}{3} = \dfrac{54}{3} = 18,$

and $\quad 80 - (a + b) = 80 - (54 + 18) = 8$

Hence length of shortest piece = 8 metres.

QUADRATIC EQUATION

If any polynomial have degree 2 called as quadratic function.

i.e. $P(x) = ax^2 + bx + c$

Eqn. will be

$ax^2 + bx + c = 0$

If roots are α and β of this equation then

$\alpha + \beta = -b/a$ $\quad\quad$ (sum of roots)

$\alpha\beta = c/a$ $\quad\quad$ (multiply of roots)

Note: 1. This is a parabolic function

Discriminant of a quadratic equation

$D = b^2 - 4ac$

Note: 2. Nature of roots:

        (i) D = 0   roots will be equal and real

        (ii) D > 0   roots will be real and un equal.

        (iii) D < 0   roots will be imaginary

*Methods for solution of quadratic equation

    (i)   Factorisation method.

    (ii)   Perfect square method.

    (iii) Quadratic formula method.

    (iv) Graphical representation method.

➢   Quadratic formula:

$$ax^2 + bx + c = 0$$

Then roots of this equation,

$$x = \frac{-b \pm \sqrt{b^2 - 4ac}}{2a}$$

$$\alpha = \frac{-b + \sqrt{b^2 - 4ac}}{2a}$$

$$\beta = \frac{-b - \sqrt{b^2 - 4ac}}{2a}$$

➢   Graphical representation of quadratic equation.

$$P(x) = ax^2 + bx + c$$

Case Ist: $a > 0, D > 0$

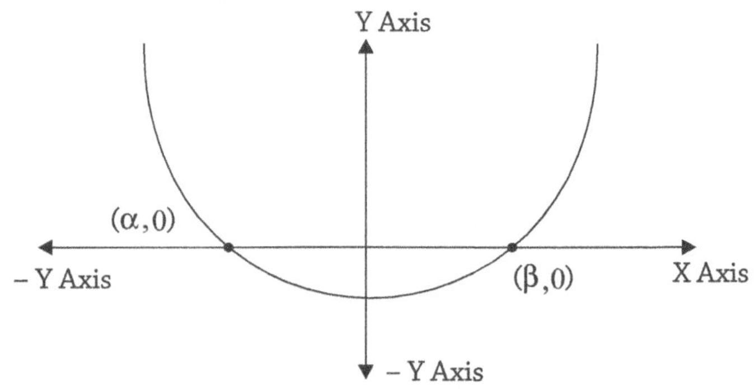

Case IInd: $a < 0, D > 0$

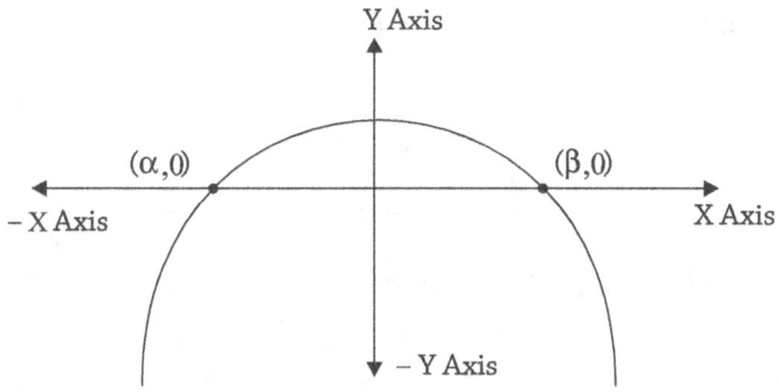

Case IIIrd: $a > 0, D = 0$

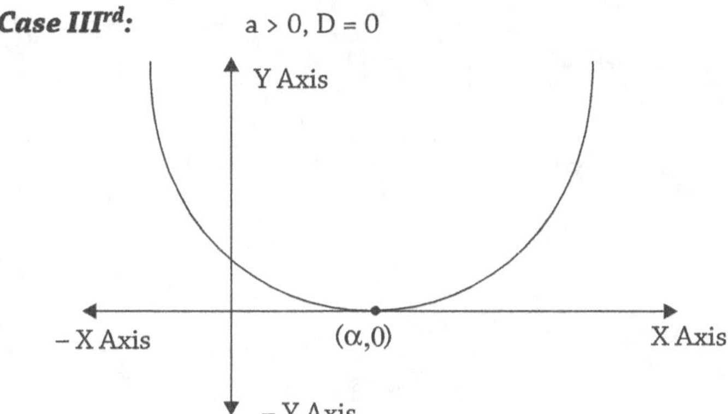

Case IVth: $a > 0, D < 0$

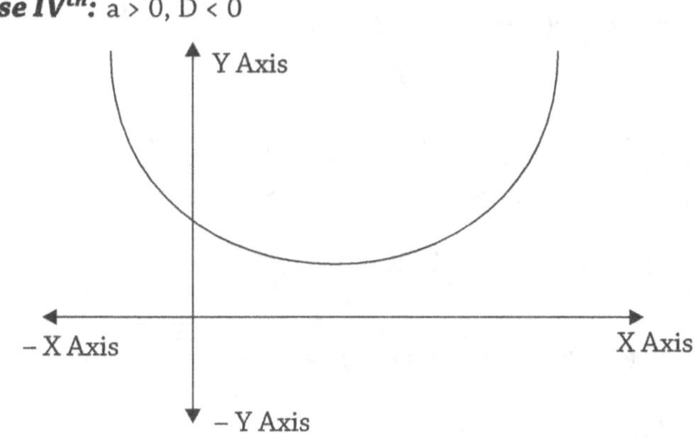

Case V^{th}: $a < 0, D = 0$

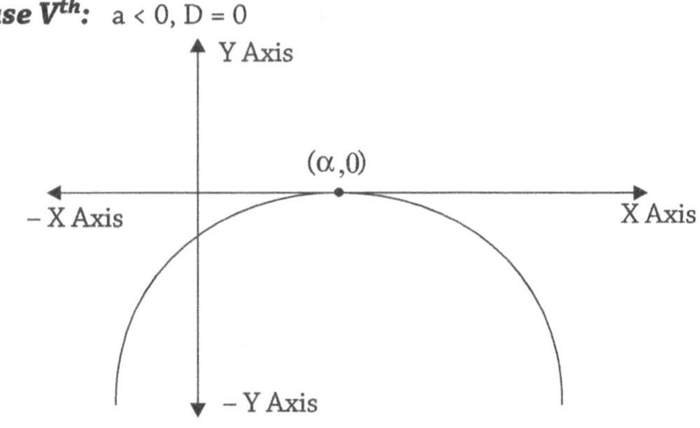

Case VIth: $a < 0, D < 0$

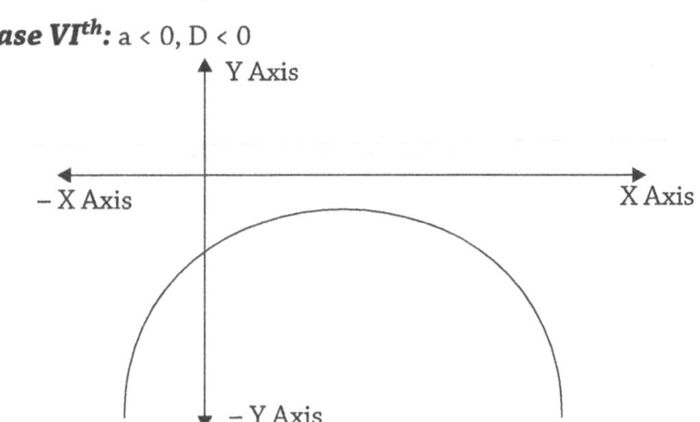

➢ Maximum/minimum value of quadratic function

Case- I: If $a > 0$ in $ax^2 + bx + c = (p(x))$ then

Maximum value $= \infty$

Minimum value $= c - \dfrac{b^2}{4a}$

Case- II: If $a < 0$ in $ax^2 + bx + c = (p(x))$ then

Minimum value $= \infty$

Maximum value $= \dfrac{b^2}{4a} + c$

Illustration 1: Find value of $\sqrt{6 + \sqrt{6 + \sqrt{6 + ...}}} = x$

Solution: $\sqrt{6 + \sqrt{6 + \sqrt{6 + ...}}} = x$

$\sqrt{6 + x} = x$

$6 + x = x^2$

$x^2 - x - 6 = 0$

$x^2 - 3x + 2x - 6 = 0$

$x(x - 3) = 2(x - 3) = 0$

$(x + 2)(x - 3) = 0 \quad x = -2$

$$x = 3$$

$x = 3$ will be correct answer b/c of under root have no negative value.

Illustration 2: The equation $x + \sqrt{x-2} = 4$ find nature of roots.

Solution: $x - 4 = -\sqrt{x-2}$

$(x - 4)^2 = \left(-\sqrt{x-2}\right)^2$

$x^2 + 16 - 8x = x - 2$

$x^2 - 9x + 18 = 0$

$$D = b^2 - 4ac$$

$$D = (-9)^2 = 4 \times 1 \times 18$$

$$= 81 - 72$$

$$\boxed{D = 9} \quad D > O$$

So that equation have unequal and real roots.

Illustration 3: Find out minimum value of $P(x) = 2x^2 - 4x + 2$

Solution: $P(x) = 2x^2 - 4x + 2$

$$P(x)_{\text{Min}} = C - \frac{b^2}{4ac}$$

$$= 2 - \frac{(4)^2}{4 \times 2 \times 2}$$

$$= 2 - \frac{16}{16} \Rightarrow 2 - 1 = 1$$

GEOMETRY

Interior and Exterior Angles of a Polygon

An angle inside a polygon between any two adjacent sides at a vertex of the polygon is called an interior angle of the polygon. An angle outside a polygon made by a side of the polygon with the its adjacent side produced is called an exterior angle of the polygon.

In the figure $ABCDEF$ is a polygon.

$\angle FAB$, $\angle ABC$, $\angle BCD$, $\angle CDE$, $\angle DEF$ and

$\angle EFA$ are interior angles of the polygon $ABCDEF$.

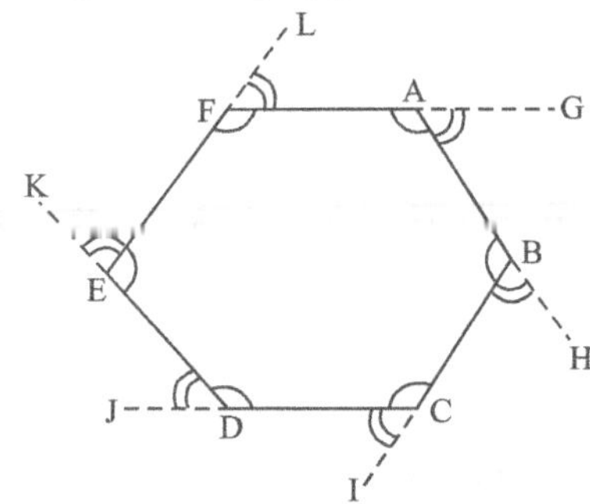

$\angle BAG$, $\angle CBH$, $\angle DCI$, $\angle EDJ$, $\angle FEK$ and $\angle AFL$ are exterior angles of the polygon $ABCDEF$.

Diagonals of a Polygon

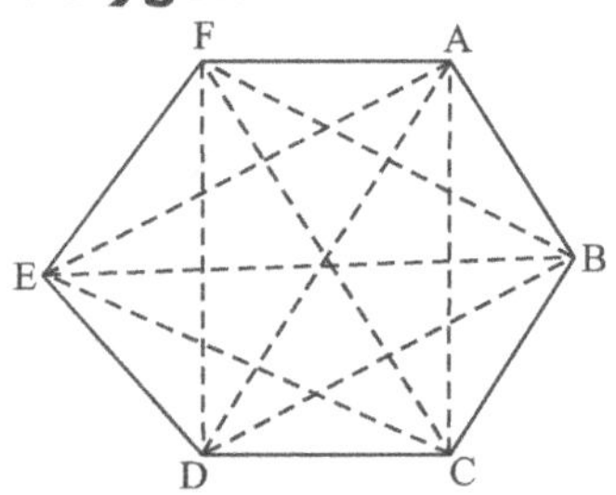

A diagonal of a polygon is a line segment connecting two non-consecutive vertices of the Polygon.

In the figure, diagonals are drawn by dotted line segments.

Properties of Polygons

(i) Sum of all the interior angles of a polygon with 'n' sides = $(n-2)\,180°$

(ii) Sum of all the exterior angles of a polygon = $360°$

$$\angle 1 + \angle 2 + \angle 3 + \angle 4 + \angle 5 + \angle 6 = 360°$$

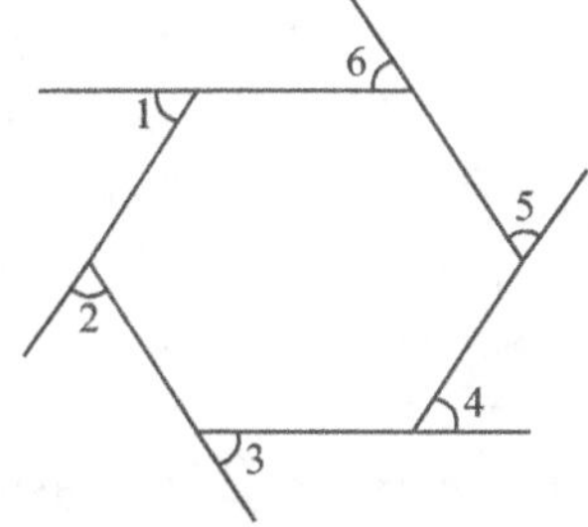

(iii) Perimeter of a regular polygon with a side length of $a = n \times a$

(iv) No. of sides of a regular polygon =

$$= \frac{360°}{\text{An enterior angle}}$$

(v) Number of diagonals of a polygon with n sides

$$= \frac{n(n-3)}{2}$$

Illustration 1: An interior angle of a regular polygon is 135°. Find the number of sides of the polygon.

Solution: Since interior angle of the regular polygon = 135°, hence exterior angle = 180° – 135° = 45°

$$\therefore \qquad \text{No. of sides} = \frac{360°}{\text{An enterior angle}} = \frac{360°}{45°} = 8°$$

$$\therefore \qquad \text{No. of sides} = 8$$

Illustration 2: An interior angle of a regular polygon is 100° more than its an exterior angle. Find the number of sides the polygon.

Solution: Let measure of each exterior angle be $x°$.

Then measure of each interior angle = $(x + 100)$

Now $\qquad x + (x + 100) = 180$

$\Rightarrow \qquad 2x = 80 \Rightarrow x = 40$

Now $\qquad$ number of sides = $\dfrac{360°}{\text{An enterior angle}} = \dfrac{360}{40} = 9$.

II. IMPORTANT TERMS RELATED TO A TRIANGLE

1. **Medians and Centroid:** We know that a line segment joining the mid point of a side of a triangle to its opposite vertex is called a median.

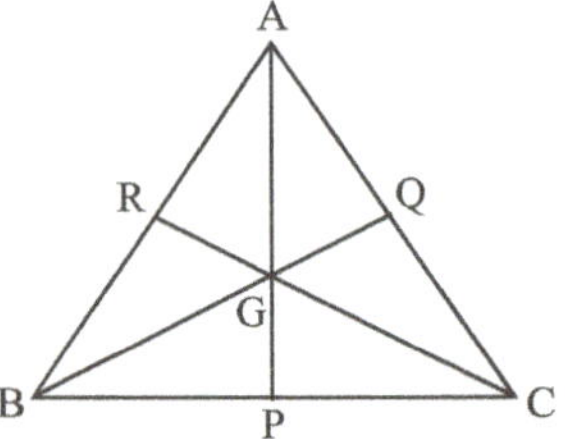

AP, BQ and CR are medians of $\triangle ABC$ where P, Q and R are mid points of sides BC, CA and AB respectively.

(i) Three medians of a triangle on concurrent. The point of concurrent of three medians is called Centroid of the triangle denoted by G.

(ii) Centroid of the triangle divides each median in the ratio 2 : 1 i.e. $AG : GP = BG : GQ = CG : GR = 2 : 1$, where G is the centroid of $\triangle ABC$.

2. **Altitudes and Orthocentre:** A perpendicular drawn from any vertex of a triangle to its opposite side is called altitude of the triangle. There are three altitudes of a triangle.

In the figure, AP, BQ and CR are altitudes of $\triangle ABC$.

The altitudes of a triangle are concurrent (meet at a point) and the point of concurrency of altitudes is called Orthocentre of the triangle, denoted by O.

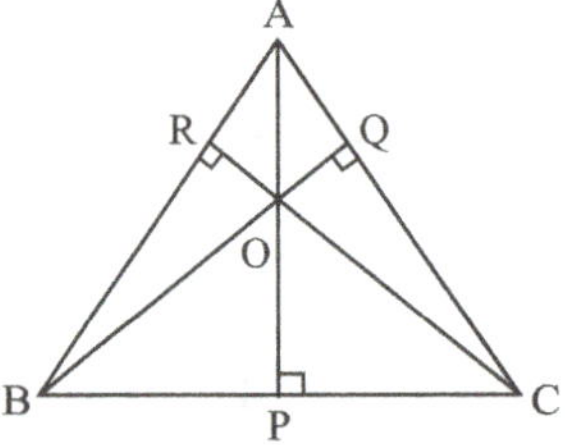

In figure, AP, BQ and CR meet at O, hence O is the orthocentre of the triangle ABC.

Note: The angle made by any side at the orthocentre and at the vertex opposite to the side are supplementary angle.

Hence, $\angle BAC + \angle BOC = \angle ABC + \angle AOC = \angle ACB + \angle AOB = 180°$.

---

3. **Perpendicular Bisectors and Circumcentre:** A line which is perpendicular to a side of a triangle and also bisects the side is called a perpendicular bisector of the side.

   (i) Perpendicular bisectors of sides of a triangle are concurrent and the point of concurrency is called circumcentre of the triangle, denoted by 'C'.

   (ii) The circumcentre of a triangle is centre of the circle that circumscribes the triangle.

   (iii) Angle formed by any side of the triangle at the circumcentre is twice the vertical angle opposite to the side.

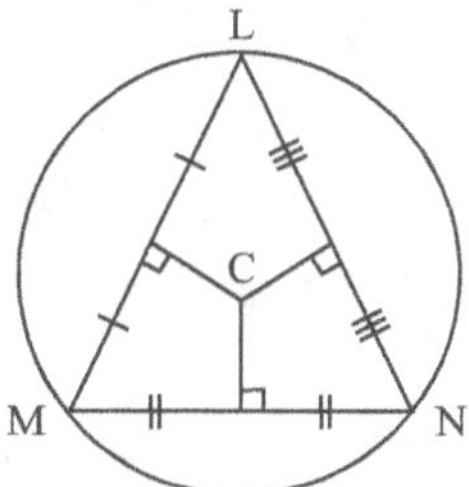

   In figure, perpendicular bisectors of sides LM, MN and NL of $\triangle LMN$ meets at C. Hence C is the circumcentre of the triangle LMN.

   $$\angle MCN = 2 \angle MLN.$$

4. **Angle Bisectors and Incentre:** Lines bisecting the interior angles of a triangle are called angle bisectors of triangle.

   (i) Angle bisectors of a triangle are concurrent and the point of concurrency is called Incentre of the triangle, denoted by I.

   (ii) With I as centre and radius equal to length of the perpendicular drawn from I to any side, a circle can be drawn touching the three sides of the triangle. So this is called incircle of the triangle. Incentre is equidistant from all the sides of the triangle.

   (iii) Angle formed by any side at the incentre is always 90° more than half the vertex angle opposite to the side.

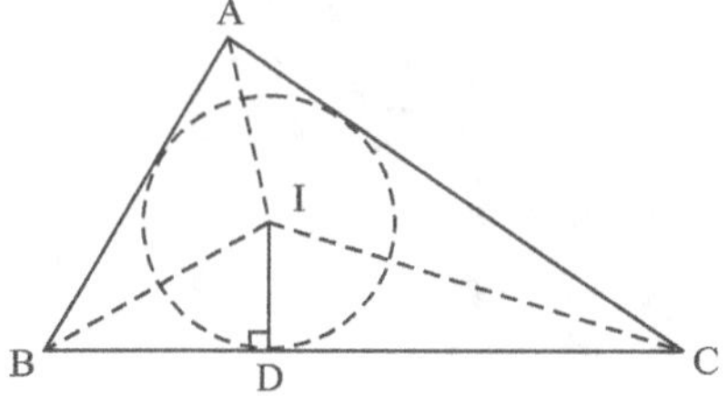

In figure *AI*, *BI*, *CI* are angle bisectors of $\triangle ABC$.

Hence *I* is the incentre of the $\triangle ABC$ and

$$\angle BIC = 90° + \frac{1}{2} \angle A, \quad \angle AIC = 90° + \frac{1}{2} \angle B$$

and $\quad \angle AIB = 90° + \frac{1}{2} \angle C$

If *BI'* and *CI'* be the angle bisectors of exterior angles at *B* and *C*, then

$$\angle BI'C = 90° - \frac{1}{2} \angle A.$$

III. PRISM

A 'prism' is a solid having identical and parallel top and bottom (or base) faces. These identical faces are regular polygon of any number of sides. The side faces of a prism are rectangular and are known as lateral faces. Number of lateral faces is equal to the number of sides in the base.

Here are some example of prisms

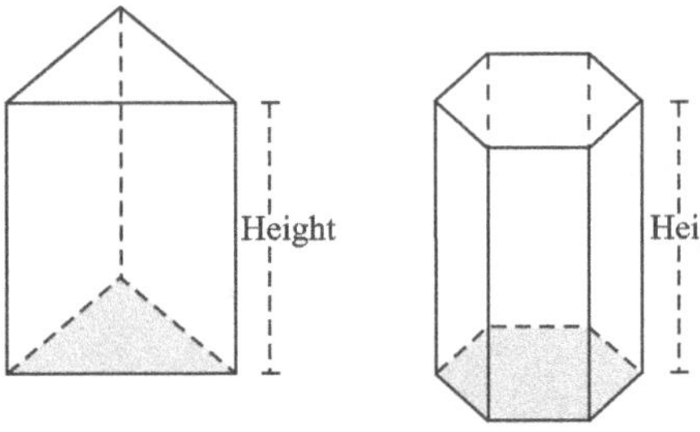

Triangular base prism   Hexagonal base prism

Lateral surface area of the prism

= (Perimeter of the base) × (Height)

Total surface area of the prism

= (Surface area of the top and bottom) + (Lateral surface area)

= 2 × Area of the base + Perimeter of base × Height

Volume of the prism = (Area of base) × (Height)

The actual formula used to find the surface area and volume will depend upon the number of sides in the base of the prism.

IV. PYRAMID

It is a three-dimensional body made up of a regular polygon shaped base and triangular lateral faces that meet at a point called vertex, which is also called the apex of the pyramid.

The number of triangular faces is equal to the number of sides in the base.

For example: A pyramid with a square base has four triangular faces, whereas a pyramid with a hexagonal face is made up of six triangular faces, and so on.

Lower face is called the base and the perpendicular distance of the vertex (or top) from the base is called the height or altitude of the pyramid.

The altitude of a lateral face of a pyramid is the slant height, which is the perpendicular distance of the vertex (or top) from the mid-point of any side of the base.

The lateral surface area of a regular pyramid is the sum of the areas of its lateral faces.

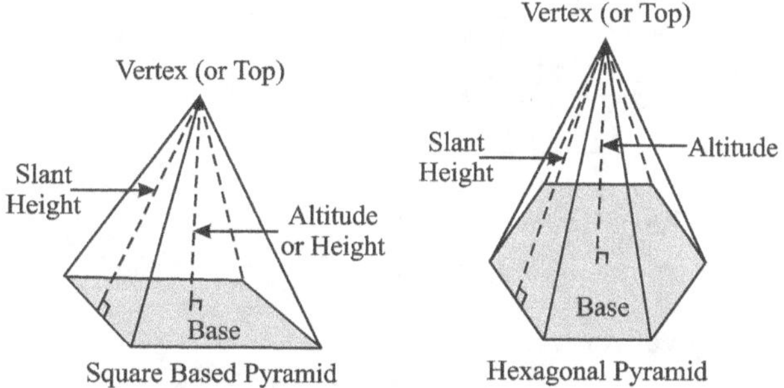

Lateral surface area of a pyramid

$$= \frac{1}{2} \times (\text{Area of the base}) \times (\text{Slant height})$$

Total surface area of a pyramid

$$= \frac{1}{2} \times \text{(Perimeter of the base)}$$

$$\times \text{(Slant height)} + \text{(Area of the base)}$$

$$\text{Volume of a pyramid} = \frac{1}{3} \times \text{Area of base} \times \text{Height}$$

Illustration 3: **Find the lateral surface area of a regular pyramid with triangular base, if each edge of the base measures 8 cm and slant height is 5 cm.**

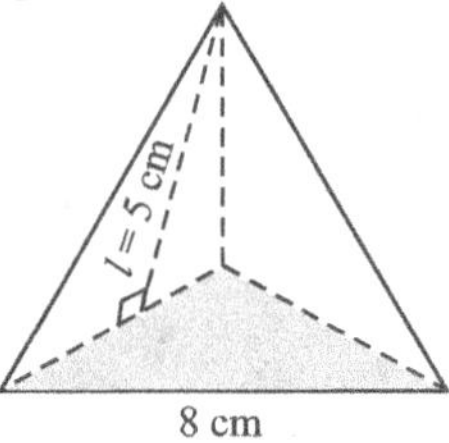

Solution: The perimeter of the base is the sum of the sides,

$$p = 3.(8) = 24 \text{ cm}$$

$$\text{L.S.A.} = \frac{1}{2} \times (24) \times (5) = 60 \text{ cm}^2$$

Illustration 4: **Find the total surface area of a pyramid with a square base if each side of the base measures 16 cm, the slant height of a side is 17 cm and the altitude is 15 cm.**

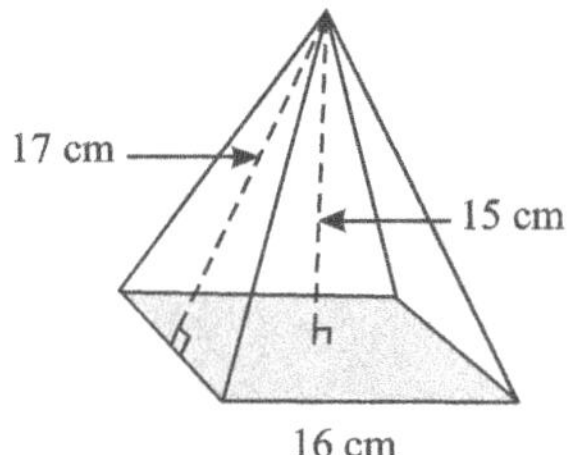

Solution: The perimeter of the base,

$$p = 4 \times 16 = 64 \text{ cm}$$

The area of the base

$$= 16^2 = 256 \text{ cm}^2$$

$$\text{T.S.A.} = \frac{1}{2}(64)(17) + 256$$

$$= 544 + 256 = 800 \text{ cm}^2$$

V. CIRCLE PACKING IN A SQUARE

Let '*a*' be the length of a side of the square and '*r*' be the radius of the circle.

Case- (i): One circle

$$2r = a \Rightarrow r = \frac{a}{2}$$

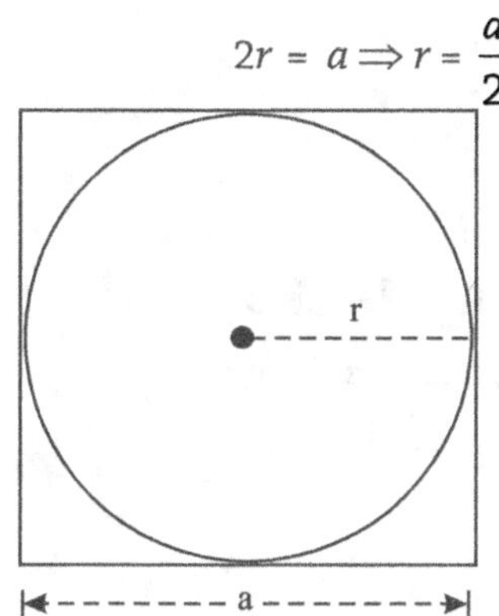

Case- (ii): Two circles

In the isosceles right angled $\triangle BCD$,

$$BD = \sqrt{2}r$$

In the isosceles right angled $\triangle DFG$,

$$DF = \sqrt{2}a$$

Now $\qquad DF = DB + BE + EF$

$$= \sqrt{2}r + 2r + \sqrt{2}r$$

$$= 2r + 2\sqrt{2}r = 2(\sqrt{2}+1)r$$

$$\therefore \quad 2(\sqrt{2}+1)r = \sqrt{2}a$$

$$\Rightarrow \qquad r = \frac{a}{\sqrt{2(\sqrt{2}+1)}} = \frac{a}{2+\sqrt{2}}$$

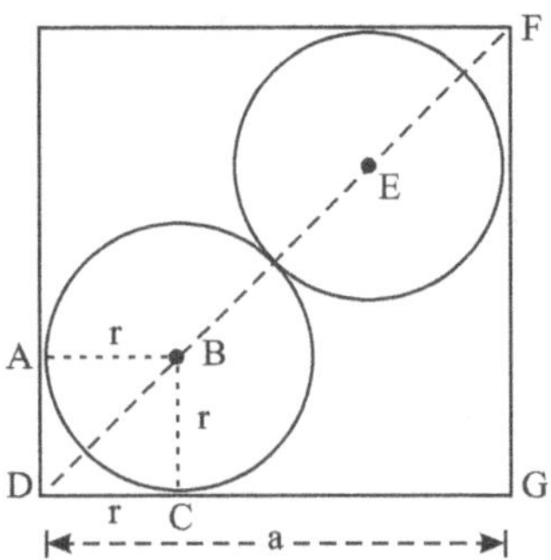

CIRCLES PACKING IN A CIRCLE

Let R be the radius of larger circle and r be the radius of smaller circle.

Case-(i): **Two circles**

$$R = 2r \;\rightarrow\; r = R/2$$

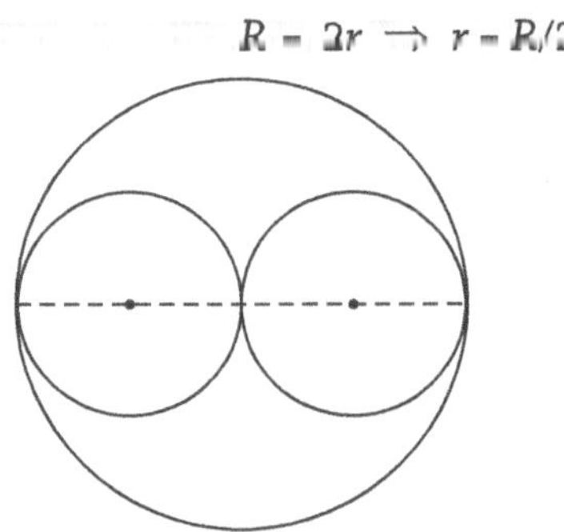

Case-(ii): **Three circles**

C is the centroid of equilateral ΔBEF

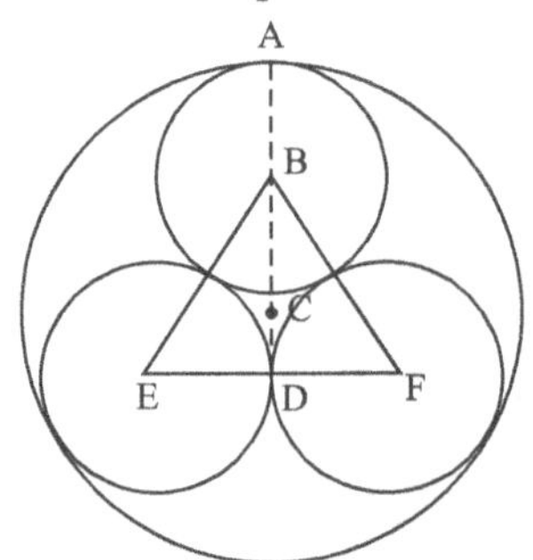

$$\therefore \quad BC : CD = 2 : 1$$

$$\therefore \qquad BC = \frac{2}{3}\,BD \qquad\qquad\qquad \text{...(1)}$$

In right angled $\Delta\, BDE$,

$$BD = \sqrt{BE^2 - DE^2}$$

$$BD = \sqrt{4r^2 - r^2} = \sqrt{3}\,r \qquad\qquad \text{...(2)}$$

From (1) and (2),

$$BC = \frac{2}{3} \times \sqrt{3}\,r = \frac{2}{\sqrt{3}}\,r$$

Now $\qquad AC = AB + BC$

$$= r + \frac{2}{\sqrt{3}}\,r = \left(\frac{\sqrt{3}+2}{\sqrt{3}}\right)r$$

Also $\qquad AC = R$

$$\therefore \quad \left(\frac{\sqrt{3}+2}{\sqrt{3}}\right)r = R \Rightarrow r = \frac{\sqrt{3}R}{\sqrt{3}+2}$$

$$\Rightarrow \qquad r = \left(2\sqrt{3} - 3\right)$$

SOME OTHER IMPORTANT CONCEPTS

1. In the figure ABC is a triangle right angled at B. Three semi-circles are drawn taking the three sides AB, BC and CA as diameter. The region enclosed by the three semi-circles is shaded.

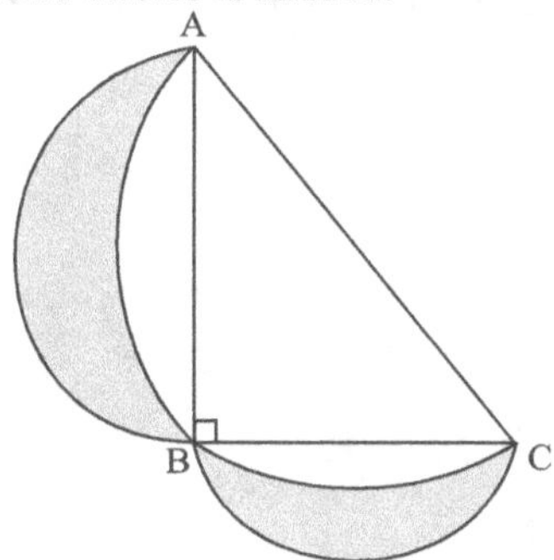

Area of the shaded region = Area of the right angled triangle.

2. In the figure given below all triangles are equilateral triangles and circles are inscribed in these triangles. If the side of triangle $ABC = a$, then the side of triangle $DEF = \dfrac{a}{2}$ and the side of triangle $GHI = \dfrac{a}{4}$

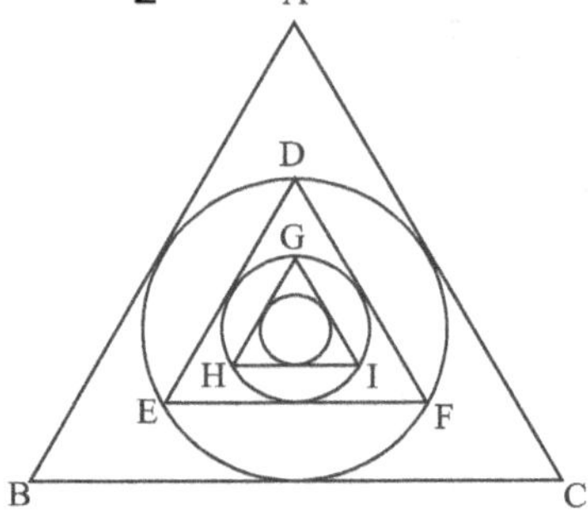

Thus length of a side of an inner triangle is half the length of immediate outer triangle. Similarly the radius of an inner circle is half the radius of immediate outer circle.

VI. COORDINATES OF SOME PARTICULAR POINTS

Let $A\,(x_1, y_1)$, $B\,(x_2, y_2)$ and $C\,(x_3, y_3)$ are vertices of any triangle ABC, then

Centroid

Centroid is the point of intersection of the medians of a triangle. Centroid divides each median in the ratio of $2 : 1$.

A median is a line segment joining the mid point of a side to its opposite vertex of a triangle.

Co-ordinates of centroid, $G = \left(\dfrac{x_1 + x_2 + x_3}{3}, \dfrac{y_1 + y_2 + y_3}{3}\right)$

Incentre

Incentre is the point of intersection of internal bisectors of the angles of a triangle. Also incentre is the centre of the circle touching all the sides of a triangle.

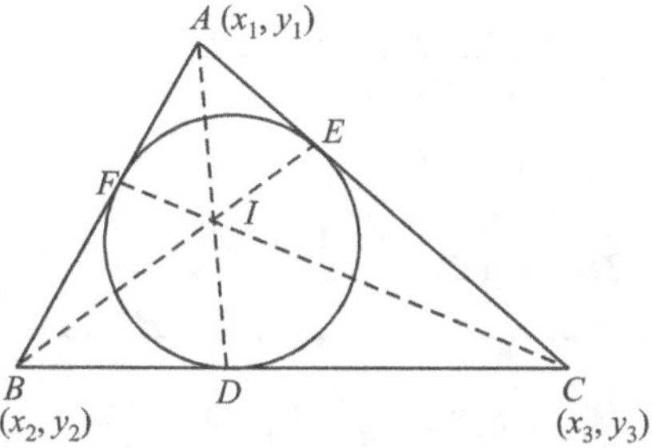

Co-ordinates of incentre,

$$I = \left(\frac{ax_1 + bx_2 + cx_3}{a+b+c}, \frac{ay_1 + by_2 + cy_3}{a+b+c} \right),$$

where a, b, c are length of the sides opposite to vertices A, B, C respectively of triangle ABC.

(i) Angle bisector divides the opposite sides in the ratio of the sides included in the angle. For example

$$\frac{BD}{DC} = \frac{AB}{AC} = \frac{c}{b}.$$

(ii) Incentre divides the angle bisectors AD, BE and CF in the ratio $(b + c) : a$, $(c + a) : b$ and $(a + b) : c$ respectively.

Circumcentre

It is the point of intersection of perpendicular bisectors of the sides of a triangle. It is also the centre of a circle passing through the vertices of the triangle. Thus if O is circumcentre of any triangle ABC, then $OA^2 = OB^2 = OC^2$.

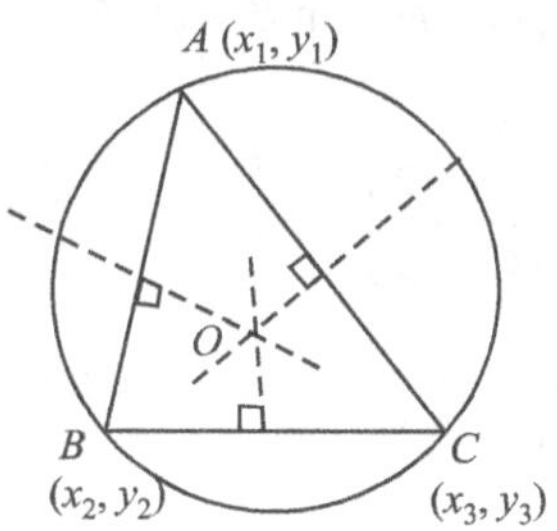

(i) If a triangle is right angle, then its circumcentre is the mid-point of hypotenuse.

(ii) If $A\,(x_1, y_1)$ $B\,(x_2, y_2)$ and $C\,(x_3, y_3)$ are the vertices of a ΔABC, then coordinates of the circumcentre of the triangle ABC is

$$\left(\frac{x_1 \sin 2A + x_2 \sin 2B + x_3 \sin 2C}{\sin 2A + \sin 2B + \sin 2C}, \right.$$

$$\left. \frac{y_1 \sin 2A + y_2 \sin 2B + y_3 \sin 2C}{\sin 2A + \sin 2B + \sin 2C} \right)$$

> **Note:** $\sin 30° = \dfrac{1}{2}$, $\sin 45° = \dfrac{1}{\sqrt{2}}$, $\sin 60° = \dfrac{\sqrt{3}}{2}$,
>
> $$\sin 90° = 1,\ \sin 120° = \frac{\sqrt{3}}{2}.$$

Orthocentre

It is the point of intersection of perpendiculars drawn from vertices on opposite sides.

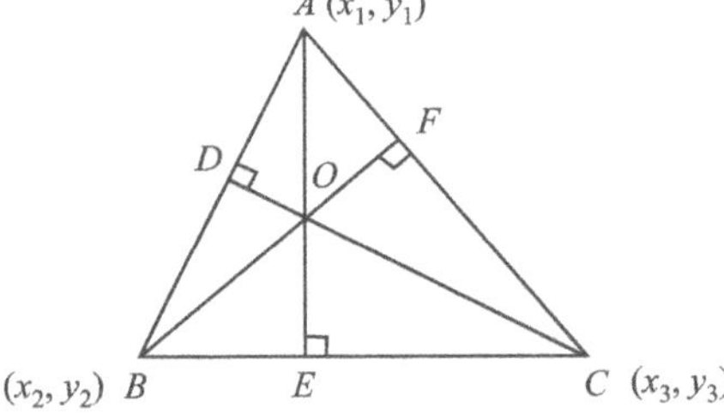

Coordinate of the orthocentre of ΔABC

$$= \left(\frac{x_1 \tan A + x_2 \tan B + x_3 \tan C}{\tan A + \tan B + \tan C}, \right.$$

$$\left. \frac{y_1 \tan A + y_2 \tan B + y_3 \tan C}{\tan A + \tan B + \tan C} \right)$$

If the triangle is right angled triangle, then orthocentre is the vertex where right angle is formed.

Note:

(i) $\tan 30° = \dfrac{1}{\sqrt{3}}$, $\tan 45° = 1$, $\tan 60° = \sqrt{3}$,

$\tan 90° = \dfrac{1}{0}$ or not defined

(ii) If the triangle is equilateral, then the centroid, incentre ortho-centre, and circumcentre coincide.

(iii) Orthocentre, centroid and circumcentre and circumcentre in the ratio $2 : 1$.

(iv) In an isosceles triangle centroid, orthocentre, incentre, and circumcentre lie on the same line.

Illustration 5: Find incentre (I) of triangle whose vertices are A (– 36, 7), B (20, 7), C (0, – 8).

Solution: Using distance formula

$$a = BC = \left| \sqrt{20^2 + (7+8)^2} \right| = 25$$

$$b = CA = \left| \sqrt{36^2 + (7+8)^2} \right| = 39$$

$$c = AB = \left| \sqrt{(36+20)^2 + (7-7)^2} \right| = 56$$

$$I = \left(\frac{25(-36) + 39(20) + 56(0)}{25 + 39 + 56}, \frac{25(7) + 39(7) + 56(-8)}{25 + 39 + 56} \right)$$

$I = (-1, 0)$.

Illustration 6: If (0, 1), (1, 1) and (1, 0) are mid-points of the sides of a triangle then find its incentre.

Solution: Let A (x_1, y_1), B (x_2, y_2) and C $(x_3 + y_3)$ are vertices of a triangle, then

$$x_1 + x_2 = 0, x_2 + x_3 = 2, x_3 + x_1 = 2$$
$$y_1 + y_2 = 2, y_2 + y_3 = 2, y_3 + y_1 = 0$$

Solving these equations, we get

$$A (0, 0), B (0, 2) \text{ and } C (2, 0)$$

Now $a = BC = 2\sqrt{2}$, $b = CA = 2$, $c = AB = 2$

Thus incentre of a $\triangle ABC$ is $(2 - \sqrt{2}, 2 - \sqrt{2})$.

Illustration 7: The two vertices of a triangle are (6, 3) and (–1, 7) and its centroid is (1, 5). Find the third vertex.

Solution: Let ABC be a triangle whose vertices are

$$A = (6, 3), \quad B = (-1, 7), \quad C = (x, y)$$

and centroid $G = (1, 5)$

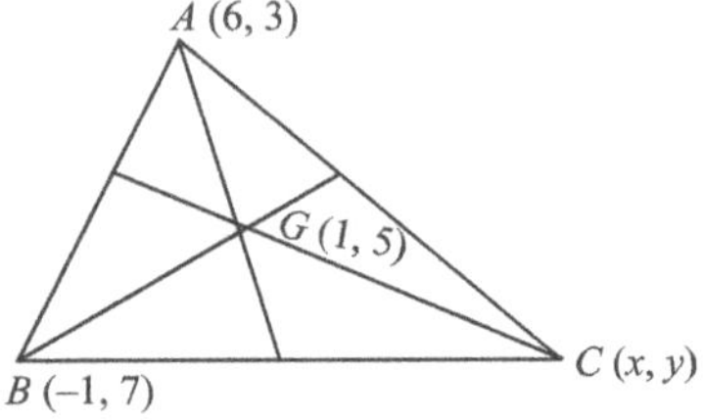

Then using the formula, for coordinates of centroid

$$1 = \frac{6 + (-1) + x}{3} \quad \text{and} \quad 5 = \frac{3 + 7 + y}{3}$$

$$\Rightarrow x = -2 \text{ and } y = 5$$

Hence, the third vertex is $C = (-2, 5)$

CO-ORDINATE GEOMETRY

$\Rightarrow$ Distance b/w two points in = 2D.

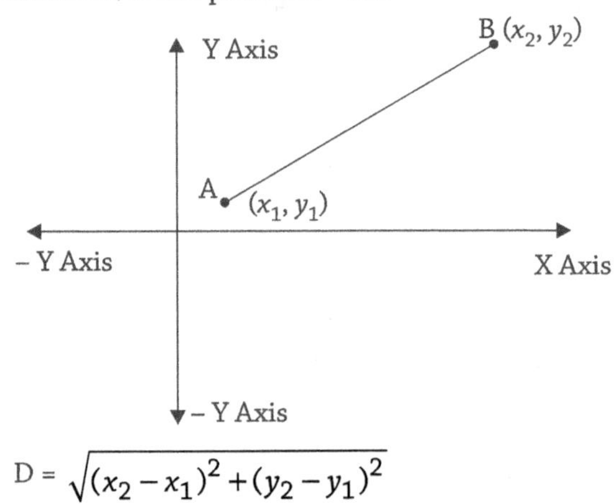

$$D = \sqrt{(x_2 - x_1)^2 + (y_2 - y_1)^2}$$

➤ Equation of line $y = mx + c$

  where m = slope of the line

  $$m = \tan\theta$$

  c = intercept at ×4 Axis.

➤ Equation of line, when it passes through given one point (x_1, y_1)

  $$y - y_1 = m(x - x_1)$$

➤ Equation of line, when passes through given two points. (x_1, y_1) and (x_2, y_2)

  $$y - y_1 = \frac{y_2 - y_1}{x_2 - x_1}(x - x_1) \qquad \therefore\ m = \frac{y_2 - y_1}{x_2 - x_1}$$

➤ Axis intercepts (a and b) then equation of line $\dfrac{x}{a} + \dfrac{y}{b} = 1$

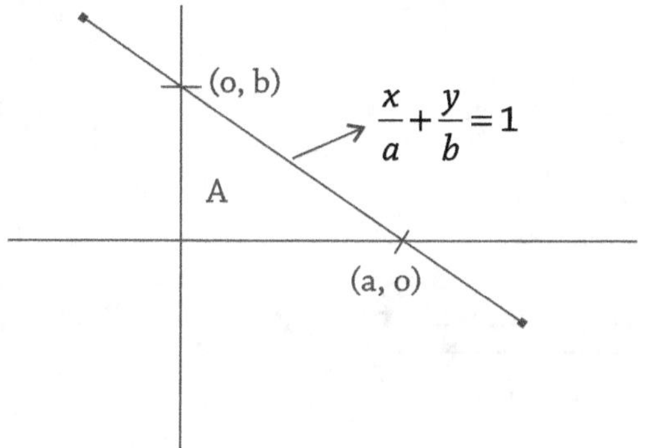

➤ Angle between two lines.

  If m_1 and m_2 are the slope of the lines then

  $$\tan\theta = \left|\frac{m_1 - m_2}{1 + m_1 m_2}\right|$$

  if lines are parallel then $m_1 = m_2$

  if lines are perpendicular then $\theta = 90°$

  $$\tan 90° = \left|\frac{m_1 - m_2}{1 + m_1 m_2}\right|$$

$$\frac{1}{0} \nearrow = \frac{m_1 - m_2}{1 + m_1 m_2}$$

$$1 + m_1 m_2 = 0$$

$$\boxed{m_1 m_2 = -1}$$

Distance b/w two parallel line

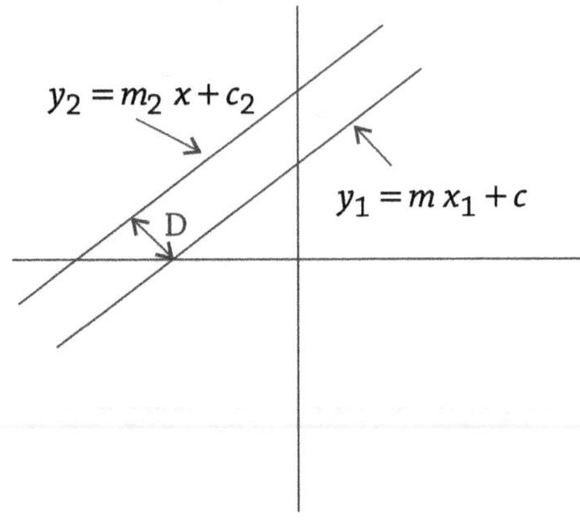

$$D = \frac{c_1 - c_2}{\sqrt{1 + m^2}}$$

Illustration 1: Find out distance between point (–2, 4) and (8, – 9)

Solution: $D = \sqrt{(x_2 - x_1)^2 (y_2 - y_1)^2}$

$$D = \sqrt{(8 - (-2))^2 + (-9 - 4)^2}$$

$$D = \sqrt{(10)^2 + (-13)^2}$$

$$D = \sqrt{100 + 169}$$

$$D = \sqrt{269}$$

Illustration 2: Find the equation of the line which passes through point (2,5) and makes 60° angle from +x Axis.

Solution: $y - y_1 = m (x - x_1)$

$y - 5 = \tan 60° (x - 2)$

$y - 5 = \sqrt{3} (x - 2)$

$$y - 5 = \sqrt{3}\,x - 2\sqrt{3}$$

$$y - \sqrt{3}\,x - 2\sqrt{3} + 5$$

Illustration 3: Which of the following equation pass through origin.

    (i) $2x + 3y = 5$ **(ii) $4x - 3y = 7$**

    (iii) $4x + ay + 8 = 0$ (iv) $4x = 11y$

Solution: Option (iv) will be correct b/c of it no have value of y. Axis intercept so that $c = 0$

Illustration 4: Find out distance b/w two parallel line $4x + 5y - 6 = 0$ and $8x + 10y + 16 = 0$

Solution: $4x + 5y - 6 = 0$

$$8x + 10y + 16 = 0 \text{ or} \qquad 2(4x + 5y + 8) = 0$$

$$4x + 5y + 8 = 0$$

$$m = -4/5$$

$$c_1 = -6$$

$$c_2 = 8$$

$$D = \frac{|c_1 - c_2|}{\sqrt{1 + m^2}} \quad \Rightarrow \quad \frac{|-6 - 8|}{\sqrt{1 + (-4/5)^2}}$$

$$= \frac{14}{\sqrt{1 + 16/25}} \Rightarrow \frac{14 \times 5}{\sqrt{41}} = \frac{70}{\sqrt{41}}$$

Illustration 5: Find out intercept on x Axis and y Axis by line $2x + 8y - 3 = 0$

Solution: $2x + 8y = 3$

Change into intercept form of equation $\dfrac{x}{3/2} + \dfrac{y}{3/8} = 1$

$a = 3/2;\ y = 3/8$

PROBABILITY

PROBABILITY REGARDING n LETTERS AND THEIR ENVELOPES

If n letters corresponding to n envelopes are placed in the envelopes at random, then

Probability that all letters are in right envelopes $= \dfrac{1}{n!}$

Probability that all letters are not in right envelopes $= 1 - \dfrac{1}{n!}$

Probability that no letters is in right envelopes

$$= \frac{1}{2!} - \frac{1}{3!} + \frac{1}{4!} - \ldots + (-1)^n \frac{1}{n!}$$

Probability that exactly r letters are in right envelopes

$$= \left[\frac{1}{2!} - \frac{1}{3!} + \frac{1}{4!} - \ldots + (-1)^{n-r} \frac{1}{(n-r)!} \right]$$

Illustration 1: There are four letters and four envelopes, the letters are placed into the envelopes at random, find the probability that all letters are placed in the wrong envelopes.

Solution: Since all letters are to be placed in wrong envelopes, hence required probability

$$= \left[\frac{1}{2!} - \frac{1}{3!} + \frac{1}{4!} \right] = \frac{1}{2} - \frac{1}{6} + \frac{1}{24} = \frac{3}{8}.$$

CHAPTER 7

GETTING READY FOR THE WAT/GD/PI

WAT: AN INTRODUCTION

Written Ability Test is akin or connected to Essay writing and WAT is being conducted with a single objective to test your language skills in areas of expression, way of writing, grammar, articulation of ideas as per the topic given and most importantly a test of how you draw a conclusion with a take away for the audience.

We all know that a manager should be well equipped with the usage of words and with putting down the thoughts on paper in a crisp and clear manner; if he wants to reach the top corporate positions. Major reason being that most of the times initial engagement with the customers/ clients would happen over emails, putting down things in a well worded manner in official documents etc. and they lead to creating a first impression on the client.

WAT ensures that everyone is able to share their thoughts on the given topic and gets a fair chance during the evaluation process.

In a way, WAT enables the panel to evaluate the candidates' inherent qualities of expression of thought, one of the major characteristics required for personnel to become a successful manager.

There is a very thin line of demarcation between Essay writing and WAT that is the body part of Essay can be generalized but in WAT you wouldn't get that liberty and you have to write in a flow, strictly to tune with the assigned topic.

WAT is only a language skill test. The experienced students advise to read Editorials of at least two National Newspapers including one Business daily. Also reading, listening or watching the news analysis of current affairs helps a great deal.

The basic selection process after qualifying the test includes Written Ability Test (WAT) and Personal Interview (PI) rounds at some Indian Institutes of Management (IIMs) and other B-schools. To start around the second week of February, the WAT and PI rounds will continue till March. The Group Discussion (GD) as a screening method has been scrapped by most IIMs and has gradually given way to the WAT.

Out of the 20 IIMs except 2 IIMs, all have replaced GD round by WAT round as their final selection process for admission to their flagship programmes. Even some of them have added WAT along with GD for admission to their various Management programmes. IIMs found WAT a better testing process to assess a candidate than GD as many candidates could not express their opinion and views during GD while who could speak louder made their presence felt during GD round.

In WAT round, a candidate can freely put down his views and thoughts on paper coherently without fear of getting disrupted.

A very important emerging theme topic during the past few WAT sessions has been the focus on Social concern. You should also be prepared to have some abstract topics on which you may be asked to write an essay in the final selection round.

Once you complete writing on the WAT topic, read it again. Try to find out the mistakes, like – punctuation, grammar, spelling errors in it. Find out at how many points you have edited by cuttings and cancellations in one paragraph of the mock WAT you have taken. Next time when you write on any WAT topic– minimize them. In a few days, you will be equipped with fine writing skills with fewer mistakes or no mistakes.

> **You fail only if you stop writing- Ray Bradbury**

Writing Ability and Time Constraint

As in the admission criteria of IIMs' essay writing is gaining importance, the main concern is the time limit. While writing an essay for admission to a top B-school, the focus should be on the time. Usually, IIM Bangalore gives 30 minutes to write the essay, while IIM Lucknow gives 15 minutes and the time for writing the essay is as little as 10 minutes in IIM Ahmedabad.

Here, the key will be to write as fast as possible in order to finish the essay. Try not to waste much time on thinking and planning the structure of the essay, else you will not be able to complete it. For this, you will need sufficient practice.

According to a student of IIM Ahmedabad, the best way to practise is by picking up one current affairs topic every day and writing as much as you can for 10 minutes. Your focus should be on starting the essay and putting in as many important points as possible. There is no compulsion to present the matter in impressive or flowery language. Instead, accuracy and correctness of spelling and grammar take precedence. The essay's evaluation is based on the number of new ideas or points you can produce in the given time, the different angles from which you can analyze the topic and the logic behind each argument.

It is important to develop the ability to think and articulate quickly. For B-school panel lists, essays are tools to see how you structure your thoughts and produce them in the least amount of time. Apart from IIMs, other prominent B-schools like XLRI and IIFT also use Essay Writing to assess candidates.

Weightage

The last CAT i.e. 2017 was conducted by IIM Lucknow. The weightage to the PI and Written Ability Test at IIM Lucknow was as follows:

Components	Weightage
Written Ability Test	10
Personal Interview	40
Total	50

(The minimum requirement for getting a pass in Personal Interview is 12 out of 40 marks.)

WAT or Written Ability Test plays a crucial role in the selection process of IIMs. Weightage to WAT in the selection process are different for different IIMs, here is the percentages of WAT in some of the IIMs'.

➤ IIM Ahmedabad -Not Disclosed (70% WAT+PI)

➤ IIM Bangalore-15%

➤ IIM Calcutta-10%

➤ IIM Lucknow-10%

➤ IIM Indore-15%

➤ IIM Kozhikode-15% (Including GD)

Looking at the percentage you can figure out that WAT plays an important role in the selection process of IIMs.

Topics for WAT

Topics generally given for WAT can be broadly classified into two categories:

1. Case Studies

2. General Topics

Case studies are nothing but a small description of a real life industry/ business scenario mentioning certain constraints, statements, targets etc. and requiring you to analyse the same and come up with the required solution.

For your practice, we are providing some current affairs topics:

➤ Demonetization in India: Decision is more appreciated than criticized

- ➢ GST: Aim to take economy on faster growth path
- ➢ "Make in India" Ground realities
- ➢ Rising Population of India could be turned into an asset
- ➢ Corruption is the root cause of current economic and social woes in India
- ➢ Ethics and morals cannot be taught in classrooms only
- ➢ Net Neutrality: Very Essential to Make India Digital
- ➢ Union Budget: Merging the General & Railway Budget will save exchequer from unnecessary spending
- ➢ E-commerce: Unrealistic Discounts are Dangerous
- ➢ Aadhar -Utility is more than perceived

HOW TO PREPARE FOR WAT

Just after getting the call, make sure you take up writing at least 10 topics every day. Time plays a major role in WAT. Keep a stopwatch in front of you while practicing WAT. It will help you a lot in managing your time on the D-Day. In a typical IIM interview the time for WAT is between **10 minutes and 30 minutes**. Remember the more you write the easier it will be for you to cope up with the time.

How to Structure your Writing?

In an IIM selection process, WAT topics can be from any field: Science and technology to Social and Cultural norms in the society. But mostly they are confined to the recent happenings and trending news around the world.

- ➢ **Introduction:** Make sure you start your WAT topic with a good introduction. The introduction should be a simple one and should be related to the topic.

- ➢ **Main Body:** In this, you have to either write for the topic or against the topic. Make up your mind on which side you want to take a stand and then try to come up with some points (around 3-4 points) and then start elaborating those points. Each point that you have chosen should end with a valid reason. Try to add a few facts and figures to validate your point then as it will add weight to what you are saying, it is very much appreciated.

- ➢ **Conclusion:** After the main body come up with a conclusion. The conclusion should be crisp and to the point. Avoid adding some extra points in this part. Just plainly conclude what you have said till now.

Time management

Time management is the key to handle properly, if you divide the time properly, you will be successful in handling this section properly. Let's take an example, to let you understand the proper division of time. Suppose the time limit for WAT is 15 minutes, divide your time as:

- **2 minutes: Understanding the topic** and deciding whether you want to write in favour or against the topic.

- **1 minute:** Make **use of the rough space**, Jot down the points that you are going to include in the main body of the essay and also make sub-bullets if you have any.

- **2 minutes:** Focus on the **introduction** part during this phase and come up with a good intro for the essay.

- **5-7 minutes:** Start **writing down the main body**. This is the time when the rough work comes handy. You can pick up your points from your rough space and start elaborating the same.

- **2 minutes: Conclusion/Summary**. Come up with a good summary/conclusion and as we cautioned avoid adding any more extra points to your conclusion.

- **1 minute: Proofreading** the essay and rectifying any spelling/ grammatical errors.

DO's and DON'Ts to remember while attempting the WAT

DO's

- If the time limit is 15 minutes, do spend a couple of minutes analyzing the topic, what exactly the topic is about and structure your writing according to the topic.

- You will get some space for rough work. Make full utilization of the rough space. You can write down the key points in the rough space provided and can also prepare a rough draft of your essay. It becomes very easy when you start writing down the essay on the main sheet.

- Keep your wristwatch in front of you. It is very important to keep an eye on the time.

- Keep a minute in the end for proofreading. It is a good habit and it will also help you to rectify spelling/grammatical errors (if any) in your essay.

- Read newspaper every day. You will get a lot of insights and ideas just by reading a newspaper. The experienced lot suggests reading 'The Hindu' (for general burning topics), Business Standard and Economic Times (for the financial and economic activities happening in India and around the world).

> While practicing, try to use simple sentences with a good mix of paragraph lengths in the write up.
> Keep reading about trending topics:

DON'Ts

> Never use jargons in your essay.
> Avoid cut/scratch. Make sure you minimize it. It always has a bad impression.
> Sometimes a WAT topic can be a difficult one. In that case do not panic. Panicking ruins your writing skills. Instead, take your time, just have a thorough look at the topic and make use of the rough space to structure your approach.
> Practice as much as you can: Try to actually write and practice for WAT, rather than just reading on varied topics. You may set up the personal target of writing on at least one topic every 2-3 days and getting it reviewed by the person who can give you a critical feedback and play the role of a facilitator in your preparation for WAT.

How to prepare Do's

> Ask questions to yourself while practicing to write: Become independent and try to evaluate yourself. Ask following questions to you and see if you may get the answers. If try to work and improve as per the answers and if not, try to get a friend or a relative or a neighbour answer those questions for you after reading your write up. The questions which can be asked are:
> Is the write up properly structured?
> Is it revolving around the topic in hand and focussed on the central theme?
> Is the write up exciting the reader and making him feel engaged with the content?
> Are there any grammar/punctuation errors?
> Am I being verbose in the write up? Can I improve upon the clarity and crisp part?
> Have I been able to cover all the relevant parameters of the ladder view?
> Did I lose track from the topic in between and/or any unclear part is present in the content?
> Am I able to reflect my managerial skills through the write up?
> If I had to reproduce the same content, what changes would I make to have a better output from the write up?

WAT as A Precursor To Personal Interview: Be Cautious!

Do not entirely forget the topic on which you have submitted the write up in WAT test. The panel evaluating you in Personal Interview round might have the copy of your submission and may ask few questions from what you have written on the topic.

In such scenarios, try to avoid a U-turn from what you have written. Your answers and point of view should be in sync with what you have written earlier in the WAT. Any deviation might reflect that you either were not serious enough while participating in WAT or you just wrote something without giving it the needed thought.

IMPORTANT TOPICS

For your practice and understanding, we have compiled a list of 100 topics for WAT, if you write down one every day, it will only take less than four months, but will make you more confident and your thinking process will be active. Maybe you won't get a topic which is similar to any of these, but still it will prepare you enough to excel. Have a look and start early.

1. Ninety-nine percent of all failures come from people who have a habit of making excuses
2. Quality performance starts with a positive attitude
3. Cowardice of gentlemen too is a factor for crime against women
4. Media Influence
5. How do you measure success in life?
6. India has the largest pool of talented manpower but very few innovations and patented products
7. Allowing Foreign Universities in India is bad for India's education system
8. How should women empower themselves?
9. More than one billion Indians: A gigantic problem or a sea of opportunities
10. The Best way to predict your Future is to create it
11. Education costs money, but then so does ignorance
12. All the world is a laboratory to the inquiring mind
13. Presidential Vs. Parliamentary Democracy: A Debate
14. Corruption is a Social Evil In India
15. Attitude is crucial for all actions
16. Application of knowledge is crucial
17. Divergent Thinking is a Stepping Stone to Creativity
18. Weakness of attitude becomes weakness of character
19. Planning and execution originate from the same stem
20. Maintaining a winning attitude is crucial
21. In writing, there is Art and in art there is Craft

22. All the efforts in the world won't matter if you're not inspired
23. The biggest adventure you can ever take is to live the life of your dreams
24. If the blind lead the blind, both shall fall in the ditch
25. Respect yourself and others will respect you
26. It is not in the stars to hold our destiny but in ourselves
27. Can cynicism and Optimism coexist?
28. A winner never stops trying
29. Weakness of attitude becomes weakness of character
30. You miss 100% of the shots you don't take
31. Action is the foundational key to all success.
32. We become what we think
33. Recession is the mother of innovation
34. Discuss the role of Public Private Partnership in India's Economic Growth
35. Foreign direct investment will revitalize the education system
36. Businesses should concentrate on making profits and not address social and environmental issues
37. Difficulties strengthen the mind as labour does the body
38. Adversity introduces a man to himself
39. If you don't try then there is no experience
40. Divergent Thinking is a Stepping Stone to Creativity
41. I aspire to be a CEO in the next 10 years
42. Interpersonal skills are asset for a manager
43. Planning and execution originate from the same stem
44. Politicans have created cobwebs of corruption
45. Delete the negative accentuate the positive
46. Are we racist by nature?
47. Scams will resurface if unpunished
48. What's measured improves
49. Start with the end in mind
50. Never mind your happiness; do your duty
51. Ethics and values are Utopian words
52. Failure is a detour, not a dead-end street
53. What will you do if you are out of competition?
54. If you are going through hell, keep going
55. Creative man is motivated by the desire to achieve
56. Attitude is crucial for all actions
57. Curiosity explores information
58. Sportsman spirit gives you confidence
59. We do best when supervised

60. You can't bask in past glory
61. We don't know how to be in a queue
62. Blowing your own trumpet will meet deaf ears
63. Only performers will survive
64. Equation is 98% hard work and 2% luck
65. Competition doesn't mean revenge
66. Self-introspection makes you honest
67. Fear of failure leads you to success
68. Aspire, Aspire and Aspire that's your right
69. Can 'Do attitude' give you an edge
70. Application of knowledge is crucial
71. Failures are stepping stones to success
72. Exams are never over
73. Maintaining a winning attitude is crucial
74. Competitive stress is good
75. Posting on social media also requires self regulation
76. Being polite means being confident
77. Being hopeful is being positive
78. Perseverance wins you success
79. Attitude is crucial for achieving success
80. Luck favors those who dare to win
81. What if I don't succeed?
82. In competent world, being ignorant is idiotic
83. Be Mature. Be successful
84. Jaundiced eye will always see yellow
85. Aspiring beyond potential
86. How to develop a positive mind
87. We have habit of wasting electricity
88. Power of Influencing
89. Etiquettes
90. We must be God fearing
91. Scams Have Tarnished The Image Of Politicians
92. Can do attitude
93. Eye to Eye Contact
94. We waste water
95. Cynicism is our DNA
96. No man was ever wise by chance
97. Aim High, And You Won't Shoot Your Foot Off
98. The True Sign of Intelligence is not Knowledge but Imagination
99. Your attitude, not your aptitude, will determine your altitude
100. Inspiration exists, but it must find you working

GD: A MAJOR COMPONENT IN SHORTLISTING

Group Discussion round is a favourite component of final selection round not only in top MBA colleges but also in various recruitment process like class 1 and 2 services, SSB, bank officers' recruitment services among others. It is a forum where people sit together, discuss a topic for a certain amount of time with the common objective of finding a solution for a problem or discuss an issue that is given to them.

Despite the fact the most of the IIMs have today given away with GD round and have replaced it by WAT, Group Discussion still holds a significant importance in many other reputed B-Schools

A GD is both a technique and an art to judge the capacity of the person and his capabilities that make him/her apt for the course.

A group of candidates are made to sit together in a circular/semi-circular fashion or in a U-shape. One person will co-ordinate the Group Discussion (called the moderator). Candidates are made to discuss on a topic or subject for a limited time and then assessed accordingly. It is a chance for the aspirant to be more vocal.

A number of people who can communicate their ideas well and discuss effectively with others in a one-to-one situation become tongue-tied in a group situation.

They will just not be able to present their ideas or discuss their ideas with the other members of the group. A Group Discussion will identify people who have such group communication skills and those who do not possess such group communication skills.

> Group Discussions measure certain attributes of the candidates that are otherwise difficult to identify and time consuming to assess.

The most current GD topics on various economic, business and social issues include the IIM Act 2017, Impact of Demonetisation, GST, Bank Merger, Bank Recapitalization, Merger of General and Railway Budget, and certain abstract topics which are more relevant to present socio-economic scenario.

A word of caution is that do not start the Group Discussions with statements like "I whole-heartedly support the topic …" or "I completely disagree with the topic …." etc.

Queries in the minds of the candidates

The selection procedure of IIMs is in multi stages, so it makes multiple queries in the minds of the aspirants. We have tried to solve a few of them here, read them and get benefitted.

- **What should I do if some other members of the group interrupt me while I am speaking?**

If you are speaking, you should try preventing others from grabbing your chance. When some other participant tries to interrupt you while you are speaking, you should tell him/her clearly and unambiguously that you would be allowed to speak. You can say, "Excuse me, please let me complete." Or, you can say, "Just a minute - let me finish my point".

- **Is it admirable to take a position in favour of the topic or against the topic?**

A Group Discussion is not a debate where you have to decide whether you would like to speak for the topic or against the topic. This is a "discussion" where you have to bring out all aspects pertaining to the topic. You have to bring out the points in favour of the topic as well as those against the topic and discuss them in the group.

- **Can we use any regional language in the middle of our discussion for better effect?**

A GD is a formal situation and therefore your entire discussion should be in proper English. There would be people from various regions, maybe many of them don't know your language and likewise you don't know theirs.

- **Will using statistics help in a GD?**

If using statistics is going to enhance the presentability of your point, then go ahead and use them. But be sure that it is correct and latest data.

- **Can I question the other group members on what they say?**

Asking questions just for the sake of asking questions, once again, is not going to get you any marks. But if you find something worth mentioning, do so in a polite and formal manner.

- **What should I do if I do not know anything about the topic?**

Make sure that you have read up about a large variety of issues. You should just keep quiet in the initial stages and listen to what the others are saying. Once you get a good enough idea about what the others are saying, use those points combined with your common sense and come up with your own points.

- **Should I be the first one to speak in the GD? Will it fetch me additional marks if I initiate the GD?**

You are going to get only a small advantage. The marks you get will depend on your overall performance. The sooner the better should not be followed, first do the preparation in your mind and only then start keeping your point.

HOW TO PREPARE FOR A GD

In a GD, the ability of a member of the group is measured on certain scales such as time limit, skills, knowledge, etc. [Few things which are considered a 'must' while preparing for Group Discussion are] discussed in this section in subsequent headings.

It's natural that the candidates actually don't have any idea about what is going to be or what will be the topic of GD. Therefore, it is necessary to keep yourself updated with the information of current affairs and historical topics and the latest happenings in Politics, Sports, Literature, etc.; have a look!!

➢ *Current Affairs:* Current affairs are very important topics that should be covered. To cover these topics, you should read the newspapers regularly.

➢ *Historical Topics:* You must have a fair knowledge about historical places and the facts behind them. These topics are not for only one area but it includes all the historical knowledge.

➢ *Sports, Arts & Literature:* You must try to have a decent idea about what is popular or not, who are the leaders in each area, the latest that has happened in these areas.

With the advent of internet, it is considered beneficial even in serious matters apart from entertainment. Some toppers suggest using YouTube; start watching and listening to some Group Discussion related session videos. You'll get some idea then start preparing for it accordingly.

When a Group Discussion is initiated and a topic is given to the group, you can think of taking any of the side for discussion. Just decide the role you want to play, think about the topic and recall the points you know about that topic. The group keeps you around the core issue while the discussion is on.

Assessment of a GD

In a GD, a candidate is evaluated on the basis of various parameters, the panel focuses on to check your:

➢ **Leadership skills:** The ability to take initiatives, to lead, to influence and carry the team.

➢ **Communication skills:** Candidates will be assessed in terms of clarity of thoughts, expression and aptness of language.

➢ **Interpersonal skills:** Interacting and managing the people is an important aspect which is tested in a GD.

➢ **Persuasive skills:** The capacity to analyze and persuade the people.

What is required in a GD?

The pre-requisites include:

➢ Your vocabulary should be strong

➢ You should be confident, and

➢ Flourish a positive image

You need to focus on few essential points in the GD, they are:

➢ Understanding the topic

➢ Having precise and sharp thoughts

➢ Taking the initiative

➢ Conquering misunderstandings

➢ Communicating your views

➢ Displaying proper knowledge about the topic

You may ask questions about the topics, which will show how much you know about the specific topic. Well, this will allow you to examine and evaluate your point of view with other candidates. It is also important for the candidates that they must avoid the quarrel or shout but don't raise your voice in any case. You should give opinions about the topics that are accurate to the comments in a decent manner.

Useful Tips & Tricks to Crack a Group Discussion

Here is a list of what should be done and what should be avoided at a Group Discussion (GD); go through it and try to follow them for leaving a lasting impression and securing your seat in one of your dream colleges.

You are expected to contribute meaningfully and help arrive at a consensus in a Group Discussion (GD). It is not a platform for you to fight your way through and dominate.

Flexibility and gelling with the group is also very important. Make a note of the following points and you'll get through with flying colors:

1. Must be on time and dressed in formals.

2. Be as natural as possible. Do not try to be someone you are not.

3. Be yourself. In an attempt to be someone else, your opinions will not be portrayed.

4. Sit in a straight and confident posture as body language is very important, so be careful!

5. Maintain eye contact with team members and you need to speak to your point. It creates more room for conversation.

6. If you have doubts go for clarifications on particular subject/ topics of the discussion.

7. Always carry a pen and a notebook. This allows you to refer to what others have said previously.

8. Be assertive yet humble. You need to stick to your values and beliefs, but learn to respect the values and opinions of others, too.

9. Grab the opportunity to speak first, i.e. to start the Group Discussion with your opinion. It generally leaves a good impression on the evaluator, but take the move only if you have complete knowledge of the subject.

10. Do not repeat a point, or be lengthy or irrelevant. Also intervene, if someone else is going on an irrelevant track.

11. Facilitate contribution from others. Do not just go on and on and on with only your opinionated view. Remember, it is a group discussion. Allow others to speak too.

12. As long as you listen and appreciate what others are saying, you will learn more understanding. So, do not interrupt. Also keep nodding, when others speak, it shows receptivity.

13. Try and sort out contradictions and arguments.

14. Be an active and dynamic participant. The examiner wants to hear you speak. So, do put forth your views.

15. Be positive and prepare your thoughts well but be cautious not to be over-confident.

16. Think well before you speak. You are being heard and judged upon.

17. When raising an objection to a point kept by another speaker, back it up with a solid reason to get your point across.

18. Use quotes, facts and figures, statements, everyday life examples to express a clear chain of thoughts. Also it might leave a good impression on the examiner and help you score well.

19. Understand that aim is not to speak a lot, a lengthy one, but to be accurate and clear with your points.

These are some basic yet very vital tips that will help you feel a bit more confident about yourself and make you ready to appear for that Group Discussion trend.

Always remember that, the quality of what you've said is actually more valuable than the quantity you've talked. Read a lot about various topics and make yourself comfortable about the latest issues and make easy to the topic.

So, to accomplish and have a successful Group Discussion always try to work well with others, improve your listening skills and understand fully the resources that will currently benefit you.

HOW TO PARTICIPATE WHEN ONE DOESN'T HAVE MUCH IDEA ABOUT THE TOPIC?

This is another question I have seen candidates asking a lot. Popping up of this question is quite obvious as no matter how much we have read, how much we have practiced with our friends offline as well as online – we are bound to not know everything under the sun. And may be on not a very good day, we end up encountering a topic for Group Discussion about which we have no idea.

Even if this happens, there is NO need to panic! Rather PATIENCE and ACTIVE LISTENING becomes demand of the time.

Let couple of people speak first on the topic, try to get an idea of the topic and then chip in with your thoughts that you have built till now. Do ensure that you are not just repeating the points already mentioned by earlier speakers, but are coming up with a value add to the discussion whose base may revolve around what you have come to know about the topic from earlier speakers.

> *Discussion is an exchange of knowledge; an argument an exchange of ignorance.*
>
> *— Robert Quillen*
>
> *Discussion is just a tool. You have to aim; the final goal must be a decision.*
>
> *— Harri Holkeri*

HOW TO PARTICIPATE IN A GD WITH AN ABSTRACT TOPIC?

At times, you may encounter an abstract topic in the Group Discussion. While one can easily get lost and beat around the bush handling such topics, there are certain intelligent ways in which these topics can be handled to one's advantage to reflect the managerial qualities to the evaluation panel.

The intelligent way to handle is nothing but to relate the abstract topic to something realistic, practical and happening around. This helps you as a candidate to think in a concrete manner and put forth the points which might not have come to your mind otherwise.

It has been observed that relating abstract topics to something real is what the panels actually look for. This enables the panel to check your thinking ability as well as stress management capability. Do not feel that just a blind creativity is expected out from you when an abstract topic is thrown at you for a group discussion.

To elaborate the above scenario with an example:

Consider that the GD topic given to you is "Everyone lives only twice". Now when it comes to correlating the above topic to something real, you can map it to the change in attitude and approach to life which one undergoes due to certain situations. A terrorist might surrender and become a good person earning a respectable life and hence get to live 2 lives.

HOW TO START A GD

If one says that starting a GD means you have got through – it is a wrong perception!

If one says that since you were third or fourth to enter a discussion, you are highly unlikely to succeed in GD – it is again a wrong perception!!

Irrespective of the umpteen myths around starting the GD, let me tell you that more than just starting a GD, what matters more is HOW YOU START A GD?

➤ Start a GD only when you believe that you are well verse with the topic and are in situation to introduce the topic to entire group

➤ The person who starts the GD is expected to let the house open for discussion after he has introduced the topic in good detail to the entire group

➤ In case the topic asks for an opinion in Yes/No, Agree/Disagree format- the person who starts the GD should not start on the note of "I agree… ", "Yes, I think…" Rather, the person who starts the GD should explain the topic to the group; introduce both sides of the topic and let others chip in with their views (can afford to allow atleast 1-2 to chip in), before the person who started the GD comes back and chips in with his view. During this second iteration in the discussion, the person who started can take a binary stand on the topic and use statements like 'I agree.'

➤ One should not speak for more than 120-150 seconds and let others speak after this duration. Continuing for long might project you as a dominating person who wants to talk and talk and not give chance to his peers

➤ The person who starts the discussion is more seen as a leader and he should try to behave like a leader and an assertive (not an aggressive) moderator and try to keep the group together, preventing any kind of deviation from the topic. These expectations arises from the fact that since you started the GD, you are considered as the person who knows the most about the topic and are in a position to gauge if the ongoing discussion is in sync with the topic or is getting deviated.

➤ Having said this, do keep in mind that do not be in a hurry to start a GD. There is no rule that if you did not start the GD, your chances of converting the discussion in your favour are gone. Rather, if you rush in to start the discussion and end up showing limited knowledge/incorrect knowledge of the subject of discussion; you have done much more harm to yourself. And this harm can be almost irreparable.

➢ So, start if and only if you believe that you can drive things ahead in the discussion and do not start just for the sake of starting.

IMPORTANT TOPICS

Generally there are three to four categories of topics given for a GD. First of all, we will discuss the categories in which the vast number of topics fall, they are:

➢ *Factual topics:* These are about practical things, which an ordinary person is aware of; they usually include the socio economic ones. For example: The education policy of India, The recent budget etc.

➢ *Controversial topics:* These are the ones which are argumentative in nature; as the name suggests, they are meant to generate controversy. For example: Women make better managers, Reservation should be removed etc.

➢ *Abstract topics:* Often these are not given, but better be prepared for any type. It is believed that they test your lateral thinking and creativity. For example: A is an alphabet

Usually, the topics given are from the field of politics or economy or general issues. Some of the topics on which you can prepare a GD, with your friends or fellow mates include:

Current

1. Data breaching in online social media accounts
2. Why are MNCs considered superior to Indian companies?
3. Private Participation in Infrastructure is Highly Desirable
4. Developing Countries need Trade, not Aid
5. Skilled Manpower Shortage in India
6. Technology Creates Income Disparities
7. Government should clean its own hands before pointing finger at the private sector for corruption.

General

8. Advertising is a Waste of Resources
9. Should India break Diplomatic Ties with Pakistan?
10. In our economic matters, there is an excessive tendency towards the thinking rather than doing.
11. Is disinvestment really that good for India or is a rethink in order?

12. Foreign aid is a dangerous drug that can stimulate in small doses but become fatally addictive in larger doses.

13. Economic freedom not old fashioned theories of development will lead to growth and prosperity

14. Water resources should be nationalized

15. Are Co-operatives relevant in today's global environment?

16. space missions are a wastage of resources for a resource-starved nation like India

17. Poverty in Third World Countries is due to Prosperity in First World Countries

18. Indian Economy: Old Wine in New Bottle!

19. Is Globalization really necessary?

20. Why can't India be a world class player in manufacturing industry as it is in IT & BPO Sectors?

21. Rise of regional blocs threatens independent nations like India

22. Brain-Drain has to be stopped

23. Doctors' accountability to improve health-care

24. Universal disarmament is a must

25. Unrest in Countries around India

26. Flexi Timings or Fixed Timings - Which is better at Work?

27. Individual Brilliance Certainly makes a Difference

28. Do NGOs in India really work for others or work for their own vested interests?

29. Can the world economy bank upon India for growth?

30. Merit or Seniority – Better criterion for promotion?

31. Start-Up India, Stand Up India - Prospering Entrepreneurial Culture

32. Gold Monetization Scheme

33. Should reservation in higher education be allowed?

34. India or Indians who is performing better?

35. Is India Ready For Ecommerce

36. Environment - What is man doing to Nature

37. Developing an entrepreneurial ecosystem in India.

38. Ensuring gender diversity in Indian work force.

39. Even a clock that does not work is right twice a day

40. How escalating pollution rate in India can be controlled?

41. What must be done to improve the education system of India?

42. India needs more implementers than Planners

43. ISRO's space missions - funds of country misused

44. Independence of Judiciary is the need of the hour

45. World's Happiness Report, 2017 has named Norway as the world's happiest nation Why is Norway the world's happiest country?

46. Are digital payments secure enough for the Indian economy to go cashless?

47. Do we really need Smart Cities?

48. Economic growth is more important than Ecological protection

49. Should Hindi be the official language of India?

50. Solution of corruption is a mirage till we catch top public figures

51. Youth in Politics

52. Are Indians Less Quality Conscious?

53. Ethics in Business are just a Passing Fad

54. Is the Consumer really the King in India?

55. Commercialization of Health Care: Good or Bad?

56. Is there any point in having a business strategy when the world changes from month to month?

57. Security Cameras & Privacy

58. Borderless World: A Myth or Reality?

59. Should voters be given a NOTA (None Of The Above) choice?

Education and Career

60. We Need More Entrepreneurs than Managers

61. Rise in MBA Salaries is Not Sustainable in the Long Run

62. Will Mumbai's Film Industry ever evolve into a Truly Modern Corporative One?

63. Indians Perform Better as Individuals than in Groups/Teams

64. Positive Attitude and not Knowledge is required for Business Success

65. Ethics in Business are just a passing fashion

66. Family owned business vs. Professionally run businesses

67. Smaller businesses and start-ups have more scope for professional growth.

68. Does Morality have an Essence in Corporate Life?

69. MBA in India is highly over-rated

70. Multinational Corporations: Are they Devils in Disguise?

71. Should the Government Set-up More IITs and IIMs, OR should it

be use the Money for Primary & Secondary Education?

72. Should Management Education be subsidized?

Discussions

73. Should sting operations be carried out?
74. Every Cloud has a Silver Lining
75. Good Things Always Come from Good Thinking
76. Men are from Mars; Women are from Venus
77. EQ (Emotional Intelligence) or IQ (Intelligence Quotient)
78. Problems unite us, Religion divides us
79. Justice delayed is justice denied
80. Do Beauty and Brains Go Together?
81. Globalization vs. Nationalism
82. Cleanliness is a Fundamental Responsibility of an Indian Citizen
83. A Person should not be too honest; Straight Trees are cut first

Imaginative

84. If I was the Finance Minister/Prime Minister
85. When I woke up in the morning I saw?

Social

86. Terrorism in India
87. Religion should not be mixed with politics
88. Should Smoking be Banned Completely?
89. Are beauty contests degrading womanhood?
90. Censorship in Movies & Our Culture
91. With Media Publishing and Telecasting Trivia, Censorship is the Need of the Hour
92. Women Empowerment - A Cause for Increasing Divorce Rate in India
93. Make in India or Made in India
94. Comment on the merits and demerits of online education versus classroom learning
95. Words are Sharper than the two-edged sword
96. Bullet train or Better trains - What does India need?

HOW TO CONCLUDE A GD

There are quite a few people who confuse conclusion of Group Discussion with the opportunity to put forth new points or their own points.

Remember that conclusion of a GD refers to the conclusion of the DISCUSSION THAT HAS ALREADY HAPPENED and the panel wants you to let them know what one can conclude from the discussion. For example: Suppose a discussion was on the topic "Should A company go for buying a company B for lateral growth?" You are expected to tell Yes or No (as the result of the discussion) and what were the major drivers arrived in the discussion that led to the respective conclusion.

You may go through the following pointers to understand the nuances of concluding a GD and strengthen your case when asked to conclude GD or when you grab an opportunity to conclude a GD.

➢   Never ever come up and mention a new point which was never discussed in GD while it was on.

➢   You are expected to present a crisp and clear conclusion. So, ensure that you are not being verbose and beating around the bush while concluding

➢   If the topic for the discussion was an opinion based, then do remember that you put forth the opinion of the group while concluding and are not repeating your personal opinion when asked to conclude. For ex: If 'yes' to the subject was your opinion but the overall discussion and group was in favour of 'no' to the subject – then while concluding mention that 'no' and not 'yes'

➢   If you feel that the group could not arrive at the conclusion, then try to infer logically from the points that were discussed by all the participants, and state a conclusion based on your inference. Do not just say that the group did not arrive at a conclusion and stop. However, if you do want to mention that the group could not arrive at a conclusion- then just do not stop there, but follow it up by saying "However/Having said that, based on the points put forth by the group we can infer the conclusion as.....".

The aim of argument, or of discussion, should not be victory, but progress.

— Joseph Joubert

Active listening, clear thinking and responsible speaking make one the effective driver of a group discussion.

— Varun Saxena

PREFERRED BODY LANGUAGE AND DRESSING ETIQUETTE

Though GD Panel mainly looks for your ability to discuss the topic analytically, precisely and in a meaningful manner coupled with display of good aptitude, body language also plays a role in facilitating your attempt to impress the panel. Reason being dressing sense, body language and the soft skills also play a major role in reflecting an individual as an effective manager while engaging with other individuals.

Going through following pointers shall help you in getting a good hold over the body language and dressing etiquette.

➢ Look simple, natural and comfortable

➢ Be sober in your gesture and body posture

➢ Do not slouch in the chair

➢ Have a comfortable posture that does not hinder anyone to look at anyone else in group. Sit as a responsible person throughout the discussion

➢ Do not stretch your legs much or keep shaking them

➢ Avoid acts like biting nails, moving fingers, shaking heads showing approval or disapproval, keeping pen or pencil in the lips or under teeth while listening very carefully and so on

➢ When you speak or listen, always have soft eye contacts. It should not appear that you are gazing at any time. You should not look down or upwards while speaking or listening to anyone

➢ Do not get conscious about the panelists watching you

➢ If there is any inconvenience due to gesture or posture of any other member, either correct yourself (if possible) OR request the respective person to address your issue so that you may get convenient sitting in the group

➢ While using hand movement for emphasizing on your point, ensure that your hands remain in your zone. Do not end up moving your hands in front of people sitting beside you. However, it is suggested that one should try to avoid the hand movement to the possible extent

➢ Be assertive, not dominating while putting forth your points in the discussion

➢ Maintain a balanced tone in your discussion and analysis. Don't lose your cool if anyone says anything you that you disagree with

➢ Stay objective. Don't take the discussion personally

Keeping all above pointers in mind, you may give practicing them a shot. Be in front of a mirror and practice the posture. And while you are observing yourself in the mirror, you can identify your own mistakes and then take corrective measures to improve the identified gaps. You may also ask your friends to evaluate you against these parameters of body posture and let you know where you are going wrong.

Last but not the least, be yourself!!

Do not get into the nervous or the panic mode due to any consciousness about appearing in a Group Discussion. Stay calm, confident and composed.

Dress Code

The generally accepted Dress code includes Business formals.

Business formals consist of shirt, trousers, tie and well-polished shoes. Blazer is not essential; however wearing a blazer helps you in reflecting even more professional look. You should prefer to wear the blazer if wearing blazer doesn't make you uncomfortable and the weather permits as well. While deciding the colour of the blazer, you may go for black/blue blazer that is either plain or has very light stripes. Avoid bright colors or distinctly visible bright patterns.

PI : AN INTRODUCTION

Personal Interview (PI) is a tool for the B-schools to question a candidate about their application, their autobiographical sketch or any issues on their transcripts or entrance test scores. They are majorly conducted to evaluate the candidate more closely.

The Interview may be the most difficult part of any selection procedure or what some other may describe the easiest one. After clearing the written exam, it is the time to face an exam where you cannot revise your answers or leave them for later review i.e. the Interview.

You have to be well aware of your strengths and weaknesses. Also, be prepared of questions like:

- What you wish to do?
- What you feel about yourself?
- What are your hobbies? etc.

The experts say that the Personal Interview can be seen as an opportunity to 'sell' yourself i.e. to present your best image in front of the interviewer. It allows you the chance not only to put a face and personality to the name and credentials on your application, but also to express your academic, personal, and professional accomplishments, experiences, and intentions in the most excellent way.

Importance of PI

The interview panel wants to learn what you are like as a person and how well you respond and communicate. They want to understand your values, how you think and how well you handle yourself under pressure. In other words, we can say that it just means that you're being sized up as a person and a future professional in all your dimensions.

The focus of a B-school interview can range from specific questions about your job to broad discussions on life. One and all B-schools are committed to admitting students who are able to handle the rigors of business schools on an academic, personal, physical and psychological basis. Your interview is your opportunity to convince the admission committee that you are up to the challenge you are expected to face in the future.

Tips and Tricks to help you in an Interview

Here we have assembled some tips and tricks from the experts to help you perform your best in an interview:

1. **Believe in yourself:** The key of a successful interview is your belief and confidence. If you believe that you are the right person for the course and are confident, then it's likely that your interviewer will believe that too. Just be confident that you will do it.

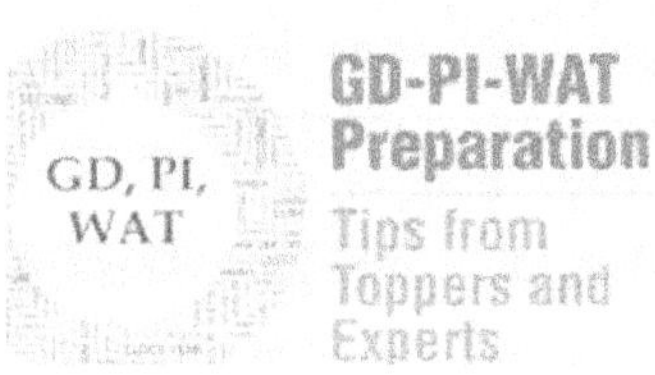

2. **The best way to improve your confidence is talk more:** Go to your friends and family and talk with them about your thoughts, it will help you in making your thoughts clear. Do a practise; you can practise by facing the mirror and talking. Talk about yourself, your dreams and your strengths. Focus on speaking fluently without stumbling or fidgeting.

3. **Have a good command over the language:** It's essential that whichever language you speak in, you should have a good command of the language. Brush up some basic grammar rules.

4. **Listen to the news in the language you will be using during the exam:** This will help you remember correct pronunciations and improve your flow of language.

5. **Remember that while it's good to talk eloquently you should not ramble on:** Speak clearly and concisely, so you express your thoughts in the best way possible.

6. **Know your resume inside out:** You should know everything about your resume as anything may be asked, your previous education, extra-curricular activities, awards, projects etc. You should be able to confidently speak about each point on your resume.

7. **Remember to maintain eye contact with the interviewer:** This is a very important point to keep in mind as an eye contact means you are confident and have a positive body language.

8. **Research the institutes before your interview:** Do so as it will make you informed and aware and prepare at least 2-3 questions that you will ask the interviewer about the course/institute. This shows your genuine interest in it.

9. **Practise positive body language:** Even if the interviewer hasn't actively studied body language, he/she will still pick up general signs. Remember not to fidget, stand still and relaxed and while sitting sit casually but in a firm position. Just be normal and relaxed; don't be in any pressure.

10. **Try planning your answers to a few questions:** It is expected that you should know some questions which will definitely come, such as:

    - Why are you interested in this course?
    - What are your strengths?
    - What are your weaknesses?
    - Why do you think you should be selected for this course?

    Do not write out any answers but jot down a few important points that you need to remember for the answers and based on the points speak impromptu.

11. **Before the interview, practise with a friend/relative** and record your answers. You will be able to listen/see where you fumble and where you need to improve.

    - On the day of the interview, make sure you are properly dressed in formal attire, are carrying copies of your resume (and relevant certificates as required) in proper case, are well rested and fresh.

    - Remember to reach the venue early and arrive for the interview on time.

12. **Focus on speaking positively and avoiding negativity:** This gives a more positive effect of your interview and will more likely get you a positive response.

13. **Be professional while you speak:** Avoid petty conversations, complaining, blaming or trying to seek pity.

14. **Be polite and calm:** Showing anger is definitely not a good idea.

15. **Include your technical knowledge wherever applicable:** This shows you are proactive and pay attention to studies.

There is no syllabus or notes on interview preparation. You won't be given answer sheets or time to revise. What you will have, however, is a clean slate to express yourself. Your power lies in your ability of expression: *how you talk, move, respond, dress, and carry yourself and how you answer questions.*

Be calm, cool and confident and you will definitely get good marks and hopefully in a year will be pursuing an MBA at a college of repute. All the best!!

THINKING PROCESS IN A PI

Personal Interview is generally the last among key components of the selection process at B-schools. While many B-schools have either replaced Group Discussion (GD) with Writing Ability Test (WAT) or some other have added another component like Group Exercise or Case Discussion in the final stages of their selection process, Personal Interview has remained intact as the key component of the selection process during MBA admissions.

It is a test where if you can feel at ease if you approach the Personal Interview as a conversation to be enjoyed, and not as a question-and-answer ordeal.

The questions may revolve around academic background, work experience, communication skills, personality traits and social behaviour etc. Prepare accordingly, keeping in mind these areas.

As we already said some of the questions may be about your hobbies or say your recent trip abroad, your adventures there and the hardships, and your choices in life. Some may be out of context; you don't have any clue about those. You simply need to be calm and professional in your approach, be confident in whatever you say. Don't mistake to think it as an informal talk as what the interviewer is doing is - watching you, evaluating you and analyzing every action of yours.

The panel may ask you anything about which they need some clarification while examining your application form or reading the essays submitted by you.

Listen carefully to the interviewer's questions and answer accordingly. Don't babble incessantly about a related topic.

Besides normal etiquettes like formal dressing, punctuality etc., your overall performance during the interview may make or break your chance into your dream B-school.

On one end PI provides you an opportunity to showcase yourself independent of other factors like chaos in GD, unawareness about topic in GD or WAT; on the other end it provides you an opportunity to know more about the B-School by asking relevant questions to the panel, including but not limited to MBA program being offered, campus life etc. It can even help you in deciding if the respective B-School is the correct destination for you or not.

Clarity of Vision

It is of high importance for a manager to be clear in his vision, goals and the strategic path needed to achieve the same.

Because of this, panel lays stress on finding out the clarity in the respective candidates with regard to the goal, what they want to achieve out of an MBA degree and how they see it as a best fit for their career goals.

Subject Knowledge

A successful manager is expected to have acumen to discuss different areas of business with anyone at any given time; be it economy, technology, ethics, social aspects, competition, strategy, vision etc. To be able to attain a level where he/she can reach the above state, it is important for the individual to cope up with the 2 year grind of a B-School when it comes to academics as well as extra-curricular. Also, it is required that the individual makes the best use of learning opportunities provided by the B-School and implements the learnings successfully.

To check the above, B-Schools ask questions on past academics, achievements and extra-curricular. They want to know how much you remember the things learnt in past academics to be assured on how much you will retain as learning after 2 years of B-School.

The strategy to score high in this parameter is to be thorough with few of your academic subjects at least and have in-depth subject knowledge of every point mentioned by you in the application form. For example: If you mentioned painting as a hobby in the application form, then be thorough on nuances of painting or if you mentioned William Words-worth as your favorites poet, then do have good knowledge about his writings and him as the person during his career.

Analytical Skills

Not only subject knowledge is what is important, but the ability to analyse the information in hand and arrive at key decisions is equally important.

Communication Skills and Attitude

A face to face interview helps in judging the candidate by engaging in talks with him/her, watching the body language, assessing the comfort level of the candidate when put under stress, seeing how is he/she able to convince the panel with their logic and determining the confidence through the frequency and assertiveness in eye contacts.

WHAT TO EXPECT IN A PI

A personal interview is aimed at knowing a candidate more intimately - assessing the clarity of thinking process, future goals and the 'fit' with the B-school.

The interviewing process can be scary if you don't know what to expect, but will be much easier if you know the basic nuances of the various skills you need to focus upon. Usually, all interviews fit a general pattern.

Though each interview will differ, yet all will share three common characteristics: *the beginning, middle and the conclusion.*

A typical interview will last almost **30 minutes,** although some may be longer. A typical structure is as follows:

- **Five minutes-** a small talk in which you introduce yourself
- **Fifteen minutes-** a mutual discussion of your background and credentials as they will be the major criteria for your selection
- **Five minutes-** the interviewer asks you for any questions from your side
- **Five minutes-** conclusion of the interview

What goes on in the mind of the Interviewer? How? When? What?

The interviewer is there to analyze you in every way, whether they ask something or not, they are judging you by your body language and gestures. We have tried to make you acquainted with the process and understand the mindset of the interviewer. Read the points and the underlying meaning of it.

- **It starts even before you say Hello!**

The typical interview starts before you even get into the inner sanctum. The recruiter begins to evaluate you the minute you are identified. You are expected to shake the recruiter's hand upon being introduced. Don't be afraid to extend your hand first. This shows assertiveness.

- **How's your small talk vocabulary?**

Many recruiters will begin the interview with some small talk. Topics may range from the weather to sports and will rarely focus on anything that brings out your skills. Nonetheless, you are still being evaluated.

- **Goal Clarity- The main Interview**

Why do you want to do an MBA? How does it fit into your career goals? What do you wish to do after your MBA? These are some hard questions that you will have to answer almost invariably in all Interviews. These questions search the 'inner motivations' of a candidate, and there are no 'right answers'. The only way to answer these questions is to introspect:

- What excites and motivates you?
- What makes you perform your best?
- What would you really like to do in your life? and
- How do you genuinely see an MBA helping in the growth of the country and yourself?

Tough questions, but answering them honestly is critical for your success.

- **The Close counts too**

The interview isn't over until you walk out of the door. The conclusion of the interview usually lasts five minutes and is very important. During this time the recruiter is assessing your overall performance.

It is important to remain enthusiastic and courteous. Often the conclusion of the interview is indicated when the interviewer stands up. However, if you feel the interview has reached its conclusion, feel free to stand up first.

- **Expect the Unexpected**

During the interview, you may be asked some unusual questions. Don't be too surprised. Many times questions are asked simply to see how you react.

For example, surprise questions could range from, "Tell me a joke" to "What time period would you like to have lived in?" These are not the kind of questions for which you can prepare in advance. Your reaction time and the response you give will be evaluated by the interviewer.

In a nutshell, some key tips are:

- Be well prepared for the conservative questions,
- Reflect confidence and stay poised,
- Very importantly, be totally honest with yourself and the interviewers, and
- Try to drive them towards your strengths.

What is expected?

You should be prepared that you may get different varieties of questions one by one by the panel members. A calm and cool attitude is expected from the interviewee.

Many a time they will interrupt in between, will divert your attention you are required to be focused and not panic. Adapt your mind to be at ease in any such situation.

They expect you to be professional in your approach and give direct and precise answers. Train your mind to be in the limitation.

Remember that you are being judged on a number of criteria. A thing of less importance to you might hold a strong position in the interviewer's mind. So, don't take things lightly.

The right preparation does not constitute only of the subject knowledge and a professional outlook but an overall set of skills and go-getter attitude. These are not the things one is born with but what can be acquired with perseverance and patience. Nourish these and rule the world.

DRESSING, ETTIQUETES AND PRESENTATION

To say precisely, 'always dress well, but keep it simple'. Dressing up for a formal ocassion is very much different from daily dressing. And that too for an interview where you are evaluated every minute needs more precaution. As it is said: The approach toward a PI should be of a very formal and conventional setup. Few of the basic tips are:

DRESS HOW YOU WANT TO BE ADDRESSED.

- ➢ Remember PIs are not based on looks, clothes or walk, they are not looking for clothes horse or alike but you should be very careful about your personality and how you present yourself.
- ➢ The clothes should be clean, ironed and matching or of proper contrast.
- ➢ Don't wear crumpled or ill-fitting clothes.
- ➢ Try to wear a solid colour, only a solid colour shirt.
- ➢ Do not wear a tie with a striped or check shirts. Strictly avoid anything that catches attention easily. Tie pin can be used.
- ➢ Wear formal shoes and sandals; better to wear either black or brown shoes according to your dress. They should be polished and it is advised to select a neat single colour socks.
- ➢ Your nails and hairs should be properly cut and groomed.
- ➢ It is advised not to keep beard or moustache a day before or few days before the final interview. Just trim them before facing the panel.

"Dont Dress To Impress Just Be The Best Unlike The Rest"

- ➢ Keep both your shirt's and trouser's pockets empty.
- ➢ Carry a neat and clean handerchief, a white coloured one should be preffered, but avoid bi-colour or flashy ones.

➢ There is no need to specify that any form of tobbaco or mouth freshner needs to be avoided, the list also includes toffes; your mouth should be clean and empty else your pronounciation and diction will get affected.

➢ Avoid being casual and clumsy in your attitude.

➢ Keep all your important papers, documents and purse in a bag. You should look organized and prepared.

➢ Drink a little water before you enter the interview room as it will keep your voice clear and lips from drying.

➢ Use a little cream on lips and face so that they do not look dry or perched.

In the Interviews:

➢ Always ask for the permission before entering the room.

➢ Do not sit until you are told to do so.

➢ Walk smartly and confidently, try to maintain a normal walk, don't feel uncomfortable.

➢ Make eye contact and smile while wishing the panel.

➢ Do not avoid eye contact, else it will make you appear less confident and consious.

➢ Look at each panelist confidently, with your head straight upright.

➢ While answering do not look upwards or downwards or scratch your chin or don't display any such negative mannerism.

➢ Do not be impolite or rude, even if you feel offended by any of the panelist breaking your argument or aking the same thing several times.

➢ Do not show your irritation or say 'I told you so', as they might not be convinced by your answer.

➢ Such things may be intentional, as they are testing your patience and concepts.

➢ They may be willing to see how you react in adverse conditions.

➢ Be patient and polite and try not to say that 'I have answered it, or my answers remains the same, or let me try to answer this differently'

➢ Do not make any sweeping and generalized statements and avoid taking sides.

- ➤ Don't be stern and too rigid in putting your views on any political matters.

- ➤ Be very specific and clear in your topics, do not talk about things half-heartedly and with half-baked knowledge.

- ➤ If you quote someone as your hero or idol, be sure you know a lot about them - everything is possible. Go through their biography, latest news, business decisions all about them. Keep yourself updated, always.

- ➤ If you are asked to comment on any problem or issue, then first try to define the problem.

- ➤ Avoid making remarks on any particular religion, sect or community.

- ➤ Be logical, do not be syrupy rather be clear, distinct and intelligent. But do not be argumentative.

- ➤ Always look for close ended questions as open ended questions lead to more questions and also expose your underpreparedness.

- ➤ Brush up your graduation subjects well, try to revise .

Do say clearly if you don't remember a thing, do not give your own definitions or create a new one.

Truth has its own beauty, try to be truthful and clear.

SOME FREQUENTLY ASKED QUESTIONS

Keeping in mind the tips from the toppers and preparing few common questions is going to help a great deal.

Justify your decision to pursue the MBA program?

Don't tell the panel that you are looking for a "challenging job in a good firm with lots of money, status and glamour". Instead, you must convey to the interview panel that you have made a rational and informed decision about your career choice and your intended course is of higher study. There are broadly four areas which your answer could touch upon:

- ➤ **Career Objectives:** You could talk about your career objectives and how the two-year MBA program will help you achieve them.

- ➤ **Value Addition:** Value addition will essentially be in two forms: knowledge and skills.

- ➤ **Background:** This is where you connect your past to your future. If you are an engineer, try and say that the MBA course and your engineering degree will help you do your job better in the company that you will join. You should be able to convincingly justify how your engineering qualification will help.

- ➢ **Opportunities and Rewards:** You could also at this stage mention the opportunities that are opening up in organizations for management graduates. At this stage mentioning superior monetary rewards for management graduates may not be a bad idea.

Why do you think you would enjoy your chosen area of study (e.g. marketing)?

Marketing is key to the success of any organization and the function has always appealed to me, because it requires a combination of creativity, strategic and analytic ability - all qualities that I feel I possess. Through discussions with some of my seniors, I have a pretty good idea of what it's like to work toward taking up a marketing job, and I know I will enjoy the work.

How do you spend your spare time?

I have a good collection of books of different genre and enjoy reading. In addition, I love driving during late evenings or on rainy weekend afternoons. Also, for the last two years I've been volunteering at the local children's hospital on Saturday mornings.

POINTERS FOR 5 MOST FREQUENTLY ASKED QUESTIONS

1. Why MBA?

   This is a make or break question in quite a few colleges, so candidates need to be very thorough with the question to this answer. Some of the major areas that a candidate should cover in this question are:

   - Identify future goals and how MBA becomes a bridge between those goals and what you have been doing till now

   - Freshers should try to include in this why they are going as a fresher for MBA and how do they find in sync with their career goals

   - Work experience candidates should put MBA as a connector between what they have done/learnt during the job and how MBA facilitates them in the dream ahead

   - Try to customize your answer as per your past and future, rather than giving a generic answer like 'to change career path', 'for faster promotion' etc. You may mention these points but do not just blatantly mention, try to put forth the relevance and link with what you want to do in future as well

- Last but not the least, despite placements and high pay packages being the major reason of you going for MBA, do not mention it at forefront. You may call it as a bye-product which is not the major reason and you are excited about MBA as a career and an opportunity to follow your passion. And money would follow as you succeed while enjoying your job.

2. What are your long term goals?

This is another one of the key answers that a candidate needs to prepare well. One needs to put forth to the panel that you are very clear with your vision and know what you want to achieve.

Remember that long term career goals tell about your destination in life, in terms of career, in terms of where you see yourself may be 15-20 years down the line.

Some of the points/questions that you may ask yourself while writing the answer to this question are:

- What do I enjoy doing?
- What am I good at?
- What characteristics I would like the most in the job?
- What kind of job suits my skill set the most?
- What kind of work life balance I want to have in long run?
- Where do I see myself 15-20 years down the line?

3. What are your short term goals?

Before we begin with the pointers on writing the answer to this question, remember that you have written your long term goals answers first and then move to this answer.

Short term goals need to be the stepping stones to achieve the long term goals. So, your answer to this question has to be prepared in a way that it is in complete sync with your long term goals (may be this question was preceded or can be succeeded by question on long term goals).

Some of the points/questions that you may ask yourself while writing the answer to this question are:

- What is my long term career goal?
- How can I break the path to achieve long term goal into small stepping stones?

- What can I do to facilitate a smooth achievement of these stepping stones?

- What are the timelines I need to set to achieve my short term goals?

- Am I able to use my analytical skills to achieve these goals?

4.   Why X B-School?

It has been observed that most of the people try to just talk about college and its placements when asked this college.

However, there are certain points which one needs to keep in mind while responding to this question because as per the evaluation of panel, this question is a make or a break in quite a few reputed colleges. Including following points in the answer shall be helpful to the candidates:

- How the respective B-School would help in achieving short term and long term goals? Talk about how industry interaction, alumni base and intra-college activities would facilitate your path to achieve goals?

- Talk about college history, how it has been a dream and how you are assured of it helping you out in carving out a successful career for you post MBA.

- You may even talk about your friends/people in your professional or social network and let the panel know about the positive image of college which you have and the reasons you trust the brand of the respective college.

5.   What are your strengths and weaknesses?

Identifying one's strengths and weaknesses is very important not from an individual's perspective but knowing that you know to identify them is important from the institution's perspective where you are aspiring to get an admit to.

Quite a few times I have seen that people get into dilemma on what to mention in strengths and weaknesses. The major reason is that people don't know how to identify the same.

To help you out in solving this dilemma, we list down a set of questions below which you may ask yourself and arrive at your strengths and weaknesses.

For Strengths

- What do most people appreciate you about?
- What is the skill set at which you are very comfortable in working with?
- What motivates you to give your best?
- What is your passion and you love doing?

For Weaknesses

- What do most people criticize you about?
- What are the areas of improvement you find in your personality and skill set?

Some General Pointers

- Do not try to bluff the panel when asked about strengths and weaknesses. The panel is experienced enough to come to know the same.
- Always couple the mentioned strengths with real life examples to elaborate why do you think them to be your strength.
- While talking about strengths, be very confident and do not take time to reflect to the panel that you are trying to build the strengths on the spot, while you actually don't know them.
- Always be ready for a cross question on how are you working to improve your weaknesses. Any example of the real life practice already put in place by you for the same shall be very helpful.

Questions are never indiscreet. Answers sometimes are.

— Oscar Wilde

OTHER MANAGEMENT EXAMS APART FROM CAT

Any management aspirant in India would be aware of CAT which is undoubtedly the most sought after entrance exam for MBA entrance in India. However, there are several other exams besides CAT that a student can and must write. We collectively call them as

➤ OMETs (Other Management Entrance Tests): The OMETs would include XAT, SNAP, CMAT, MAT etc.

➤ Institute specific exams which include NMAT, TISSNET, IRMA, and IIFT etc.

Many top B-schools require you to write their own exams. The key reasons why a candidate should write other exams besides CAT are as follows:

➤ It helps to diversify your risks.

➤ It is an opportunity to capitalize on your strengths.

➤ Some exams give you some extra time to prepare.

Awareness and adequate preparation for these exams is essential, as these tests have patterns which are different from CAT. Let us look at the major Other management Entrance Tests (OMETs) and some exams conducted by Individual Institutes.

➤ **Other management Entrance Tests (OMETs)**

✓ **Xavier Aptitude Test (XAT)**

XAT is the second most popular management entrance examination after CAT. XAT is conducted by XLRI, Jamshedpur on behalf of Xavier Association of Management Institutes. Apart from XLRI, which is among the top-5 B-schools in India according to latest rankings by various independent agencies, XAT scores are used by more than 100 institutes across India.

✓ **Common Management Admissions Test (CMAT)**

CMAT is an online computer-based test conducted by the All

India Council for Technical Education (AICTE), India. From its launch in 2011 as a one-stop test for admission into all the AICTE approved B-schools in the country, CMAT has come a long way. The exam is proposed to be conducted twice a year.

Till 2015, CMAT was held twice in a year but in 2016 the practice was abolished as AICTE decided to hold the exam once a year on the third Sunday of January. An additional CMAT was conducted twice few years back so as to provide a chance to candidates who missed out on applying earlier.

✓ Management Aptitude Test (MAT)

MAT is conducted by All India Management Association four times a year – February, May, September, and December in both the formats- Paper Based Test (PBT) or Computer Based Test (CBT) or Both the Tests i.e. PBT & CBT. Even though the paper has a section on General Awareness, the score in this section is rarely used by any B-school for short listing candidates for the GD-PI process.

✓ Symbiosis National Aptitude Test (SNAP)

SNAP is an aptitude test conducted by the Symbiosis society as a first entry requirement for all the B schools under Symbiosis International University which has 12 B schools under its umbrella, 3 General management and the others - sectoral or specialized MBAs. The list of institutes which come under its domain includes SIBM Pune, SCMHRD Pune, SIBM Bangalore, SIIB Pune etc. The exam is considered a must for MBA aspirants, thanks to this eclectic mix of colleges using its scorecard as a part of their selection processes.

➢ Exams conducted by Individual Institutes

A lot of institutes hold their individual entrance exams to shortlist candidates as per their requirements. Few of them are:

- ✓ **IIFT** entrance test for (Indian Institute of Foreign Trade with its branches in) New Delhi and Kolkata.
- ✓ **TISSNET** for Tata Institute of Social Sciences, Mumbai offering specialization in a range of areas from HRM & IR to Social Entrepreneurship to Women empowerment etc. Like MAT, TISSNET is also conducted in both paper-pencil and online format. The exam is usually conducted in the month of January.
- ✓ **NMAT** for Narsee Monjee Institute of Management Studies, Mumbai, Hyderabad and Bangalore offering General MBA,

Banking, Capital Markets and HRM. It is conducted in online format and that students can take maximum of three attempts and the best of the three is taken as their final performance while short-listing for GDPI.

- ✓ **MICAT** for Mudra Institute of Communications, Ahmedabad.
- ✓ **IBSAT** for ICFAI Business School, Hyderabad and several other locations in the country.

These are some of the major exams conducted for admission into management schools. However, why is it that everyone is giving CAT the status not achieved by any of these?.

What makes CAT special is the quality of opportunities it opens for you and therefore the nature of competition. The exam is quite rightly seen by many as the mother of all management entrance exams. However, this also means that your preparation for CAT will prepare you for a good part of a lot of other exams as well. Your preparation for CAT will adequately prepare you for any of these exams as well. But still a lot of other things need to be focused upon, according to the syllabus provided by them. For example in MAT, there is also a section on Indian and Global environment.

Also, the sound of IIM does take an entirely different meaning for an MBA aspirant than any other college. It always has had an edge over other B-schools for several reasons like its faculty, campus, placements and a brand value that is incomparable. This makes the aspirants yearn for a place in these premier institutes that can only be made possible by sitting for CAT. Also, it covers IITs, IISc, NITs, FMS and other top colleges.

"MBA is not always just finance. It teach management principles, which are useful to manage every part of your life'.   -Says Neha Manglik, CAT Topper

HOW TO CHOOSE THE BEST B-SCHOOL FOR ONESELF?

With the B-school application season kicking in, it is important for the students to decide on the number of B-schools that they would like to apply to, the exams they would like to write etc.

Students need to look at the following criteria carefully and then decide on which B-Schools to apply to.

> **Placement:** A large number of management institutes boast of a 100% placement record for their students. With management institutes mushrooming all over the country these claims should not be taken at face value, and should be scrutinised more closely.

> **Location of the B-School:** B-schools located in larger cities, with a better industry interface would score over the small-city counterparts as they would tend to have better opportunities for internships, better quality part-time faculty members and also a little edge in final placements.

> **Brand Name:** You do your MBA only once and the brand name of the B-school you went to will stay with you for the rest of your career.

> **Return on Investment:** Look very closely at the fee you will need to pay. With the B-school expenses for the two years of MBA reaching as much as 15 lakhs, it is important for you to consider how much money you will need to pay and what kind of salary you will get.

Also certain attributes have been suggested to help one choose the best b-school for oneself, which includes the following :

> *Quality of Student Life*
> *Prestige of the MBA School*
> *MBA Starting Salary*
> *Teaching Methodology (Case vs. Quantitative)*
> *Reputation of Quality of Teaching*
> *Faculty Orientation (Research vs. Teaching)*
> *Net Cost (Tuition Less Financial Aid)*
> *Size of Program (Number of Students)*
> *Proximity to Home.*

WHAT ARE TOP B-SCHOOLS LOOKING FOR EXCEPT THE CAT SCORE?

If one looks at the profiles of the CAT aspirants through the years, it reveals an interesting trend. While candidates from the engineering discipline continue to dominate, their percentage has declined to some extent, paving the way for more candidates from agriculture and architecture backgrounds.

Many other factors affect a candidate's selection, which includes:

It is being felt gradually that the CAT score is not the only indicator of managerial potential. There are many other significant aspects of managerial aptitude that are not adequately captured by CAT.

(1) Work Experience

A number of applicants have two to three years' working experience. This reflects a trend that more working professionals are gradually seeking management degrees for career growth and development. It is needless to say that there is a need for a wider talent pool across disciplines and industry requires the best minds.

(2) Innovation Diverse Knowledge

Today, there is an increasing dependence on innovation and a requirement for managers with a diverse knowledge-base.

In many cases, candidates with a low CAT score have shown exceptional managerial potential during personal interviews. There is also a poor connection between the CAT score and academic performance of a student in the PGDM programme. The recruiters hardly look at the CAT score while recruiting for their organisations. Although a good CAT score ensures entry into top-line business schools and IIMs, it does not necessarily measure the academic worth of students.

> Top-line B Schools often give weightage to other skill-sets, like

> analytical reasoning,

> decision-making skills,

> problem-solving attitude,

> creativity, communications and

> other positive attributes.

Aspects such as leadership abilities, communication skills, creativity and responsiveness to the environment are taken into account in the selection process. As a result, candidates who are strong in these abilities have a better chance to get selected.

Today, attempts are also made to keep the selection process more comprehensive and balanced rather than giving too much of weightage to any particular criterion like the CAT score. The weightage is also distributed between academic performance, work experience, communication skills and other personal attributes.

MBA IN INDIA VS. MBA ABROAD

MBA has been in trend since past many years and till date is the favourite option of graduates from all streams. Pursuing MBA from India or abroad is a dilemma which many students face.

There are a lot of factors that need your attention while deciding the place and the college from where you want to do your MBA.

1. Do you have any work experience?
2. What is the amount of money you are willing to spend on an MBA?
3. How fast do you need an ROI?
4. Are you doing an MBA only to gain some knowledge?
5. Do you have any specific colleges or countries in mind?
6. If you do not get into the college that you want, what will you do next?
7. Are you afraid of giving entrance test?
8. Have you given any mock test for any of the following CAT, GMAT, GRE?

Answer these 8 questions and you may somewhat have an idea of where you want to do an MBA from India or some other country. After that you have to decide which institute? and which course to choose?

Both of these options have their own advantages and disadvantages; let's make a comparative analysis below:

MBA IN INDIA

Management education in India is booming. There are over 1,250 approved business schools, 1,25,000 full-time and 1,00,000 distance MBA students and 1,30,000 MBA aspirants taking the Common Admission Test every year. The end-users the recruiters seem to be facing a constant supply crunch, and are always on the lookout for the talent graduating from the top B-schools. Thus, an MBA in India is considered a valuable commodity that insures a quick return on investment.

- In India, the majority of students pursue it directly after graduation. Won't matter a lot if you don't have experience (Although experience is always beneficial). But a work experience helps you take matured decisions.
- An MBA abroad falls only in the domain of people with quite well off, whereas in India, you have some economical options as well such as FMS Delhi which offer quality education at a low cost. MBA in India from tier I colleges like the IIMs would cost you around ₹ 10-15 lakhs, the same from tier I colleges abroad would fall in the price bracket of ₹ 30- 50 lakhs.
- You get good opportunities after an MBA in India and a possibility of abroad opportunities too.

MBA FROM ABROAD

- Studying abroad is a great learning experience- you get to discover a new culture and increase your knowledge. You may meet people from different corners of the world, will get to know multiple languages and cultures. Apart from the management course, you can learn a lot of other things also.
- An MBA abroad will cost you more than an MBA in India but once you complete your course you will get better returns. Many people suggest about taking a loan, doing the course and within a few years, being able to repay and also being in a position to have a decent bank balance. Just try and research the cost revenue analysis before thinking of joining any such.
- You will find great opportunities abroad and your resume will be valued more back home also. You will get much better packages and even extra emoluments facilities after doing one.

"It's about working hard and let the institute be your driving force. Irrespective of from where you do MBA, you'll have to grill yourself for a job. Thinking that foreign MBA would make things easier is a myth.

- Samuel John, MBA in Marketing and Finance,
SCMS Cochin

It entirely depends upon your personal goals to arrive at a decision as both the options have their own pros and cons. It is suggested that you first prioritize your objectives and what you want to achieve and then discuss it with your family and mentors. This will help you to arrive at a decision which will be in alignment with everything and you will end up choosing the option which is best for you.

Some other experts suggest that both the scenarios are ideal but it depends on the University and the Institute you are doing your MBA from. If you are doing your MBA from a Foreign University then there are fewer chances of getting duped because Foreign Universities are affiliated by their respective authoritative bodies.

In India, there are few colleges which are not certified by AICTE/UGC. If you are applying for such colleges you won't get an educational loan from the bank and if you somehow get a degree from these colleges, then your degree won't be worthy. If you want to do your MBA from India, make sure that you are doing it from a reputed Institute or University.

Some foreign universities have created programs in which you start earning from day one. They have an intense focus on evolving nature of the global business and to enhance the professional skills of the students, demanded by the 21st century corporate world.

What Other Aspirants Say

Let's read few testimonials about the benefits of doing an MBA from abroad.

After gaining work experience of around two years, Neha Arya wanted to groom her managerial skills for which she decided to do MBA. She wanted to be taught in a more practical way with a case study approach.

"The options that fit my expectations were available only abroad. In India, we are more traditional and the course content we have has been the same since ages. Barring a few institutes, the lecture method here is focused on one way communication wherein students are forced to think in a particular way." - Neha Arya

If you aim to settle abroad then you must go ahead for an MBA degree from a foreign school. It just proves to be an added advantage.

Your degree might be the gate pass for your journey but it is your skills that prove to be the flight that takes you to the destination. Both Indian universities and universities abroad offer good placements these days.

Mansie Dewan, an MBA consulting expert says, "I know many MBA graduates from India who want to do another MBA from abroad to learn from a diverse peer group."

Indian universities are also placing students in countries other than India. There are companies that might give importance to a degree from a particular country but then the skills of the person are what can take them through.

It is a myth that it is just your university that shapes up your career. Yes, placements might help you get placed but it is your 'attitude and the skills' that help you sustain in the company.

The job market for MBA graduates is always hungry for good individuals; all you need to do is brush up your expertise for the job market.

Well, these are the factors that usually lay the foundation of whether you get an MBA degree from India or an MBA degree abroad. Now, it is up to you to prioritize these things and then whatever suits you, should be your pick.

PROSPECTS ABROAD

A Global MBA in which you study in a foreign country might be costlier but worth it for the exposure that it gives you. MBA studies abroad gives you an edge over others as they help you gain the global business perspective and international experience that is going to make you an invaluable asset to your future employers.

An MBA abroad provides you a lot of global network and practical outlook. Your overall personality and the approach towards life changes a lot with the resourcefulness it provides. In fact, you could expect not only technical skills (that are easier to gain in junior roles), but also managerial skills like team leading, planning and coordination.

The top business schools abroad give a new dimension to your career path. Such an MBA bestows upon you the opportunity of exploring a new country. Such a crucial decision cannot be taken on the basis of a few digits alone.

You need to delve into a lot of things to fit in; they include:

- ➢ Connect your aspirations to the offerings of the country

- ➢ Study the types of MBA offered as they usually have a global coverage of topics in their syllabus

- ➢ Have a clear idea of your investment - scholarships, types of funding, insurance, etc.

> Evaluate the long term prospects- have the vision of settling in that place while selecting your B-school. Some of them have only local or country specific fame.

Several countries have remarkable universities that offer a wide array of courses to choose from. A number of them need you to sit for GMAT as they accept only that score and not CAT. However, some of them even have their own entrance tests.

Global MBA is about leadership and decision making and these skills are imparted as a part of the curriculum. In addition to a good GMAT score, the screening process to crack an MBA itself is very rigorous in comparison to Indian universities.

- Dr Chavi Bhargava, Director, Faculty of Management Studies,
Manav Rachna International University

Internationalization is done in order to enhance the quality of research, education and international exposure for each student. Today's managers require being equipped with skills to perform effectively across different markets; managerial education is going through a pattern shift both in terms of approach and ideology across the world.

There are a growing number of countries vying for a place at the top of the table in terms of MBAs. In Europe, you can find excellent courses at

universities in Spain, Germany and Switzerland. Further afield, the best business schools in Canada and Australia are strong contenders for your attention.

A number of institutes abroad have study and work facilities. This is an attractive option for lots of candidates since settling in a far off place requires a lot of money. Most of them demand some work experience too, so the people who are in the habit of earning and spending on their own find this option a lucrative one.

"Foreign institutes have stringent rules and regulations which are unheard of in India. They are very strict when it comes to plagiarism issues. There is no human intervention but software to catch plagiarism and the guilty students are immediately failed from the examination and made to take the exam again."

- Neha, MBA in International Business, Birmingham City University,
UK

MEET THE TOPPERS

SUCCESS STORIES

CAT is a national level management aptitude test. Lakhs of aspirants fill the form for around 4300 seats; this statistics in itself portrays the toughness of the competition. CAT toppers get into the top institutes of repute only with firm determination and their consistent efforts.

A total of 20 candidates have scored an overall 100 percentile in CAT 2017. While in CAT 2016 all the top 20 candidates were male and engineers, this year the top 20 list contains two female candidates and three non-engineers.

Who doesn't enjoy reading success stories, and what if they also guide and motivate you? Read and enhance your knowledge to excel.

TOPPER NO. 1: FIRST RANK HOLDER SAI PRANEETH REDDY

Ever since the results of the Common Admission Test (CAT) 2017 had been declared, Sai Praneeth Reddy hailing from Andhra Pradesh became a hero, having secured the first rank and a 100 percentile in the exam. Sai Praneeth Reddy, a student of the Indian Institute of Technology, Madras (IITM) is from Andhra Pradesh's Anantapur village.

To understand the strategy required for the preparation of such a level of exam, it is advisable to go through his schedule and planning and get benefitted.

Here are Some Excerpts from the Interviews.

What was your schedule? On which segment did you focus more?

I used to write mock tests from 9 am to 12 noon without fail and this was proved very crucial in cracking the test. I was very good with quantitative and DILR sections. I concentrated more on English in the last one month. These are the basic things I followed during preparation and it did pay well.

How is the feeling of being the topper and which is your dream B school?

I am feeling very excited that I have achieved 100 percentile, I hope to perform well in the upcoming rounds of Group Discussion (GD) and Personal Interview (PI) with the same spirit and get into IIM-A.

Being from a technical background, an IITian, why do you want to do a management course?

I realized that I can excel in the technical field but there are areas where you have to get your work done by others. For which you need to have team management skills and there is no other better place to learn those skills than IIM in India.

Plans for the future all set? What next?

I won't say I'll be going to IIM right now, I also have a job offer in hand, so I haven't decided yet what to do first but both the options are opened for me.

A few words for the aspirants

Learning from mistakes is the main thing that will help you get better in life. Don't miss the mock tests. For English, start reading novels and articles, it helps a lot. For quantitative ability section, be strong with basics.

Topper No. 2: A 99.98 Percentiler Family Boy Shikhar

SHIKHAR SACHDEVA

Shikhar Sachdeva has topped CAT 2017 with 99.98 percentile, even more than his expectation of around 99.8 percentile. Shikhar credits his success in the country's most competitive management entrance exam to his family.

What were your overall and sectional percentiles in CAT 2017?

My overall percentile is 99.98 (222.81). My sectional percentiles are 98.15 (71.07) in VARC, 99.76 (53.68) in LRDI and 100 (98.09) in QA.

Were you sure that you'll be able to score 99.99 percentile?

Not at all. I mean there were two sides to me all through the waiting period. One side was realistic, wherein I was expecting not more than 99.8. And there was another side that was wishing for an amazing result, and that side of me was constantly praying for 99.98. That exact figure. And it's an amazing coincidence that I got just that.

How was your exam day?

As far as the actual exam goes, I'd given a lot of mocks, so I wasn't really worried about any eventuality. Quant was my forte, so I knew that even if I had mediocre scores in other sections I could've made up in quant. So yes, a tough LRDI definitely didn't faze me as much as other people.

What according to you were the toughest and easiest sections?

I felt the toughest section was VARC. It seemed easy at first glance but definitely had a lot of tricks up its sleeves. This prompted a lot of people to answer more questions than were necessary, and hence they accumulated negative scores. LRDI may have had tougher questions on the whole, but everyone expected that, and so it wasn't much of a surprise. QA was the easiest section, easy questions using simple concepts. Nothing too tricky at all.

How did you tackle your strong and weak areas?

I think practice is the key. Coaching will go only so far. After that, it all comes down to your own motivation. What I did was work on my strong areas early on during my preparation. Later on, I focused my attention solely on my weak zone (LRDI) and developed my own unique strategies that helped me counter it, one of which was to go through all the sets, before I attempted even one question. This helped me prioritize on which question I felt comfortable, and which I wanted to leave.

What was your time management strategy during the test?

There isn't enough time to do all 100 questions. So, one has to prioritize. Focus on doing questions from your strong areas at first and later get on to your weak areas. Don't waste time on a question that you feel you're not getting ahead with.

Did you take coaching? How helpful was it? Is it possible to succeed through self study?

I took coaching. I was part of the classroom course at one of the most renowned institutes. And personally, I've come to feel that classroom coaching is not necessary for CAT. There are amazing web courses available, at a fraction of the price of the classroom courses. The best strategy for an aspirant would be to take 2 mock series from renowned institutes, 1 booklet series, and then make use of any one web course.

What is your family's contribution in your success?

They were always there for me. They've supported me in all of my endeavours. One of the incidents comes to my mind. I was always a night owl. So during my CAT preparation, I often gave my mocks late at night. So, often if I was up till 4 or 5 in the morning, and felt hungry, I could just knock on my parent's door, and my mom would cook something for me. Not a lot of parents are as supportive as they are.

Whom do you want to dedicate your success to?

The people around me. My family, with all their support. My friends, with all the motivation they gave me to keep pushing forward. And my mentors, who taught me everything I know.

Tell us something about your hobbies and inspirations.

My hobbies are playing cricket, watching and collecting movies, and reading. As far as heroes go, as odd as it sounds, I've always been inspired by Adolf Hitler, not the genocidal psychopath but the leader.

IIMs released CAT question paper and answer key for the first time. Did you find any wrong questions/answers?

Well there were a few, especially in VARC. But then at the end of the day, VARC is something that is very subjective and open to interpretation. I'm satisfied with the way the entire process was carried out by the organizing authorities.

Which B-School do you wish to join?

Among the Indian B-Schools, I'd love to be a student at IIM Ahmedabad if given a chance. As one of my seniors said, "IIM A is not a college, it's a feeling". I'd love to be a part of that feeling.

Please give a few words of advice to aspirants who are preparing for entrance exams?

Don't take the undue pressure. Enjoy your preparation, and don't give up on your dreams, ever. Nothing is bigger than your dreams.

Topper No. 3: A Risk Taker 100 Percentiler

MADHUR GUPTA

An aspiring entrepreneur, Madhur left his job as Operations Manager at Amazon in August 2017 to focus on CAT. His mantra for cracking the CAT was **cracking all kinds of mock tests**. Madhur attempted more than 70 mock tests to ensure there is no loose end left to tie by the time CAT arrived.

He has scored **100 percentile** and has already been selected by **IIM Ahmedabad, IIM Bangalore and IIM Calcutta** for the interview round.

He loves to read entrepreneurial books and watches TV series 'Friends' to unwind. He is a Bal Bharati Public School, Pitampura alumnus and a Mechanical Engineering graduate from Delhi Technological University, Delhi.

During DTU days, he was the team leader of the formula Student team of DTU (known as Team Defianz Racing which is a 40 member's team). The team designs and fabricates a fully functional, single-seater formula race car every year and participates in world-wide Formula Student competitions organized by Institute of Mechanical Engineers (ImechE). He shared his CAT prep strategy and future plans, which are as follows:

Were you expecting such a score? A 100 percentile?

"It was my first attempt and I had expected around 99.9 percentile. So scoring 100 percentile was really great. I was naturally elated."

What was the strategy you adopted for the rigorous preparation?

I started preparing for CAT 2017 from January and joined a reputed coaching. I ramped up my preparation only in August after quitting my job at Amazon, as Operations Manager. I joined a small start-up alongside CAT preparation from August onwards. In the last-three to four months I gave over 70 mock tests, of different mock series from renowned and established centres, as I believe, the number of mocks don't matter alone. What is important is that one attempts variety of questions so that the possibility of surprise questions in the actual exam is negated. To be able to handle surprise questions is important and that can be done only by attempting a wide variety of mock tests.

Secondly, VARC was my weak area and I was really worried about it. CAT 2017 is the only test among all the mocks and actual tests I attempted in which I scored 99.78. My VARC score was low in mocks and this gave me considerable stress.

Since I belong to GEM (General, Engineering, Male) category, the cut-offs are very high for this category so I was really stressed about whether I will make it to the select 200 or not. So, on the advice of my mentor, I started focusing on my strengths first and once I had saturated my preparation of those subjects, I moved to VARC. I took 3-4 days off and devised a strategy to tackle VARC. I would spend 2-3 hours on the RC part to ensure my weakness turned into strength.

Do you think joining a coaching institute is necessary?

I would say coaching institutes are helpful but not necessary. In the sense, that they give regularity and structure to your exam preparation and provide you a competitive environment so that you don't slow down. However, many aspirants score 100 percentile without joining a coaching institute. Among twenty 100 percentilers this year, 4-5 are the ones who didn't join any coaching institute and still managed cent percent score.

How much did your family support in taking the risk of leaving such a flourishing job?

I had a lucrative job at Amazon. I was the youngest Operations Manager at Amazon across India so it was not only lucrative but reputable as well. But when I expressed my desire to prepare for CAT, my parents were totally supportive of my decision. They told me to pursue higher studies without worrying about giving up my job. "Jobs will come and go, but you do what you wish to do", they told me. The confidence your parents show in you helps you take risks. So, I'd say my family played a pivotal role in my success in CAT 2017.

What are your plans for the future?

I have got interview calls from IIM Ahmedabad, IIM Bangalore and IIM Calcutta. I hope to join any one of these to pursue management. I am interested in entrepreneurship so I plan to foray into that post my MBA. If not entrepreneurship, then I will go for consulting.

What valuable tips can you give to future CAT aspirants?

They should really focus on attempting lot of mocks but do so only at the later stage when they have completed the course. If they start attempting mocks in the initial stages, without completing the course, they will not score well and that will make them anxious. So don't start with mock test series before you have completed your course.

Also, analyzing your performance is really important as it will help you judge yourself. You'll know what's to be done next.

Do as many mocks as you can, I did above 70. There are many aspirants who relied just on the mock tests and scored very well in CAT.

Few Words from the Toppers

Nothing can serve as well as human experience. In spite of various online portals, magazines and journals suggesting several ways to prepare for a competitive exam, nothing can beat the value of advices given by people who have actually taken the exam, especially the ones you can conveniently trust. One can get handy tips that make the preparation smoother, removing many of the unnecessary fears one builds within. This can be a great source in building of confidence and motivation and in boosting your morale.

However, you should be extremely careful about where the information comes from? Is it authentic, worthy of your trust or not? You should not mandatorily adapt every idea provided; only listen to such things, but don't adapt without analyzing. What may work for others may not necessarily be favourable for you.

You are the best judge who can decide when, how and what to start and follow.

Moreover, teachers and those who have done well earlier can provide great source of help by giving valuable tips, even before you start the preparation. For your benefit, we have collected few tips from the toppers which can surely guide you in a better way.

> In the first 2-3 months focus on the few basic concepts you need to be familiar with for taking CAT 2018. Building the basics should be the first step according to Sanuj Mittal, 100 percentiler in CAT.

S. P. Reddy (a B. Tech from IIT Madras) and a CAT topper advises the aspirants to focus more on Mocks and the preparatory tests for CAT from renowned institutes.

> "I was very punctual in writing a mock daily from 9AM to 12noon and analyzed it later well after evaluation for the errors. This strategy has helped to crack CAT 2017 with 100 percentile" - S. P. Reddy

The only advice to CAT 2018 aspirants from *Sai P. R.* who scored 100 percentile in CAT 2017, is to learn from mistakes and don't miss the mocks.

> To improve in VARC the best way is to start reading novels and articles. And to further strengthen the Quant, a CAT 2018 aspirant should have the clarity on basics and strong fundamentals. – Sai P.

Gyayak advises CAT aspirants to believe in themselves. In his view, CAT is an easy exam but you need to believe in yourself. A 100 percentile, Gyayak Jain, a student of PGP 2017-19 batch at IIM Ahmedabad.

> As per Gyayak, a CAT topper "My overall preparation strategy for CAT revolved around giving mock tests, reviewing my performance and improving in the areas where the performance was not good enough. Try to be mentally involved in the preparations all the time."

> "I made sure on a daily basis to study for two-three hours and on Friday (weekend in Algeria), six-eight hours. I utilized even the travel time to office for some meaningful activity like revising formulae," Prateek Bajpai, a CAT topper.

Avoid spending too much time on one question. Instead try more questions of a lesser platform. The time management is the key to success in such exams.

> "Time spent in solving two very difficult questions could have been better utilized in solving three medium/easy nature questions"- Shashank Heda, a CAT topper and now an IIM Bangalore student.

According to Neha, a CAT topper during your preparation for CAT exam you should search for more than one way to attempt and solve the questions with accuracy. This is also greatly recommended by the experts.

> "I took 86 mock tests for preparation and trusted almost 90 per cent on the analysis." says Avidipto Chakraborty, a former BITS Pilani student who scored a perfect 100 percentile in CAT.

> "It is important to take mock exams. They give you a good idea of where you stand with respect to others. I was not a consistently good performer during my coaching for CAT, but I had faith in myself. We would take mock exams sincerely and spend hours analyzing them," said Kartik, a chemical engineer from IIT Delhi.

Students usually try to switch to a different book once they're done with one. Sticking to the same book will help you a lot more as it gives you "depth". Revising one material repeatedly will help you more than switching between three-four books," says Rahul Sharma, a teacher in a private coaching institute who scored 100 percentile in CAT.

GENERAL TIPS TO FOLLOW FOR SUCCESS

Tip 1

Rather than focusing on all the topics, students should try to select those topics with which they are more comfortable. Even in the final test, students shouldn't try to solve each and every question and waste their energy; just spend 5 minutes in scanning a section and then select questions from their area of expertise and skill.

Tip2

It is of utmost importance that the students look at questions from previous years' CAT and understand its syllabus. After that doing an analysis to judge their level is very much required. They should assess whether they are proficient, average or need improvement in each of the areas. The areas that fall in the third category should be focused on a priority basis followed by the second and then the first.

Tip3

The aspirants should always start early in preparing for the exams as an early start would benefit them in gaining knowledge about the kind of questions to be asked. Another advantage is that the additional time can be spent in developing extra reading habits and increasing the vocabulary.

Tip4

The best way to go on with the CAT preparations is to evaluate oneself in every 10-15 days, which is done by mock tests. The one thing that students should be careful about is to not to repeat the mistakes made by them in either the mock CATs or while practising at home else the whole purpose of taking mock tests would be lost.

Tip5

One thing that is a must while preparing for CAT is practice on calculations attentively on a daily basis. CAT doesn't have long equations the only thing which works is the smart way of calculations which can be mastered by practising the tricks given by experts and available in books and internet.

Tip6

One must keep in mind that management schools seek to test understanding of basic concepts that the one possesses. So, students should stop looking for the toughest material to practise and realize that their competence needs to be focused upon.

Tip7

Some experts advise that the aspirants must study a minimum of 10 hours each day especially 6 months before the last date of the exams. The list further includes preparation of minimum 10,000 words to enhance the vocabulary, reading the newspapers and editorials for 2 hours every day regularly and reading at least two magazines and one novel each week.

Tip8

Time management is an essential ingredient to crack the CAT exam and make it to your favourite college. Managing one's time includes balancing speed with accuracy, handling the pressure and uncertainty and the apt decision making.

Tip9

Try not to forget that CAT has negative marking; for every wrong answer one mark will be deducted. The aspirants are advised not to take wild guesses in the Exam. If you are doubtful, try the elimination route, but only if the student is able to eliminate 2-3 choices, than he should take a guess.

Tip10

Last but not the least, students are advised to keep calm, relax, and believe in themselves throughout the process and especially on the day of the test. Be ready with all your stuff like admit card, pencils, pen etc. well in advance to avoid last minute hassle and give your best shot.